THE COMPLETE WORKS

OF

JAMES WHITCOMB RILEY

IN SIX VOLUMES

From A Child-World

THE COMPLETE WORKS

OF

JAMES WHITCOMB RILEY

IN WHICH THE POEMS, INCLUDING A NUMBER HERETOFORE UNPUBLISHED,
ARE ARRANGED IN THE ORDER IN WHICH THEY WERE WRITTEN,
TOGETHER WITH PHOTOGRAPHS, BIBLIOGRAPHIC NOTES,
AND A LIFE SKETCH OF THE AUTHOR

COLLECTED AND EDITED BY
EDMUND HENRY EITEL

BIOGRAPHICAL EDITION
VOLUME FOUR

INDIANAPOLIS
THE BOBBS-MERRILL COMPANY
PUBLISHERS

PRESS OF
BRAUNWORTH & CO.
BOOKBINDERS AND PRINTERS
BROOKLYN, N. Y.

CONTENTS

CONTENTS

CONTENTS

CONTENTS

CONTENTS

CONTENTS

CONTENTS

THE COMPLETE WORKS

OF

JAMES WHITCOMB RILEY

IN SIX VOLUMES

THE POET OF THE FUTURE

O THE Poet of the Future! He will come to us
as comes
The beauty of the bugle's voice above the roar of
drums—
The beauty of the bugle's voice above the roar and
din
Of battle-drums that pulse the time the victor
marches in.
His hands will hold no harp, in sooth; his lifted
brow will bear
No coronet of laurel—nay, nor symbol anywhere,
Save that his palms are brothers to the toiler's at the
plow,
His face to heaven, and the dew of duty on his
brow.

He will sing across the meadow,—and the woman
at the well
Will stay the dripping bucket, with a smile
ineffable;
And the children in the orchard will gaze wistfully
the way
The happy songs come to them, with the fragrance
of the hay;

1

The barn will neigh in answer, and the pasture-
　　lands behind
Will chime with bells, and send responsive lowings
　　down the wind;
And all the echoes of the wood will jubilantly call
In sweetest mimicry of that one sweet voice
　　　　of all.

O the Poet of the Future! He will come as man to
　　man,
With the honest arm of labor, and the honest face
　　of tan,
The honest heart of lowliness, the honest soul of
　　love
For human-kind and nature-kind about him and
　　above.
His hands will hold no harp, in sooth; his lifted
　　brow will bear
No coronet of laurel—nay, nor symbol anywhere,
Save that his palms are brothers to the toiler's at
　　the plow,
His face to heaven, and the dew of duty on his
　　brow.

NAUGHTY CLAUDE

WHEN Little Claude was naughty wunst
   At dinner-time, an' said
He won't say *"Thank you"* to his Ma,
   She maked him go to bed
An' stay two hours an' not git up,—
   So when the clock struck Two,
Nen Claude says,—"Thank you, Mr. Clock,
   I'm much obleeged to you!"

THE ARTEMUS OF MICHIGAN

GRAND HAVEN is in Michigan, and in
     possession, too,
Of as many rare attractions as our party ever
     knew :—
The fine hotel, the landlord, and the lordly bill of
     fare,
And the dainty-neat completeness of the pretty
     waiters there ;
The touch on the piano in the parlor, and the trill
Of the exquisite soprano—in our fancy singing still ;
Our cozy room, its comfort, and our thousand
     grateful thoughts,
And at our door the gentle face
       Of
         H.
           Y.
              Potts !

His artless observations, and his drollery of style,
Bewildered with that sorrowful serenity of smile—
The eye's elusive twinkle, and the twitching of the
     lid,

Like he didn't go to say it and was sorry that he did.
O Artemus of Michigan! so worthy of the name,
Our manager indorses it, and Bill Nye does the
    same,—
You tickled our affection in so many tender spots
That even Recollection laughs
        At
          H.
            Y.
              Potts!

And hark ye! O Grand Haven! count your rare at-
    tractions o'er—
The commerce of your ships at sea, and ships along
    the shore;
Your railroads, and your industries, and interests
    untold,
Your Opera-house—our lecture, and the gate-
    receipts in gold!—
Ay, Banner Town of Michigan! count all your
    treasures through—
Your crowds of summer tourists, and your
    Sanitarium, too;
Your lake, your beach, your drives, your breezy
    groves and grassy plots,
But head the list of all of these
        With
          H.
            Y.
              Potts!

WAITIN' FER THE CAT TO DIE

LAWZY! don't I rickollect
    That-air old swing in the lane!
Right and proper, I expect,
    Old times *can't* come back again;
But I want to state, ef they
Could come back, and I could say
What *my* pick 'ud be, i jing!
I'd say, Gimme the old swing
'Nunder the old locus' trees
On the old place, ef you please!—
Danglin' there with half-shet eye,
Waitin' fer the cat to die!

I'd say, Gimme the old gang
    O' barefooted, hungry, lean,
Ornry boys you want to hang
    When you're growed up twic't as mean!
The old gyarden-patch, the old

6

Truants, and the stuff we stol'd!
The old stompin'-groun', where we
Wore the grass off, wild and free
As the swoop o' the old swing,
Where we ust to climb and cling,
And twist roun', and fight, and lie—
Waitin' fer the cat to die!

'Pears like I most allus could
    Swing the highest of the crowd—
Jes' sail up there tel I stood
    Down-side up, and screech out loud,—
Ketch my breath, and jes' drap back
Fer to let the old swing slack,
Yit my towhead dippin' still
In the green boughs, and the chill
Up my backbone taperin' down,
With my shadder on the groun'
Slow and slower trailin' by—
Waitin' fer the cat to die!

Now my daughter's little Jane's
    Got a kind o' baby-swing
On the porch, so's when it rains
    She kin play there—little thing!
And I'd limped out t'other day
With my old cheer thisaway,
Swingin' *her* and rockin' too,
Thinkin' how *I* ust to do

At *her* age, when suddenly,
"Hey, Gran'pap!" she says to me,
"Why you rock so slow?" . . . Says I,
"Waitin' fer the cat to die!"

THE ALL-KIND MOTHER

LO, whatever is at hand
   Is full meet for the demand:
Nature ofttimes giveth best
When she seemeth chariest.
She hath shapen shower and sun
To the need of every one—
Summer bland and winter drear,
Dimpled pool and frozen mere.
All thou lackest she hath still
Near thy finding and thy fill.
Yield her fullest faith, and she
Will endow thee royally.

Loveless weed and lily fair
She attendeth here and there—
Kindly to the weed as to
The lorn lily teared with dew.
Each to her hath use as dear
As the other; an thou clear
Thy cloyed senses thou may'st see
Haply all the mystery.
Thou shalt see the lily get
Its divinest blossom; yet
Shall the weed's tip bloom no less
With the song-bird's gleefulness.

9

Thou art poor, or thou art rich—
Never lightest matter which;
All the glad gold of the noon,
All the silver of the moon,
She doth lavish on thee, while
Thou withholdest any smile
Of thy gratitude to her,
Baser used than usurer.
Shame be on thee an thou seek
Not her pardon, with hot cheek,
And bowed head, and brimming eyes
At her merciful "Arise!"

TO HATTIE—ON HER BIRTHDAY

WRITTEN IN "A CHILD'S GARDEN OF VERSES"

WHEN your "Uncle Jim" was
    younger,
In the days of childish hunger
For the honey of such verses
As this little book rehearses
    In such sweet simplicity,—
Just the simple gift that this is
Would have brimmed his heart with blisses
Sweet as Hattie's sweetest kisses,
    On her anniversary,

DOWN TO THE CAPITAL

I'BE'N down to the Capital at Washington,
   D. C.,
Where Congerss meets and passes on the pensions
   ort to be
Allowed to old one-legged chaps, like me, 'at sence
   the war
Don't wear their pants in pairs at all—and yit how
   proud we are!

Old Flukens, from our deestrick, jes' turned in and
   tuck and made
Me stay with him while I was there; and longer 'at
   I stayed
The more I kep' a-wantin' jes' to kind o' git away,
And yit a-feelin' sociabler with Flukens ever' day.

You see I'd got the idy—and I guess most folks
   agrees—
'At men as rich as him, you know, kin do jes' what
   they please;
A man worth stacks o' money, and a Congerssman
   and all,
And livin' in a buildin' bigger'n Masonic Hall!

Now mind, I'm not a-faultin' Fluke—he made his
    money square:
We both was Forty-niners, and both bu'sted gittin'
    there;
I weakened and onwindlassed, and he stuck and
    stayed and made
His millions; don't know what *I'm* worth untel my
    pension's paid.

But I was goin' to tell you—er a-ruther goin' to try
To tell you how he's livin' now: gas burnin' mighty
    nigh
In ever' room about the house; and all the night,
    about,
Some blame reception goin' on, and money goin' out.

They's people there from all the world—jes' ever'
    kind 'at lives,
Injuns and all! and Senaters, and Ripresentatives;
And girls, you know, jes' dressed in gauze and roses,
    I *de*clare,
And even old men shamblin' round and waltzin' with
    'em there!

And bands a-tootin' circus-tunes, 'way in some other
    room
Jes' chokin' full o' hothouse plants and pinies and
    perfume;
And fountains, squirtin' stiddy all the time; and
    statutes, made
Out o' puore marble, 'peared-like, sneakin' round
    there in the shade.

And Fluke he coaxed and begged and pled with
    me to take a hand
And sashay in amongst 'em—crutch and all, you
    understand;
But when I said how tired I was, and made fer
    open air,
He follered, and tel five o'clock we set a-talkin'
    there.

"My God!" says he—Fluke says to me, "I'm
    tireder'n you;
Don't putt up yer tobacker tel you give a man a
    chew.
Set back a leetle furder in the shadder—that'll do;
I'm tireder'n you, old man; I'm tireder'n you.

"You see that-air old dome," says he, "humped up
    ag'inst the sky?
It's grand, first time you see it; but it changes, by
    and by,
And then it stays jes' thataway—jes' anchored high
    and dry
Betwixt the sky up yender and the achin' of yer
    eye.

"Night's purty; not so purty, though, as what it
    ust to be
When my first wife was livin'. You remember her?"
    says he.
I nodded-like, and Fluke went on, "I wonder now
    ef she
Knows where I am—and what I am—and what
    I ust to be?

"That band in there!—I ust to think 'at music
    couldn't wear
A feller out the way it does; but that ain't music
    there—
That's jes' a' *imitation,* and like ever'thing, I swear,
I hear, er see, er tetch, er taste, er tackle anywhere!

"It's all jes' *artificial,* this-'ere high-priced life of
    ours;
The theory, *it's* sweet enough, tel it saps down and
    sours.
They's no *home* left, ner *ties* o' home about it. By
    the powers,
The whole thing's artificialer'n artificial flowers!

"And all I want, and could lay down and *sob* fer,
    is to know
The homely things of homely life; fer instance, jes'
    to go
And set down by the kitchen stove—Lord! that
    'u'd rest me so,—
Jes' set there, like I ust to do, and laugh and joke,
    you know.

"Jes' set there, like I ust to do," says Fluke,
    a-startin' in,
'Peared-like, to say the whole thing over to his-
    se'f ag'in;
Then stopped and turned, and kind o' coughed,
    and stooped and fumbled fer
Somepin' o' 'nuther in the grass—I guess his hand-
    kercher.

Well, sence I'm back from Washington, where I
　　left Fluke a-still
A-leggin' fer me, heart and soul, on that-air pen-
　　sion bill,
I've half-way struck the notion, when I think o'
　　wealth and sich,
They's nothin' much patheticker'n jes' a-bein' rich!

JAP MILLER

JAP MILLER down at Martinsville's the blamed-
    est feller yit!
When *he* starts in a-talkin' other folks is apt to
    quit!—
'Pears like that mouth o' his'n wuzn't made fer
    nothin' else
But jes' to argify 'em down and gether in their
    pelts:
He'll talk you down on tariff; er he'll talk you down
    on tax,
And prove the pore man pays 'em all—and them's
    about the fac's!—
Religen, law, er politics, prize-fightin' er baseball—
Jes' tetch Jap up a little and he'll post you 'bout 'em
    all.

And the comicalist feller ever tilted back a cheer
And tuk a chaw tobacker kind o' like he didn't
    keer.—
There's where the feller's stren'th lays,—he's so
    common-like and plain,—
They hain't no dude about old Jap, you bet you—
    nary grain!

17

They 'lected him to Council and it never turned his
    head,
And didn't make no differunce what anybody said,—
He didn't dress no finer, ner rag out in fancy
    clothes;
But his voice in Council-meetin's is a turrer to his
    foes

He's fer the pore man ever' time! And in the last
    campaign
He stumped old Morgan County, through the sun-
    shine and the rain,
And helt the banner up'ards from a-trailin' in the
    dust,
And cut loose on monopolies and cuss'd and cuss'd
    and cuss'd!
He'd tell some funny story ever' now and then, you
    know,
Tel, blame it! it wuz better'n a Jack-o'-lantern
    show!
And I'd go furder, yit, to-day, to hear old Jap
    norate
Than any high-toned orater 'at ever stumped the
    State!

W'y, that-air blame Jap Miller, with his keen sir-
    castic fun,
Has got more friends than ary candidate 'at ever
    run!

Don't matter what *his* views is, when he states the
same to you,

They allus coincide with yourn, the same as two and
two:

You *can't* take issue with him—er, at least, they
hain't no sense

In startin' in to down him, so you better not com-
mence.—

The best way's jes' to listen, like your humble servant does,

And jes' concede Jap Miller is the best man ever
wuz!

JOHN TARKINGTON JAMESON

JOHN JAMESON, my jo John!
  Ye're bonnie wee an' sma';
Your ee's the morning violet,
  Wi' tremblin' dew an' a';
Your smile's the gowden simmer-sheen,
  Wi' glintin' pearls aglow
Atween the posies o' your lips,
  John Jameson, my jo!

Ye hae the faither's braidth o' brow,
  An' synes his look benign
Whiles he hings musin' ower the burn,
  Wi' leestless hook an' line;
Ye hae the mither's mou' an' cheek
  An' denty chin—but O!
It's maist ye're like your ain braw sel',
  John Jameson, my jo!

John Jameson, my jo John,
  Though, wi' sic luvers twain,
Ye dance far yont your whustlin' frien'
  Wha laggart walks his lane,—

20

Be mindet, though he naps his last
　　Whaur kirkyird thistles grow,
His ghaist shall caper on wi' you,
　　John Jameson, my jo!

HENRY W. GRADY

ATLANTA, DECEMBER 23, 1889

TRUE-HEARTED friend of all true friendli-
    ness!—
  Brother of all true brotherhoods!—Thy hand
  And its late pressure now we understand
Most fully, as it falls thus gestureless
And Silence lulls thee into sweet excess
  Of sleep. Sleep thou content!—Thy loved South-
    land
  Is swept with tears, as rain in sunshine; and
Through all the frozen North our eyes confess
  Like sorrow—seeing still the princely sign
Set on thy lifted brow, and the rapt light
  Of the dark, tender, melancholy eyes—
  Thrilled with the music of those lips of thine,
And yet the fire thereof that lights the night
  With the white splendor of thy prophecies.

IN THE EVENING

I

IN the evening of our days,
  When the first far stars above
Glimmer dimmer, through the haze,
  Than the dewy eyes of love,
Shall we mournfully revert
  To the vanished morns and Mays
Of our youth, with hearts that hurt,—
  In the evening of our days?

II

Shall the hand that holds your own
  Till the twain are thrilled as now,—
Be withheld, or colder grown?
  Shall my kiss upon your brow
Falter from its high estate?
  And, in all forgetful ways,
Shall we sit apart and wait—
  In the evening of our days?

III

Nay, my wife—my life!—the gloom
  Shall enfold us velvet-wise,
And my smile shall be the groom
  Of the gladness of your eyes:
Gently, gently as the dew
  Mingles with the darkening maze,
I shall fall asleep with you—
  In the evening of our days.

THOUGHTS ON THE LATE WAR

I WAS for Union—you, ag'in' it.
  'Pears like, to me, each side was winner,
Lookin' at now and all 'at's in it.
        Le' 's go to dinner.

Le' 's kind o' jes' set down together
And do some pardnership forgittin'—
Talk, say, for instunce, 'bout the weather,
        Or somepin' fittin'.

The war, you know, 's all done and ended,
And ain't changed no p'ints o' the compass;
Both North and South the health's jes' splendid
        As 'fore the rumpus.

The old farms and the old plantations
Still ockipies the'r old positions.
Le' 's git back to old situations
        And old ambitions.

Le' 's let up on this blame', infernal
Tongue-lashin' and lap-jacket vauntin',
And git back home to the eternal
        Ca'm we're a-wantin'.

Peace kind o' sort o' suits my diet—
When women does my cookin' for me;
Ther' wasn't overly much pie et
          Durin' the army.

THE OLD BAND

IT 'S mighty good to git back to the old town,
  shore,
Considerin' I've b'en away twenty year and more.
Sence I moved then to Kansas, of course I see a
  change,
A-comin' back, and notice things that's new to me
  and strange;
Especially at evening when yer new band-fellers
  meet,
In fancy uniforms and all, and play out on the
  street—
. . . What's come of old Bill Lindsey and the Saxhorn fellers—say?
    I want to hear the *old* band play.

What's come of Eastman, and Nat Snow? And
  where's War Barnett at?
And Nate and Bony Meek; Bill Hart; Tom Richa'-
  son and that
Air brother of him played the drum as twic't as big
  as Jim;
And old Hi Kerns, the carpenter—say, what's become o' him?

27

I make no doubt yer *new band* now's a *competenter*
  band,
And plays their music more by note than what they
  play by hand,
And stylisher and grander tunes; but somehow—
  *any*way,
  I want to hear the *old* band play.

Sich tunes as "John Brown's Body" and "Sweet
  Alice," don't you know;
And "The Camels Is A-Comin'," and "John Ander-
  son, My Jo";
And a dozent others of 'em—"Number Nine" and
  "Number 'Leven"
Was favo-*rites* that fairly made a feller dream o'
  Heaven.
And when the boys 'u'd saranade, I've laid so still
  in bed
I've even heerd the locus'-blossoms droppin' on the
  shed
When "Lilly Dale," er "Hazel Dell," had sobbed
  and died away—
  . . . I want to hear the *old* band play.

Yer *new* band ma'by beats it, but the *old band's*
  what I said—
It allus 'peared to kind o' chord with somepin' in my
  head;

And, whilse I'm no musicianer, when my blame'
    eyes is jes'
Nigh drownded out, and Mem'ry squares her jaws
    and sort o' says
She *won't* ner *never will* fergit, I want to jes' turn in
And take and light right out o' here and git back
    West ag'in
And *stay* there, when I git there, where I never haf'
    to say
      I want to hear the *old* band play.

BY ANY OTHER NAME

FIRST the teacher called the roll,
   Clos't to the beginnin',
"Addeliney Bowersox!"
   Set the school a-grinnin'.
Winter-time, and stingin' cold
   When the session took up—
Cold as *we* all looked at *her,*
   Though *she* couldn't look up!

Total stranger to us, too—
   Country folks ain't allus
Nigh so shameful unpolite
   As some people call us!—
But the honest facts is, *then,*
   Addeliney Bower-
Sox's feelin's was so hurt
   She cried half an hour!

My dest was acrost from hern:
   Set and watched her tryin'
To p'tend she didn't keer,
   And a kind o' dryin'

Up her tears with smiles—tel I
  Thought, "Well, *'Addeliney*
Bowersox' is plain, but *she's*
  Purty as a piney!"

.   .   .   .

It's be'n many of a year
  Sence that most oncommon
Cur'ous name o' *Bowersox*
  Struck me so abomin-
Nubble and outlandish-like!—
  I changed it to Adde-
Liney *Daubenspeck*—and *that*
  Nearly killed her Daddy!

LINES FER ISAAC BRADWELL, OF INDAN-
OPLIS, IND., COUNTY-SEAT
OF MARION

*[Writ on the fly-leaf of a volume of the author's
poems that come in one of gittin' burnt up in the
great Bowen-Merrill's fire of March 17, 1890.]*

THROUGH fire and flood this book has
    passed.—
Fer what?—I hardly dare to ast—
Less'n it's still to pamper me
With extry food fer vanity;—
Fer, since it's fell in hands as true
As *yourn* is—and a *Hoosier* too,—
I'm prouder of the book, I jing!
Than 'fore they tried to burn the thing!

32

"THE LITTLE MAN IN THE TIN-SHOP"

WHEN I was a little boy, long ago,
  And spoke of the theater as the "show,"
The first one that I went to see,
Mother's brother it was took me—
(My uncle, of course, though he seemed to be
Only a boy—I loved him so!)
And ah, how pleasant he made it all!
And the things he knew that *I* should know!—
The stage, the "drop," and the frescoed wall;
The sudden flash of the lights; and oh,
The orchestra, with its melody,
And the lilt and jingle and jubilee
    Of "The Little Man in the Tin-shop"!

For Uncle showed me the "Leader" there,
With his pale, bleak forehead and long, black hair;
Showed me the "Second," and "'Cello," and "Bass,"
And the "B-Flat," pouting and puffing his face
At the little end of the horn he blew
Silvery bubbles of music through;
And he coined me names of them, each in turn,

33

Some comical name that I laughed to learn,
Clean on down to the last and best,—
The lively little man, never at rest,
Who hides away at the end of the string,
And tinkers and plays on everything,—
 That's "The Little Man in the Tin-shop"!

Raking a drum like a rattle of hail,
Clinking a cymbal or castanet;
Chirping a twitter or sending a wail
Through a piccolo that thrills me yet;
Reeling ripples of riotous bells,
And tipsy tinkles of triangles—
Wrangled and tangled in skeins of sound
Till it seemed that my very soul spun round,
As I leaned, in a breathless joy, toward my
Radiant uncle, who snapped his eye
And said, with the courtliest wave of his hand,
"Why, that little master of all the band
 Is 'The Little Man in the Tin-shop'!

"And I've heard Verdi the Wonderful,
And Paganini, and Ole Bull,
Mozart, Handel, and Mendelssohn,
And fair Parepa, whose matchless tone
Karl, her master, with magic bow,
Blent with the angels', and held her so
Tranced till the rapturous Infinite—
And I've heard arias, faint and low,
From many an operatic light

Glimmering on my swimming sight
Dimmer and dimmer, until, at last,
I still sit, holding my roses fast
    For 'The Little Man in the Tin-Shop.' "

Oho! my Little Man, joy to you—
And *yours*—and *theirs*—your lifetime through!
Though *I've* heard melodies, boy and man,
Since first "the show" of my life began,
Never yet have I listened to
Sadder, madder, gladder glees
Than your unharmonied harmonies;
For yours is the music that appeals
To all the fervor the boy's heart feels—
All his glories, his wildest cheers,
His bravest hopes, and his brightest tears;
And so, with his first bouquet, he kneels
    To "The Little Man in the Tin-shop."

A SOUTHERN SINGER

WRITTEN IN MADISON CAWEIN'S "LYRICS AND IDYLS"

HEREIN are blown from out the South
Songs blithe as those of Pan's pursed
mouth—
As sweet in voice as, in perfume,
The night-breath of magnolia-bloom.

Such sumptuous languor lures the sense—
Such luxury of indolence—
The eyes blur as a nymph's might blur,
With water-lilies watching her.

You waken, thrilling at the trill
Of some wild bird that seems to spill
The silence full of winy drips
Of song that Fancy sips and sips.

Betimes, in brambled lanes wherethrough
The chipmunk stripes himself from view,
You pause to lop a creamy spray
Of elder-blossoms by the way.

Or where the morning dew is yet
Gray on the topmost rail, you set
A sudden palm and, vaulting, meet
Your vaulting shadow in the wheat.

On lordly swards, of suave incline,
Entessellate with shade and shine,
You shall misdoubt your lowly birth,
Clad on as one of princely worth:

The falcon on your wrist shall ride—
Your milk-white Arab side by side
With one of raven-black.—You fain
Would kiss the hand that holds the rein.

Nay, nay, Romancer! Poet! Seer
Sing us back home—from there to here:
Grant your high grace and wit, but we
Most honor your simplicity.—

Herein are blown from out the South
Songs blithe as those of Pan's pursed mouth—
As sweet in voice as, in perfume,
The night-breath of magnolia-bloom.

JUNE AT WOODRUFF

OUT at Woodruff Place—afar
From the city's glare and jar,
With the leafy trees, instead
Of the awnings, overhead;
With the shadows cool and sweet,
For the fever of the street;
With the silence, like a prayer,
Breathing round us everywhere.

Gracious anchorage, at last,
From the billows of the vast
Tide of life that comes and goes,
Whence and where nobody knows—
Moving, like a skeptic's thought,
Out of nowhere into naught.
Touch and tame us with thy grace,
Placid calm of Woodruff Place!

Weave a wreath of beechen leaves
For the brow that throbs and grieves
O'er the ledger, bloody-lined,
'Neath the sunstruck window-blind!

Send the breath of woodland bloom
Through the sick man's prison-room,
Till his old farm-home shall swim
Sweet in mind to hearten him!

Out at Woodruff Place the Muse
Dips her sandal in the dews,
Sacredly as night and dawn
Baptize lilied grove and lawn:
Woody path, or paven way—
She doth haunt them night and day,—
Sun or moonlight through the trees,
To her eyes, are melodies.

Swinging lanterns, twinkling clear
Through night-scenes, are songs to her—
Tinted lilts and choiring hues,
Blent with children's glad halloos;
Then belated lays that fade
Into midnight's serenade—
Vine-like words and zithern-strings
Twined through all her slumberings.

Blessèd be each hearthstone set
Neighboring the violet!
Blessèd every roof-tree prayed
Over by the beech's shade!
Blessèd doorway, opening where
We may look on Nature—there
Hand to hand and face to face—
Storied realm, or Woodruff Place.

IRY AND BILLY AND JO

A TINTYPE

IRY an' Billy an' Jo!—
　　Iry an' Billy's *the boys,*
An' *Jo's* their *dog,* you know,—
Their pictur's took all in a row.
　　　Bet they kin kick up a noise—
　　Iry an' Billy, the boys,
An' that-air little dog Jo!

Iry's the one 'at stands
　　Up there a-lookin' so mild
An' meek—with his hat in his hands,
　　Like such a *'bediant* child—
(*Sakes-alive!*)—An' *Billy* he sets
In the cheer an' holds on to Jo an' *sweats*
Hisse'f, a-lookin' so good! Ho-ho!
　　　Iry an' Billy an' Jo!

Yit the way them boys, you know,
　　Usen to jes' turn in
An' fight over that dog Jo
　　Wuz a burnin'-shame-an'-a-sin!—

40

Iry *he'd* argy 'at, by gee-whizz!
That-air little Jo-dog wuz *his!*—
An' Billy *he'd* claim it wuzn't so—
'Cause the dog wuz *hisn!*—An' at it they'd go,
Nip-an'-tugg, tooth-an'-toe-nail, you know—
      Iry an' Billy an' Jo!

But their Pa—(He wuz the marshal then)—
   He 'tended-like 'at he *jerked 'em up;*
An' got a jury o' Brick-yard men
   An' helt *a trial* about the pup:
An' *he* says *he* jes' like to 'a' died
When the rest o' us town-boys *testified*—
      Regardin', you know,
      Iry an' Billy an' Jo.—

'Cause we all knowed, when *the Gipsies* they
   Camped down here by the crick last Fall,
They brung Jo with 'em, 'an' give him away
   To Iry an' Billy fer nothin' at all!—
So the jury fetched in the *verdick* so
      Jo he ain't *neether* o' theirn fer *shore*—
      He's *both* their dog, an' jes' no more!
      An' so
      They've quit quarrelin' long ago,
      Iry an' Billy an' Jo.

UNCLE SIDNEY'S VIEWS

I HOLD that the true age of wisdom is when
  We are boys and girls, and not women and
    men,—
When as credulous children we *know* things because
We *believe* them—however averse to the laws.
It is *faith,* then, not science and reason, I say,
That is genuine wisdom.—And would that to-day
We, as then, were as wise and ineffably blest
As to live, love and die, and trust God for the rest!

So I simply deny the old notion, you know,
That the wiser we get as the older we grow!—
For *in youth* all we know we are *certain* of.—*Now*
The greater our knowledge, the more we allow
For skeptical margin.—And hence I regret
That the world isn't flat, and the sun doesn't set,
And we may not go creeping up home, when we die,
Through the moon, like a round yellow hole in the
    sky.

BEREAVED

LET me come in where you sit weeping,—ay,
　　Let me, who have not any child to die,
Weep with you for the little one whose love
　　　　I have known nothing of.

The little arms that slowly, slowly loosed
Their pressure round your neck; the hands you used
To kiss.—Such arms—such hands I never knew.
　　　　May I not weep with you?

Fain would I be of service—say some thing,
Between the tears, that would be comforting,—
But ah! so sadder than yourselves am I,
　　　　Who have no child to die.

THE RIDER OF THE KNEE

KNIGHTLY Rider of the Knee
Of Proud-prancing Unclery!
Gaily mount, and wave the sign
Of that mastery of thine.

Pat thy steed and turn him free,
Knightly Rider of the Knee!
Sit thy charger as a throne—
Lash him with thy laugh alone:

Sting him only with the spur
Of such wit as may occur,
Knightly Rider of the Knee,
In thy shriek of ecstasy.

Would, as now, we might endure,
Twain as one—thou miniature
Ruler, at the rein of me—
Knightly Rider of the Knee!

THE LITTLE-RED-APPLE TREE

THE Little-red-apple Tree!—
    O the Little-red-apple Tree!
When I was the little-est bit of a boy
    And you were a boy with me!
The bluebird's flight from the topmost boughs,
    And the boys up there—so high
That we rocked over the roof of the house
    And whooped as the winds went by!

Hey! The Little-red-apple Tree!
    With the garden-beds below,
And the old grape-arbor so welcomely
    Hiding the rake and hoe!
Hiding, too, as the sun dripped through
    In spatters of wasted gold,
Frank and Amy away from you
    And me in the days of old!

The Little-red-apple Tree!—
    In the edge of the garden-spot,
Where the apples fell so lavishly
    Into the neighbor's lot;—

So do I think of you alway,
    Brother of mine, as the tree,—
Giving the ripest wealth of your love
    To the world as well as me.

Ho! The Little-red-apple Tree!
    Sweet as its juiciest fruit
Spanged on the palate spicily,
    And rolled o'er the tongue to boot,
Is the memory still and the joy
    Of the Little-red-apple Tree,
When I was the little-est bit of a boy
    And you were a boy with me!

UNCLE SIDNEY

SOMETIMES, when I bin bad,
　　An' Pa "currecks" me nen,
An' Uncle Sidney he comes here,
　I'm allus good again;

'Cause Uncle Sidney says,
　　An' takes me up an' smiles,—
*The goodest mens they is ain't good
　As baddest little childs!*

IN THE NIGHT

WHEN it's night, and no light, too,
    Wakin' by yourse'f,
With the old clock mockin' you
    On the mantel-she'f;
In the dark—so still and black,
    You're afeard you'll hear
Somepin' awful pop and crack,—
    "Go to sleep, my dear!"

That's what *Mother* says.—And *then's*
    When we ain't *afeard!*
Wunder, when we be big mens,
    Then 'ul we be skeerd?—
Some night Mother's goned away,
    And ist *us* is here,
Will The Good Man wake and say,
    "Go to sleep, my dear"?

THE DREAM OF THE LITTLE PRINCESS

'TWAS a curious dream, good sooth!—
　　The dream of The Little Princess;
It seemed a dream, yet a truth,
Long years ago in her youth.—
　　It *came* as a dream—no less
　　It was *not* a dream, she says.

(She is singing and saying things
　　Musical as the wile
Of the eery quaverings
That drip from the grievèd strings
　　Of her lute.—We weep or smile
　　Even as she, meanwhile.)

In a day, long dead and gone,
　　When her castle-turrets threw
Their long, sharp shadows on
The sward like lances,—wan
　　And lone, she strayed into
　　Strange grounds where lilies grew.

49

There, late in the afternoon,
    As she sate in the terrace shade,
Rav'ling a half-spun tune
From a lute like a wee new-moon,—
        High off was a bugle played,
        And a sound as of steeds that neighed.

And the lute fell from her hands,
    As her eyes raised, half in doubt,
To the arch of the azure lands
Where lo! with the fluttering strands
        Of a rainbow reined about
        His wrist, rode a horseman out.

And The Little Princess was stirred
    No less at his steeds than him;—
A jet-black span of them gird
In advance, he bestrode the third;
        And the troop of them seemed to swim
        The skies as the Seraphim.

Wingless they were, yet so
    Upborne in their wondrous flight—
As their master bade them go,
They dwindled on high; or lo!
        They curved from their heavenmost height
        And swooped to her level sight.

And the eyes of The Little Princess
    Grow O so bright as the chants
Of the horseman's courtliness,—

Saluting her low—Ah, yes!
    And lifting a voice that haunts
    Her own song's weird romance.

For (she sings) at last he swept
    As near to her as the tips
Of the lilies, that whitely slept,
As he leaned o'er one and wept
    And touched it with his lips—
    Sweeter than honey-drips!

And she keeps the lily yet—
    As the horseman bade (she says)
As he launched, with a wild curvet,
His steeds toward the far sunset,
    Till gulfed in its gorgeousness
    And lost to The Little Princess:

But O my master sweet!
    He is coming again! (she sings)
My Prince of the Coursers fleet,
    With his bugle's echoings,
    And the breath of his voice for the wings
Of the sandals of his feet!

THE SQUIRT-GUN UNCLE MAKED ME

UNCLE SIDNEY, when he was here,
    Maked me a squirt-gun out o' some
Elder-bushes 'at growed out near
Where wuz the brick-yard—'way out clear
        To where the Toll-Gate come!

So when we walked back home again,
    He maked it, out in our woodhouse where
Wuz the old work-bench, an' the old jack-plane,
An' the old 'poke-shave, an' the tools all lay'n'
        Ist like he wants 'em there.

He sawed it first with the old hand-saw;
    An' nen he peeled off the bark, an' got
Some glass an' scraped it; an' told 'bout Pa,
When *he* wuz a boy an' fooled his Ma,
        An' the whippin' 'at he caught.

Nen Uncle Sidney, he took an' filed
    A' old arn ramrod; an' one o' the ends
He screwed fast into the vise; an' smiled,
Thinkin', he said, o' when he wuz a child,
        'Fore him an' Pa wuz mens.

52

He punched out the peth, an' nen he putt
    A plug in the end with a hole notched through;
Nen took the old drawey-knife an' cut
An' maked a hande 'at shoved clean shut
      But ist where yer hand held to.

An' he wropt th'uther end with some string an'
    white
    Piece o' the sleeve of a' old tored shirt;
An' nen he showed me to hold it tight,
An' suck in the water an' work it right.—
      An' it 'ud ist squirt an' squirt!

THE YOUTHFUL PRESS

LITTLE Georgie Tompers, he
  Printed some fine cards for me;
But his press had "J" for *James*—
By no means the choice of names.—

Yet it's proper, none the less,
That his little printing-press
Should be taught that *James* for "J"
Always is the better way.

For, if left to its own whim,
Next time it might call me "Jim,"—
Then THE CULTURED PRESS would be
Shocked at such a liberty.

Therefore, little presses all
Should be trained, while they are small,
To develop *taste* in these
Truths that shape our destinies.

MAX AND JIM

MAX an' Jim,
    They're each other's
Fat an' slim
    Little brothers.

Max is thin,
    An' Jim, the fac's is,
Fat ag'in
    As little Max is!

Their Pa 'lowed
    He don't know whuther
He's most proud
    Of one er th'other!

Their Ma says
    They're both so sweet—'*m!*—
That she guess
    She'll haf to eat 'em!

THE OLD HAYMOW

THE Old Haymow's the place to play
   Fer boys, when it's a rainy day!
I good 'eal ruther be up there
Than down in town, er anywhere!

When I play in our stable-loft,
The good old hay's so dry an' soft,
An' feels so fine, an' smells so sweet,
I 'most ferget to go an' eat.

An' one time onc't I *did* ferget
To go tel dinner was all et,—
An' they had shortcake—an'—Bud he
Hogged up the piece Ma saved fer me!

Nen I won't let him play no more
In our haymow where I keep store
An' got hen-eggs to sell,—an' shoo
The cackle-un old hen out, too!

An' nen, when Aunty she was here
A-visitun from Rensselaer,
An' bringed my little cousin,—*he*
Can come up there an' play with me.

But, after while—when Bud he bets
'At I can't turn no summersetts,
I let him come up, ef he can
Ac' ha'f-way like a gentleman!

GUINEY-PIGS

GUINEY-PIGS is awful cute,
  With their little trimbly snoot
Sniffin' at the pussly that
We bring 'em to nibble at.
  Looks like they're so clean an' white,
  An' so dainty an' polite,
  They could eat like you an' me
    When they's company!

Tiltin' down the clover-tops
Till they spill, an' overdrops
The sweet morning dew—Don't you
Think they might have napkins, too?
  Ef a guiney-pig was big
  As a *shore-an'-certain* pig,
  Nen he wouldn't ac' so fine
    When he come to dine.

Nen he'd chomp his jaws an' eat
Things out in the dirty street,
Dirt an' all! An' nen lay down
In mud-holes an' waller roun'!
  So the *guiney-pigs* is best,
  'Cause they're nice an' tidiest;
  They eat 'most like you an' me
    When they's company!

BUSCH AND TOMMY

LITTLE Busch and Tommy Hays—
  Small the theme, but large the praise,—
  For two braver brothers,
Of such toddling years and size,
Bloom of face, and blue of eyes,
Never trampled soldier-wise
  On the rights of mothers!

Even boldly facing their
Therapeutic father's air
  Of complex abstraction,
But to kindle—kindlier gaze,
Wake more smiles and gracious ways—
Ay, nor find in all their days
  Ampler satisfaction!

Hail ye, then, with chirp and cheer,
All wan patients, waiting here
  Bitterer medications!—
Busch and Tommy, *tone* us, too.—
How our life-blood leaps anew,
Under loving touch of you
  And your ministrations!

59

THE LUGUBRIOUS WHING-WHANG

THE rhyme o' The Raggedy Man's 'at's best
  Is Tickle me, Love, in these Lonesome Ribs,
'Cause that-un's the strangest of all o' the rest,
An' the worst to learn, an' the last one guessed,
An' the funniest one, an' the foolishest.—
  Tickle me, Love, in these Lonesome Ribs!

I don't know what in the world it means—
  Tickle me, Love, in these Lonesome Ribs!—
An' nen when I *tell* him I don't, he leans
Like he was a-grindin' on some machines
An' says: Ef I *don't,* w'y, I don't know *beans!*
  Tickle me, Love, in these Lonesome Ribs!

Out on the margin of Moonshine Land,
  Tickle me, Love, in these Lonesome Ribs!
Out where the Whing-Whang loves to stand,
Writing his name with his tail in the sand,
And swiping it out with his oogerish hand;
  Tickle me, Love, in these Lonesome Ribs!

Is it the gibber of Gungs or Keeks?
    Tickle me, Love, in these Lonesome Ribs!
Or what *is* the sound that the Whing-Whang
    seeks?—
Crouching low by the winding creeks,
And holding his breath for weeks and weeks!
    Tickle me, Love, in these Lonesome Ribs!

Aroint him the wraithest of wraithly things!
    Tickle me, Love, in these Lonesome Ribs!
'Tis a fair Whing-Whangess, with phosphor rings,
And bridal-jewels of fangs and stings;
And she sits and as sadly and softly sings
As the mildewed whir of her own dead wings,—
    Tickle me, Dear,
        Tickle me here,
    Tickle me, Love, in me Lonesome Ribs!

LITTLE MANDY'S CHRISTMAS-TREE

LITTLE Mandy and her Ma
   'S porest folks you ever saw!—
Lived in porest house in town,
Where the fence 'uz all tore down.

And no front-door steps at all—
Ist a' old box 'g'inst the wall;
And no door-knob on the door
Outside.—*My!* but they 'uz pore!

Wuz no winder-shutters on,
And some of the *winders* gone,
And where they 'uz broke they'd pas'e
Ist brown paper 'crost the place.

Tell you! when it's *winter there,*
And the snow ist ever'where,
Little Mandy's Ma she say
'Spec' they'll freeze to death some day.

Wunst my Ma and me—when we
Be'n to church, and's goin' to be
Chris'mus purty soon,—we went
There—like the Committee sent.

And-sir! when we're in the door,
Wuz no carpet on the floor,
And no fire—and heels-and-head
Little Mandy's tucked in bed!

And her Ma telled *my* Ma she
Got no coffee but ist tea,
And fried mush—and's all they had
Sence her health broke down so bad.

Nen Ma hug and hold me where
Little Mandy's layin' there;
And she kiss her, too, and nen
Mandy kiss my Ma again.

And my Ma she telled her *we*
Goin' to have a Chris'mus-Tree,
At the Sund'y-School, 'at's fer
ALL the childern, and fer *her*.

Little Mandy *think*—nen she
Say, "What *is* a Chris'mus-Tree?"
Nen my Ma she give *her* Ma
Somepin' 'at I never saw,

And say she *must* take it,—and
She ist maked her keep her hand
Wite close shut,—and nen she *kiss*
Her hand—shut ist like it is.

Nen we comed away. . . . And nen
When it's Chris'mus Eve again,
And all of us childerns be
At the Church and Chris'mus-Tree—

And all git toys and things
'At old Santy Claus he brings
And puts on the Tree;—wite where
The *big* Tree 'uz standin' there,

And the things 'uz all tooked down,
And the childerns, all in town,
Got their presents—nen we see
They's a *little* Chris'mus-Tree

Wite *behind* the *big* Tree—so
We can't see till *nen,* you know,—
And it's all ist loaded down
With the purtiest things in town!

And the teacher smile and say:
"This-here Tree 'at's hid away
It's marked *'Little Mandy's Tree.'*—
Little Mandy! Where is she?"

Nen nobody say a word.—
Stillest place you ever heard!—
Till a man tiptoe up where
Teacher's still a-waitin' there.

Nen the man he whispers, so
Ist the *Teacher* hears, you know.
Nen he tiptoe back and go
Out the big door—ist so slow!

.   .   .   .

Little Mandy, though, *she* don't
Answer—and Ma say "she won't
Never, though each year they'll be
'Little Mandy's Chris'mus-Tree'

Fer pore childern"—my Ma says—
·And *Committee* say they guess
"Little Mandy's Tree" 'ull be
Bigger than the *other* Tree!

THE FUNNIEST THING IN THE WORLD

THE funniest thing in the world, I know,
 Is watchin' the monkeys 'at's in the show!—
Jumpin' an' runnin an' racin' roun',
'Way up the top o' the pole; nen down!
First they're here, an' nen they're there,
An' ist a'most any an' ever'where!—
Screechin' an' scratchin' wherever they go,
They're the funniest thing in the world, I know!

They're the funniest thing in the world, I think:—
Funny to watch 'em eat an' drink;
Funny to watch 'em a-watchin' us,
An' actin' 'most like grown folks does!—
Funny to watch 'em p'tend to be
Skeered at their tail 'at they happen to see;—
But the funniest thing in the world they do
Is never to laugh, like me an' you!

THE BUMBLEBEE

YOU better not fool with a Bumblebee!—
Ef you don't think they can sting—you'll see!
They're lazy to look at, an' kind o' go
Buzzin' an' bummin' aroun' so slow,
An' ac' so slouchy an' all fagged out,
Danglin' their legs as they drone about
The hollyhawks 'at they can't climb in
'Ithout ist a-tumble-un out ag'in!
Wunst I watched one climb clean 'way
In a jimson-blossom, I did, one day,—
An' I ist grabbed it—an' nen let go—
An' *"Ooh-ooh! Honey! I told ye so!"*
Says The Raggedy Man; an' he ist run
An' pullt out the stinger, an' don't laugh none,
An' says: "They *has* be'n folks, I guess,
'At thought I wuz predjudust, more er less,—
Yit I still muntain 'at a Bumblebee
Wears out his welcome too quick fer me!"

A PROSPECTIVE GLIMPSE

JANEY PETTIBONE'S the best
  Little girl an' purtiest
In this town! an' lives next door,
Up-stairs over their old store.

Little Janey Pettibone
An' her Ma lives all alone,—
'Cause her Pa broke up, an' nen
Died 'cause they ain't rich again.

Little Janey's Ma she sews
Fer my Ma sometimes, an' goes
An' gives music-lessuns—where
People's got pianers there.

But when Janey Pettibone
Grows an' grows, like I'm a-growin',
Nen *I'm* go' to keep a store,
An' sell things—an' sell some more—

Till I'm ist as rich!—An' nen
Her Ma can be rich again,—
Ef *I'm* rich enough to own
Little Janey Pettibone!

THE OLD TRAMP

A'OLD Tramp slep' in our stable wunst,
  An' The Raggedy Man he caught
An' roust him up, an' chased him off
  Clean out through our back lot!

An' th' old Tramp hollered back an' said,—
  "You're a *purty* man!—*You* air!—
With a pair o' eyes like two fried eggs,
  An' a nose like a Bartlutt pear!"

THE PET COON

NOEY BIXLER ketched him, an' fetched him
    in to me
  When he's ist a little teenty-weenty baby-coon
'Bout as big as little pups, an' tied him to a tree;
    An' Pa gived Noey fifty cents, when he come
      home at noon.
Nen he buyed a chain fer him, an' little collar, too,
    An' sawed a hole in a' old tub an' turnt it upside
      down;
An' little feller'd stay in there and won't come out
    fer you—
    'Tendin' like he's kind o' skeered o' boys 'at lives
      in town.

Now he ain't afeard a bit! he's ist so fat an' tame,
    We on'y chain him up at night, to save the little
      chicks.
Holler "Greedy! Greedy!" to him, an' he knows his
    name,
    An' here he'll come a-waddle-un, up fer any
      tricks!
He'll climb up my leg, he will, an' waller in my lap,
    An' poke his little black paws 'way in my pockets
      where
They's beechnuts, er chinkypins, er any little scrap
    Of anything 'at's good to eat—an' *he* don't care!

An' he's as spunky as you please, an' don't like dogs
    at all.—
  Billy Miller's black-an'-tan tackled him one day,
An' "Greedy" he ist kind o' doubled all up like a
    ball,
  An' Billy's dog he gived a yelp er two an' runned
    away!
An' nen when Billy fighted me, an' hit me with a
    bone,
  An' Ma she purt' nigh ketched him as he dodged
    an' skooted through
The fence, she says, "You better let my little boy
    alone,
  Er 'Greedy,' next he whips yer dog, shall whip
    you, too!"

AN IMPETUOUS RESOLVE

WHEN little Dickie Swope's a man,
　　He's go' to be a Sailor;
An' little Hamey Tincher, he's
　　A-go' to be a Tailor:
Bud Mitchell, he's a-go' to be
　　A stylish Carriage-Maker;
An' when *I* grow a grea'-big man,
　　I'm go' to be a Baker!

An' Dick'll buy his sailor-suit
　　O' Hame; an' Hame'll take it
An' buy as fine a double-rig
　　As ever Bud kin make it:
An' nen all three'll drive roun' fer me,
　　An' we'll drive off togevver,
A-slingin' pie-crust 'long the road
　　Ferever an' ferever!

THE HUNTER BOY

HUNTER Boy of Hazelwood—
Happier than Robin Hood!
Dance across the green, and stand
Suddenly, with lifted hand
Shading eager eyes, and be
Thus content to capture me!—
Cease thy quest for wilder prey
Than my willing heart to-day!

Hunter Boy! with belt and bow,
Bide with me, or let me go,
An thou wilt, in wake of thee,
Questing for mine infancy!
With thy glad face in the sun,
Let thy laughter overrun
Thy ripe lips, until mine own
Answer, ringing, tone for tone!

O my Hunter! tilt the cup
Of thy silver bugle up,
And like wine pour out for me
All its limpid melody!

Pout thy happy lips and blare
Music's kisses everywhere—
Whiff o'er forest, field and town,
Tufts of tune like thistle-down!
    O to go, as once I could,
    Hunter Boy of Hazelwood!

BILLY GOODIN'

A big piece o' pie, and a big piece o' puddin'—
I laid it all by fer little Billy Goodin'!

—BOY POET

LOOK so neat an' sweet in all yer frills an' fancy
  pleatin'!
Better shet yer kitchen, though, afore you go to
  Meetin'!—
 Better hide yer mince-meat an' stewed fruit an'
  plums!
 Better hide yer pound-cake an' bresh away the
  crumbs!
 Better hide yer cubbord-key when Billy Goodin'
  comes,
    A-eatin'! an' a-eatin'! an' a-eatin'!

Sight o' Sund'y-doin's done 'at ain't done in
  Meetin'!
Sun acrost yer garden-patch a-pourin' an' a-beatin';

Meller apples drappin' in the weeds an' roun' the
   groun'—
Clingstones an' sugar-pears a-ist a-plunkin'
   down!—
Better kind o' comb the grass 'fore Billy comes
   aroun',
         A-eatin'! an' a-eatin'! an' a-eatin'!

Billy Goodin' ain't a-go' to go to any Meetin'!
We 'ull watch an' ketch an' give the little sneak a
   beatin'!—
Better hint *we* want'o stay 'n' snoop yer grapes
   an' plums!
Better eat 'em all yerse'f an' suck yer stingy
   thumbs!–
Won't be nothin' anyhow when Billy Goodin'
   comes!—
         A-eatin'! an' a-eatin'! an' a-eatin'!

SONG—FOR NOVEMBER

WHILE skies glint bright with bluest light
    Through clouds that race o'er field and
town,
And leaves go dancing left and right,
    And orchard apples tumble down;
While schoolgirls sweet, in lane or street,
    Lean 'gainst the wind and feel and hear
Its glad heart like a lover's beat,—
    So reigns the rapture of the year.

    Then ho! and hey! and whoop-hooray!
      Though winter clouds be looming,
    Remember a November day
    Is merrier than mildest May
      With all her blossoms blooming.

While birds in scattered flight are blown
    Aloft and lost in bosky mist,
And truant boys scud home alone
    'Neath skies of gold and amethyst;
While twilight falls, and echo calls
    Across the haunted atmosphere,
With low, sweet laughs at intervals,—
    So reigns the rapture of the year.

Then ho! and hey! and whoop-hooray!
  Though winter clouds be looming,
Remember a November day
Is merrier than mildest May
  With all her blossoms blooming.

AT AUNTY'S HOUSE

ONE time, when we'z at Aunty's house—
　　'Way in the country!—where
They's ist but woods—an' pigs, an' cows—
　　An' all's outdoors an' air!—
An' orchurd-swing; an' churry trees—
An' *churries* in 'em!—Yes, an' these-
Here redhead birds steals all they please,
　　An' tetch 'em ef you dare!—
W'y, wunst, one time, when we wuz there,
　　We et out on the porch!

Wite where the cellar door wuz shut
　　The table wuz; an' I
Let Aunty set by me an' cut
　　My vittuls up—an' pie.
'Tuz awful funny!—I could see
The redheads in the churry tree;
An' beehives, where you got to be
　　So keerful, goin' by;—
An' "Comp'ny" there an' all!—an' we—
　　We et out on the porch!

79

An' I ist et *p'surves* an' things
  'At Ma don't 'low me to—
An' *chickun-gizzurds*—(don't like *wings*
  Like *Parunts* does! do *you?*)
An' all the time the wind blowed there,
An' I could feel it in my hair,
An' ist smell clover *ever'*where!—
  An' a old redhead flew
Purt' nigh wite over my high-chair,
    When we et on the porch!

LIFE AT THE LAKE

THE green below and the blue above!—
The waves caressing the shores they love:
Sails in haven, and sails afar
And faint as the water-lilies are
In inlets haunted of willow wands,
Listless lovers, and trailing hands
With spray to gem them and tan to glove.—
The green below and the blue above.

The blue above and the green below!
Would that the world were always so!—
Always summer and warmth and light,
With mirth and melody day and night!
Birds in the boughs of the beckoning trees,
Chirr of locusts and whiff of breeze—
World-old roses that bud and blow.—
The blue above and the green below.

The green below and the blue above!
Heigh! young hearts and the hopes thereof!—
Kate in the hammock, and Tom sprawled on
The sward—like a lover's picture, drawn

By the lucky dog himself, with Kate
To moon o'er his shoulder and meditate
On a fat old purse or a lank young love.—
The green below and the blue above.

The blue above and the green below!
Shadow and sunshine to and fro.—
Season for dreams—whate'er befall
Hero, heroine, hearts and all!
Wave or wildwood—the blithe bird sings,
And the leaf-hid locust whets his wings—
Just as a thousand years ago—
The blue above and the green below.

JOHN BOYLE O'REILLY

SEPULTURE—BOSTON, AUGUST 13, 1890

DEAD? this peerless man of men—
Patriot, Poet, Citizen!—
  Dead? and ye weep where he lies
    Mute, with folded eyes!

Courage! All his tears are done;
Mark him, dauntless, face the sun!
  He hath led you.—Still, as true,
    He is leading you.

Folded eyes and folded hands
Typify divine commands
  He is hearkening to, intent
    Beyond wonderment.

'Tis promotion that has come
Thus upon him. Stricken dumb
  Be your moanings dolorous!
    God knows what He does.

83

Rather, as your chief, *aspire!*—
Rise and sieze his toppling lyre,
 And sing Freedom, Home and Love,
 And the rights thereof!

Ere in selfish grief ye sink,
Come! catch rapturous breath and think—
 Think what sweep of wing hath he,
 Loosed in endless liberty.

THE BOYS' CANDIDATE

LAS' time 'at Uncle Sidney come,
    He bringed a watermelon home—
An' half the boys in town
Come taggin' after him.—An' he
Says, when we et it,—*"Gracious me!*
    'S the boy-house fell down?"

CHRISTINE

Two strangers meeting at a festival;
Two lovers whispering by an orchard wall.
                                    —TENNYSON

MOST quaintly touching, in her German
            tongue—
  Haply, had he but mastered that as well
  As she his English, this were not to tell:—
Touring through her dear Fatherland, the young
American first found her, as she sung
  "Du bist mir nah' und doch so fern," while fell
  Their eyes together, and the miracle
Of love and doom was wrought. Her father wrung
The lovers from each other's arms forever—
  Forgive him, all forgiving souls that can!
    She died that selfsame hour—just paused to
            write
Her broken heart's confession thus: "I never
  Was O so loving in a young gentleman
    Than yet I am to you. So ist Good night."

OLD JOHN CLEVENGER ON BUCKEYES

OLD John Clevenger lets on,
    Allus, like he's purty rough
Timber.—He's a grate old John!—
    "Rough?"—don't swaller no sich stuff!
Moved here, sence the war was through,
    From Ohio—somers near
Old Bucyrus,—loyal, too,
    As us "Hoosiers" is to *here!*
Git old John stirred up a bit
    On his old home stompin'-ground—
Talks same as he lived thare yit,
    When some subject brings it round—
Like, fer instunce, Sund'y last,
    Fetched his wife, and et and stayed
All night with us.—Set and gassed
    Tel plum midnight—'cause I made
Some remark 'bout "buckeyes" and
    "What was buckeyes good fer?"—So,
Like I 'lowed, he waved his hand
    And lit in and let me know:—

" 'What is Buckeyes good fer?'—What's
Pineys and *fergit-me-nots?*—
Honeysuckles, and sweet peas,
And sweet-williamsuz, and these
Johnny-jump-ups ev'rywhare,
Growin' round the roots o' trees
In Spring-weather?—what air *they*
Good fer?—kin you tell me—*Hey?*
'Good to look at?' Well they air!
'Specially when *Winter's* gone,
Clean *dead-cert'in!* and the wood's
Green again, and sun feels good's
June!—and shed your blame boots on
The back porch, and lit out to
Roam round like you ust to do,
Bare-foot, up and down the crick,
Whare the buckeyes growed so thick,
And witch-hazel and pop-paws,
And hackberries and black-haws—
With wild pizen-vines jis knit
Over and *en-nunder* it,
And wove round it all, I jing!
Tel you couldn't hardly stick
A durn *case-knife* through the thing!
Wriggle round through *that;* and then—
All het-up, and scratched and tanned,
And muskeeter-bit and mean-
Feelin'—all at onc't again,
Come out suddent on a clean
Slopin' little hump o' green
Dry soft grass, as fine and grand

As a pollor-sofy!—And
Jis pile down thare!—and tell *me*
Anywhares you'd ruther be—
'Ceptin' *right thare,* with the wild-
Flowrs all round ye, and your eyes
Smilin' with 'em at the skies,
Happy as a little child!
Well!—right here, *I* want to say,
Poets kin talk all they please
'Bout 'wild-flowrs, in colors gay,'
And 'sweet blossoms flauntin' theyr
Beauteous fragrunce on the breeze'—
But the sight o' *buckeyes* jis
Sweet to me as *blossoms* is!

"I'm *Ohio-born*—right whare
People's *all* called 'Buckeyes' *thare*—
'Cause, I s'pose, our buckeye crap's
Biggest in the world, perhaps!—
Ner my head don't stretch my hat
Too much on account o' *that!*—
'Cause it's Natchur's ginerus hand
Sows 'em broadcast ore the land,
With eye-single fer man's good
And the gineral neghborhood!
So *buckeyes* jis natchurly
'Pears like *kith-and-kin* to *me!*
'S like the good old sayin' wuz,
'Purty *is* as purty *does!*'—
We can't *eat* 'em, cookd er raw—
Yit, I mind, *tomattusuz*

Wuz considerd pizenus
Onc't—and dasen't eat 'em!—*Pshaw*—
'Twouldn't take *me* by supprise,
Some day, ef we et *buckeyes!*
That, though, 's nuther here ner thare! —
Jis the Buckeye, whare we air,
In the present times, is what
Ockuppies my lovin' care
And my most perfoundest thought!
. . . Guess, this minute, what I got
In my pocket, 'at I've packed
Purt' nigh forty year.—A dry,
Slick and shiny, warped and cracked,
Wilted, weazened old *buckeye!*
What's it *thare* fer? What's my hart
In my *brest* fer?—'Cause it's part
Of my *life*—and 'tends to biz—
Like this *buckeye's* bound to act—
'Cause *it* 'tends to *Rhumatiz!*

". . . Ketched more *rhumatiz* than *fish,*
Seinen', onc't—and pants froze on
My blame legs!—And ust to wish
I wuz well er *dead and gone!*
Doc give up the case, and shod
His old hoss again and stayed
On good roads!—*And thare I laid!*
Pap he tuck some bluegrass sod
Steeped in whisky, bilin'-hot,
And socked *that* on! Then I got
Sorto' holt o' him, *somehow*—

Kindo' crazy-like, they say—
And I'd *killed* him, like as not,
Ef I hadn't swooned away!
Smell my scortcht pelt purt' nigh now!
Well—to make a long tale short—
I hung on the blame disease
Like a shavin'-hoss! and sort
O' wore it out by slow degrees—
Tel my legs wuz straight enugh
To poke through my pants again
And kick all the doctor-stuff
In the fi-er-place! Then turned in
And tuck Daddy Craig's old cuore—
Jis a buckeye—and that's *shore.*—
Hain't no case o' rhumatiz
Kin subsist whare buckeyes is!"

MEREDITH NICHOLSON

KEATS, and Kirk White, David Gray and the
   rest of you
  Heavened and blest of you young singers gone,—
Slender in sooth though the theme unexpressed of
   you,
  Leave us this like of you yet to sing on!
Let your Muse mother him and your souls brother
   him,
  Even as now, or in fancy, you do:
Still let him sing to us ever, and bring to us
  Musical musings of glory and—you.

Never a note to do evil or wrong to us—
  Beauty of melody—beauty of words,—
Sweet and yet strong to us comes his young song
   to us,
  Rippled along to us clear as the bird's.
No fame elating him falsely, nor sating him—
  Feasting and fêting him faint of her joys,
But singing on where the laurels are waiting him,
  Young yet in art, and his heart yet a boy's.

MY RUTHERS

[Writ durin' State Fair at Indanoplis, whilse visitin' a Soninlaw then residin' thare, who has sence got back to the country whare he says a man that's raised there ort to a-stayed in the first place.]

I TELL you what I'd ruther do—
  Ef I only had my ruthers,—
I'd ruther work when I wanted to
  Than be bossed round by others;—
    I'd ruther kindo' git the swing
    O' what was *needed,* first, I jing!
    Afore I *swet* at anything!—
  Ef I only had my ruthers;—
In fact I'd aim to be the same
  With all men as my brothers;
And they'd all be the same with *me*—
  Ef I only had my ruthers.

I wouldn't likely know it all—
  Ef I only had my ruthers;—
I'd know *some* sense, and some baseball—
  Some *old* jokes, and—some others:
    I'd know *some politics,* and 'low
    Some tarif-speeches same as now,
    Then go hear Nye on "Branes and How

To Detect Theyr Presence." *T'others*,
That stayed away, I'd *let* 'em stay—
　　All my dissentin' brothers
Could chuse as shore a kill er cuore,
　　Ef I only had my ruthers.

The pore 'ud git theyr dues *some*times—
　　Ef I only had my ruthers,—
And be paid *dollars* 'stid o' *dimes,*
　　Fer childern, wives and mothers:
　　　　Theyr boy that slaves; theyr girl that sews—
　　　　Fer *others*—not herself, God knows!—
　　　　The grave's *her* only change of clothes!
　　. . . Ef I only had my ruthers,
They'd all have "stuff" and time enugh
　　To answer one-another's
Appealin' prayer fer "lovin' care"—
　　Ef I only had my ruthers.

They'd be few folks 'ud ast fer trust,
　　Ef I only had my ruthers,
And blame few business men to bu'st
　　Theyrselves, er harts of others:
　　　　Big Guns that come here durin' Fair-
　　　　Week could put up jest anywhare,
　　　　And find a full-and-plenty thare,
　　Ef I only had my ruthers:
The rich and great 'ud 'sociate
　　With all theyr lowly brothers,
Feelin' *we* done the honorun—
　　Ef I only had my ruthers.

GOD'S MERCY

BEHOLD, one faith endureth still—
Let factions rail and creeds contend,
God's mercy *was,* and *is,* and *will*
Be with us, foe and friend.

THE WHITHERAWAYS

Set Sail October 15, 1890

THE Whitheraways!—That's what I'll have to
    call
You—sailing off, with never word at all
Of parting!—sailing 'way across the sea,
With never one good-by to *me*—to ME!

Sailing away from me, with no farewell!—
Ah, Parker Hitt and sister Muriel—
And Rodney, too, and little Laurance—all
Sailing away—just as the leaves, this Fall!

Well, then, *I* too shall sail on cheerily
As now you all go sailing o'er the sea:
I've *other* little friends with me on shore—
Though they but make me yearn for *you* the more!

And so, sometime, dear little friends afar,
When this faint voice shall reach you, and you are
All just a little homesick, you must be
As brave as I am now, and think of me!

Or, haply, if your eyes, as mine, droop low,
And would be humored with a tear or so,—
Go to your *Parents,* Children! let *them* do
The *crying*—'twill be easier for them to!

A BOY'S MOTHER

MY mother she's so good to me,
  Ef I was good as I could be,
I couldn't be as good—no, sir!—
Can't any boy be good as her!

She loves me when I'm glad er sad;
She loves me when I'm good er bad;
An', what's a funniest thing, she says
She loves me when she punishes.

I don't like her to punish me.—
That don't hurt,—but it hurts to see
Her cryin'.—Nen *I* cry; an' nen
We both cry an' be good again.

She loves me when she cuts an' sews
My little cloak an' Sund'y clothes;
An' when my Pa comes home to tea,
She loves him most as much as me.

She laughs an' tells him all I said,
An' grabs me up an' pats my head;
An' I hug *her,* an' hug my Pa
An' love him purt' nigh as much as Ma.

THE RUNAWAY BOY

WUNST I sassed my Pa, an' he
    Won't stand that, an' punished me,—
Nen when he wuz gone that day,
I slipped out an' runned away.

I tooked all my copper-cents,
An' clumbed over our back fence
In the jimpson-weeds 'at growed
Ever'where all down the road.

Nen I got out there, an' nen
I runned some—an' runned again,
When I met a man 'at led
A big cow 'at shooked her head.

I went down a long, long lane
Where wuz little pigs a-playin';
An' a grea'-big pig went *"Booh!"*
An' jumped up, an' skeered me too.

Nen I scampered past, an' they
Was somebody hollered *"Hey!"*
An' I ist looked ever'where,
An' they wuz nobody there.

I *want* to, but I'm 'fraid to try
To go back. . . . An' by an' by
Somepin' hurts my th'oat inside—
An' I want my Ma—an' cried.

Nen a grea'-big girl come through
Where's a gate, an' telled me who
Am I? an' ef I tell where
My home's at she'll show me there.

But I couldn't ist but tell
What's my *name;* an' she says "well,"
An' ist tooked me up an' says
"She know where I live, she guess."

Nen she telled me hug wite close
Round her neck!—an' off she goes
Skippin' up the street! An' nen
Purty soon I'm home again.

An' my Ma, when she kissed me,
Kissed the big girl too, an' *she*
Kissed me—ef I p'omise shore
I won't run away no more!

THE FISHING-PARTY

WUNST we went a-fishin'—Me
   An' my Pa an' Ma, all three,
When they wuz a picnic, 'way
Out to Hanch's Woods, one day.

An' they wuz a crick out there,
Where the fishes is, an' where
Little boys 'taint big an' strong
Better have their folks along!

My Pa he ist fished an' fished!
An' my Ma she said she wished
Me an' her was home; an' Pa
Said he wished so worse'n Ma.

Pa said ef you talk, er say
Anything, er sneeze, er play,
Hain't no fish, alive er dead,
Ever go' to bite! he said.

Purt' nigh dark in town when we
Got back home; an' Ma, says she,
Now she'll have a fish fer shore!
An' she buyed one at the store.

Nen at supper, Pa he won't
Eat no fish, an' says he don't
Like 'em.—An' he pounded me
When I choked! . . .Ma, didn't he?

THE RAGGEDY MAN

O THE Raggedy Man! He works fer Pa;
An' he's the goodest man ever you saw!
He comes to our house every day,
An' waters the horses, an' feeds 'em hay;
An' he opens the shed—an' we all ist laugh
When he drives out our little old wobble-ly calf;
An' nen—ef our hired girl says he can—
He milks the cow fer 'Lizabuth Ann.—
    Ain't he a' awful good Raggedy Man?
      Raggedy! Raggedy! Raggedy Man!

W'y, The Raggedy Man—he's ist so good,
He splits the kindlin' an' chops the wood;
An' nen he spades in our garden, too,
An' does most things 'at *boys* can't do.—
He clumbed clean up in our big tree
An' shooked a' apple down fer me—
An' 'nother 'n', too, fer 'Lizabuth Ann—
An' 'nother 'n', too, fer The Raggedy Man.—
    Ain't he a' awful kind Raggedy Man?
      Raggedy! Raggedy! Raggedy Man!

An' The Raggedy Man one time say he
Pick' roast' rambos from a' orchurd-tree,
An' et 'em—all ist roast' an' hot!—
An' it's so, too!—'cause a corn-crib got
Afire one time an' all burn' down
On "The Smoot Farm," 'bout four mile from
      town—
On "The Smoot Farm"! Yes—an' the hired han'
'At worked there nen 'uz The Raggedy Man!—
  Ain't he the beatin'est Raggedy Man?
    Raggedy! Raggedy! Raggedy Man!

The Raggedy Man's so good an' kind
He'll be our "horsey," an' "haw" an' mind
Ever'thing 'at you make him do—
An' won't run off—'less you want him to!
I drived him wunst way down our lane
An' he got skeered, when it 'menced to rain,
An' ist rared up an' squealed and run
Purt' nigh away!—an' it's all in fun!
Nen he skeered *ag'in* at a' old tin can . . .
  Whoa! y' old runaway Raggedy Man!
    Raggedy! Raggedy! Raggedy Man!

An' The Raggedy Man, he knows most rhymes,
An' tells 'em, ef I be good, sometimes:
Knows 'bout Giunts, an' Griffuns, an' Elves,
An' the Squidgicum-Squees 'at swallers the'rselves!
An', wite by the pump in our pasture-lot,
He showed me the hole 'at the Wunks is got,

'At lives 'way deep in the ground, an' can
Turn into me, er 'Lizabuth Ann!
Er Ma, er Pa, er The Raggedy Man!
  Ain't he a funny old Raggedy Man?
    Raggedy! Raggedy! Raggedy Man!

An' wunst, when The Raggedy Man come late,
An' pigs ist root' thue the garden-gate,
He 'tend like the pigs 'uz *bears* an' said,
"Old Bear-shooter'll shoot 'em dead!"
An' race' an' chase' 'em, an' they'd ist run
When he pint his hoe at 'em like it's a gun
An' go "Bang!—Bang!" nen 'tend he stan'
An' load up his gun ag'in! Raggedy Man!
  He's an old Bear-shooter Raggedy Man!
    Raggedy! Raggedy! Raggedy Man!

An' sometimes The Raggedy Man lets on
We're little *prince*-children, an' old King's gone
To git more money, an' lef' us there—
And *Robbers* is ist thick ever'where;
An' nen—ef we all won't cry, fer *shore*—
The Raggedy Man he'll come and "'splore
The Castul-halls," an' steal the "gold"—
An' steal *us,* too, an' grab an' hold
An' pack us off to his old "Cave"!—An'
  Haymow's the "cave" o' The Raggedy Man!—
    Raggedy! Raggedy! Raggedy Man!

The Raggedy Man—one time, when he
Wuz makin' a little bow-'n'-orry fer me,
Says "When you're big like your Pa is,
Air *you* go' to keep a fine store like his—
An' be a rich merchunt—an' wear fine clothes?—
Er what *air* you go' to be, goodness knows?"
An' nen he laughed at 'Lizabuth Ann,
An' I says "'M go' to be a Raggedy Man!—
   I'm ist go' to be a nice Raggedy Man!"
      Raggedy! Raggedy! Raggedy Man!

OUR HIRED GIRL

OUR hired girl, she's 'Lizabuth Ann;
   An' she can cook best things to eat!
She ist puts dough in our pie-pan,
   An' pours in somepin' 'at's good an' sweet;
An' nen she salts it all on top
With cinnamon; an' nen she'll stop
   An' stoop an' slide it, ist as slow,
In th' old cook-stove, so's 'twon't slop
   An' git all spilled; nen bakes it, so
     It's custard-pie, first thing you know!
       An' nen she'll say,
        "Clear out o' my way!
   They's time fer work, an' time fer play!
    Take yer dough, an' run, child, run!
    Er I cain't git no cookin' done!"

When our hired girl 'tends like she's mad,
   An' says folks got to walk the chalk
When *she's* around, er wisht they had!
   I play out on our porch an' talk
To Th' Raggedy Man 'at mows our lawn;
An' he says, *"Whew!"* an' nen leans on
   His old crook-scythe, and blinks his eyes,

An' sniffs all 'round an' says, "I swawn!
  Ef my old nose don't tell me lies,
  It 'pears like I smell custard-pies!"
       An' nen *he'll* say,
        "Clear out o' my way!
  They's time fer work, an' time fer play!
    Take yer dough, an' run, child, run!
    Er she cain't git no cookin' done!"

Wunst our hired girl, when she
  Got the supper, an' we all et,
An' it wuz night, an' Ma an' me
  An' Pa went wher' the "Social" met,—
An' nen when we come home, an' see
A light in the kitchen door, an' we
  Heerd a maccordeun, Pa says, "Lan'-
O'-Gracious! who can *her* beau be?"
    An' I marched in, an' 'Lizabuth Ann
    Wuz parchin' corn fer The Raggedy Man!
       Better say,
        "Clear out o' the way!
  They's time fer work, an' time fer play!
    Take the hint, an' run, child, run!
    Er we cain't git no courtin' done!"

THE BOY LIVES ON OUR FARM

THE Boy lives on our Farm, he's not
    Afeard o' horses none!
An' he can make 'em lope, er trot,
    Er rack, er pace, er run.
Sometimes he drives *two* horses, when
    He comes to town an' brings
A wagonful o' 'taters nen,
    An' roastin'-ears an' things.

Two horses is "a team," he says,—
    An' when you drive er hitch,
The *right* un's a "near horse," I guess,
    Er "off"—I don't know which.—
The Boy lives on our Farm, he told
    Me, too, 'at he can see,
By lookin' at their teeth, how old
    A horse is, to a T!

I'd be the gladdest boy alive
    Ef I knowed much as that,
An' could stand up like him an' drive,
    An' ist push back my hat,
Like he comes skallyhootin' through
    Our alley, with one arm
A-wavin' Fare-ye-well! to you—
    The Boy lives on our Farm!

SONG OF THE BULLET

IT whizzed and whistled along the blurred
   And red-blent ranks ; and it nicked the star
Of an epaulette, as it snarled the word—
                    War !

On it sped—and the lifted wrist
   Of the ensign-bearer stung, and straight
Dropped at his side as the word was hissed—
                    Hate !

On went the missile—smoothed the blue
   Of a jaunty cap and the curls thereof,
Cooing, soft as a dove might do—
                    Love !

Sang !—sang on !—sang hate—sang war—
   Sang love, in sooth, till it needs must cease,
Hushed in the heart it was questing for.—
                    Peace !

CHRISTMAS GREETING

A WORD of Godspeed and good cheer
To all on earth, or far or near,
Or friend or foe, or thine or mine—
In echo of the voice divine,
Heard when the star bloomed forth and lit
The world's face, with God's smile on it.

From an Early Photograph

UNCLE WILLIAM'S PICTURE

UNCLE WILLIAM, last July,
   Had his picture took.
"Have it done, of course," says I,
   "Jes' the way you look!"
(All dressed up, he was, fer the
Barbecue and jubilee
The old settlers helt.)   So he—
   Last he had it took.

Lide she'd coaxed and begged and pled,
   Sence her mother went;
But he'd cough and shake his head
   At all argyment;
Mebby clear his th'oat and say,
"What's *my* likeness 'mount to, hey,
Now with *Mother* gone away
   From us, like she went?"

But we projicked round, tel we
   Got it figgered down
How we'd git him, Lide and me,
   Drivin' into town;

Bragged how well he looked and fleshed
Up around the face, and freshed
With the morning air; and breshed
    His coat-collar down.

All so providential! W'y,
    Now he's dead and gone,
Picture 'pears so lifelike I
    Want to start him on
Them old tales he ust to tell,
And old talks so sociable,
And old songs he sung so well—
    'Fore his voice was gone!

Face is sad to *Lide,* and they's
    Sorrow in the eyes—
Kisses it sometimes, and lays
    It away and cries.
I smooth down her hair, and 'low
He is happy, anyhow,
Bein' there with Mother now,—
    Smile, and wipe my eyes.

ERASMUS WILSON

'RAS WILSON, I respect you, 'cause
    You're common, like you allus was
Afore you went to town and s'prised
The world by gittin' "reckonized,"
And yit perservin', as I say,
Your common hoss-sense ev'ryway!
And when that name o' yourn occurs
On hand-bills, er in newspapers,
Er letters writ by friends 'at ast
About you, same as in the past,
And neghbors and relations 'low
You're out o' the tall timber now,
And "gittin' thare" about as spry's
The next!—as *I say*, when my eyes,
Er ears, lights on your name, I mind
The first time 'at I come to find
You—and my Rickollection yells,
Jest jubilunt as old sleigh-bells—
"'Ras Wilson! Say! Hold up! and shake
A paw, fer old acquaintance sake!"

My *Rickollection,* more'n like,
Hain't overly too apt to strike
The what's-called "cultchurd public eye"
As wisdum of the deepest dye,—
And yit my *Rickollection* makes
So blame lots fewer bad mistakes,
Regardin' human-natur' and
The fellers 'at I've shook theyr hand,
Than my *best jedgemunt's* done, the day
I've met 'em—'fore I got away,—
'At—Well, 'Ras Wilson, let me grip
Your hand in warmest pardnership!

Dad-burn ye!—Like to jest haul back
A' old flat-hander, jest che-whack!
And take you 'twixt the shoulders, say,
Sometime you're lookin' t'other way!—
Er, maybe whilse you're speakin' to
A whole blame Court-house-full o' 'thu-
Syastic friends, I'd like to jest
Come in-like and break up the nest
Afore you hatched another cheer,
And say: "'Ras, *I* can't stand hitched here
All night—ner wouldn't ef I could!—
But Little Bethel Neghborhood,
You ust to live at, 's sent some word
Fer you, ef ary chance occurred
To git it to ye,—so ef you
Kin stop, I'm waitin' fer ye to!"

You're common, as I said afore—
You're common, yit oncommon *more.*—
You allus kindo' 'pear, to me,
What all mankind had ort to be—
Jest *natchurl,* and the more hurraws
You git, the less you know the cause—
Like as ef God Hisse'f stood by,
Where best on earth hain't half knee-high,
And *seein'* like, and knowin' *He*
'S the Only Grate Man really,
You're jest content to size your hight
With any feller man's in sight.—
And even then they's scrubs, like me,
Feels stuck-up, in your company!

Like now :—I want to go with you
Plum out o' town a mile er two
Clean past the Fair-ground whare's some
    hint
O' pennyrile er peppermint,
And bottom-lands, and timber thick
Enugh to sorto' shade the crick!
I want to *see* you—want to set
Down somers, whare the grass hain't wet,
And kindo' *breathe* you, like puore air—
And taste o' your tobacker thare,
And talk and chaw! Talk o' the birds
We've knocked with cross-bows.—After-
    wards
Drop, mayby, into some dispute
'Bout "pomgrannies," er cal'mus-root—

And how *they* growed, and *whare?*—on tree
Er vine?—Who's best boy-memory!—
And wasn't it *gingsang,* insted
O' cal'mus-root, growed like you said?—
Er how to tell a coon-track from
A mussrat's;—er how milksick come—
Er ef *cows* brung it?—Er why now
We never see no "muley"-cow—
Ner "frizzly"-chicken—ner no "clay-
Bank" mare—ner nothin' thataway!—
And what's come o' the *yeller*-core
Old wortermelons?—hain't no more.—
Tomattusus, the same—all *red*-
Uns nowadays—All past joys fled—
Each and all jest gone k-whizz!
Like our days o' childhood is!

Dag-gone it, 'Ras! they hain't no friend,
It 'pears-like, left to comperhend
Sich things as these but you, and see
How dratted sweet they air to me!
But you, 'at's loved 'em allus, and
Kin sort 'em out and understand
'Em, same as the fine books you've read,
And all fine thoughts you've writ, er said,
Er worked out, through long nights o' rain,
And doubts and fears, and hopes, again,
As bright as morning when she broke,—
You know a tear-drop from a joke!
  And so, 'Ras Wilson, stop and shake
  A paw, fer old acquaintance sake!

BACK FROM TOWN

OLD friends allus is the best,
  Halest-like and heartiest:
Knowed us first, and don't allow
We're so blame much better now!
They was standin' at the bars
When we grabbed "the kivvered kyars"
And lit out fer town, to make
Money—and that old mistake!

We thought then the world we went
Into beat "The Settlement,"
And the friends 'at we'd make there
Would beat any anywhere!—
And they *do*—fer that's their biz:
They beat all the friends they is—
'Cept the raal old friends like you
'At staid at home, like *I'd* ort to!

W'y, of all the good things yit
I ain't shet of, is to quit
Business, and git back to sheer
These old comforts waitin' here—

These old friends; and these old hands
'At a feller understands;
These old winter nights, and old
Young-folks chased in out the cold!

Sing "Hard Times'll come ag'in
No More!" and neighbers all jine in!
Here's a feller come from town
Wants that-air old fiddle down
From the chimbly!—Git the floor
Cleared fer one cowtillion more!—
It's poke the kitchen fire, says he,
And shake a friendly leg with me!

TUGG MARTIN

I

TUGG MARTIN'S tough.—No doubt o' that!
    And down there at
The camp he come from word's bin sent
Advisin' this-here Settle-ment
  To kind o' *humor* Tugg, and not
      To git him hot.—
Jest pass his imperfections by,
And he's as good as pie!

II

They claim he's *wanted* back there.—Yit
The officers they mostly quit
    Insistin' when
They notice Tugg's so *back'ard,* and
Sort o' gives 'em to understand
  He'd ruther not!—A Deputy
  (The slickest one you ever see!)
Tackled him *last*—"disguisin' then,"
As Tugg says, "as *a gentleman*"!—
  You'd ort 'o hear *Tugg* tell it—*My!*
    I thought I'd *die!*

119

III

The way it wuz :—Tugg and the rest
        The boys wuz jest
A-kind o' gittin' thawed out, down
At "Guss's Place," fur-end o' town,
    One night,—when, first we knowed,
            Some feller rode
Up in a buggy at the door,
    And hollered fer some one to come
            And fetch him some
Red-licker out—And whirped and swore
That colt he drove wuz *"Thompson's"*—shore !

IV

Guss went out, and come in ag'in
    And filled a pint and tuk it out—
Stayed quite a spell—then peeked back in,
    Half-hid-like where the light wuz dim,
            And jieuked his head
            At Tugg and said,—
"Come out a minute—here's a gent
    Wants you to take a drink with him."

V

Well—Tugg laid down his cards and went—
        In fact, *we all*
            Got up, you know,
            Startin' to go—

When in reels Guss ag'inst the wall,
  As white as snow,
Gaspin',—*"He's tuk Tugg!—Wher' 's my gun?"*
 And-sir, outside we heerd
The hoss snort and kick up his heels
 Like he wuz skeerd,
And then the buggy-wheels
Scrape—and then *Tugg's* voice hollerun,—
  "I'm bested!—Good-by, fellers!" . . . 'Peared
   S' all-fired suddent,
   Nobody couldn't
Jest git it fixed,—tel hoss and man,
 Buggy and Tugg, off through the dark
Went like the devil beatin' tan-
   Bark!

VI

What *could* we do? . . . We filed back to
 The bar: And Guss jest *looked* at us,
And we looked back "The same as you,"
 Still *sayin'* nothin'—And the sap
  It stood in every eye,
And every hat and cap
Went off, as we teched glasses solemnly,
  And Guss says-he:
"Ef it's 'good-by' with Tugg, fer *shore,*—I say
 God bless him!—Er ef they
 Ain't railly no *need* to pray,
I'm not *reniggin'*—board's the play,
And here's God bless him, anyway!"

VII

It must 'a' bin an hour er so
   We all set there,
 Talkin' o' pore
   Old Tugg, you know,
 'At never wuz ketched up before,—
 When—all slow-like—the door-
Knob turned—and Tugg come shamblin' in
Handcuffed!—'at's what he wuz, I swear!—
   Yit smilin', like he hadn't bin
Away at all! And when we ast him where
The *Deputy* wuz at,—"I don't know *where,*"
   Tugg said,—
    "All *I* know is—he's dead."

TO RUDYARD KIPLING

TO do some worthy deed of charity
  In secret and then have it found out by
Sheer accident, held gentle Elia—
  That—that was the best thing beneath the sky!
Confirmed in part, yet somewhat differing—
  (Grant that his gracious wraith will pardon me
If impious!)—I think a better thing
  Is: being found out when one strives to be.

So, Poet and Romancer—old as young,
  And wise as artless—masterful as mild,—
If there be sweet in any song I've sung,
  'Twas savored for thy palate, O my Child!
For thee the lisping of the children all—
  For thee the youthful voices of old years—
For thee all chords untamed or musical—
  For thee the laughter, and for thee the tears.

And thus, borne to me o'er the seas between
  Thy land and mine, thy Song of certain wing
Circles above me in the "pure serene"
  Of our high heaven's vast o'er-welcoming;

While, packeted with joy and thankfulness,
    And fair hopes many as the stars that shine,
And bearing all love's loyal messages,
    Mine own goes homing back to thee and thine.

DECORATION DAY ON THE PLACE

IT'S lonesome—sorto' lonesome,—it's a *Sund'y-*
    day, to me,
It 'pears-like—more'n any day I nearly ever see!—
Yit, with the Stars and Stripes above, a-flutterin' in
    the air,
On ev'ry Soldier's grave I'd love to lay a lily thare.

They say, though, Decoration Days is giner'ly
    observed
'Most *ev'rywheres*—espeshally by soldier-boys
    that's served.—
But me and Mother's never went—we seldom git
    away,—
In p'int o' fact, we're *allus* home on *Decoration
Day.*

They say the old boys marches through the streets
    in colum's grand,
A-follerin' the old war-tunes they're playin' on the
    band—
And citizuns all jinin' in—and little childern, too—
All marchin', under shelter of the old Red White
    and Blue.—

With roses! roses! roses!—ev'rybody in the
    town!—
And crowds o' little girls in white, jest fairly loaded
    down!—

Oh! don't THE BOYS know it, from theyr camp
    acrost the hill?—
Don't they see theyr com'ards comin' and the old
    flag wavin' still?

Oh! can't they hear the bugul and the rattle of the
    drum?—
Ain't they no way under heavens they can rickollect
    us some?
Ain't they no way we can coax 'em, through the
    roses, jest to say
They know that ev'ry day on earth's theyr Decora-
    tion Day?

We've tried that—me and Mother,—whare Elias
    takes his rest,
In the orchurd—in his uniform, and hands acrost
    his brest,
And the flag he died fer, smilin' and a-ripplin' in the
    breeze
Above his grave—and over that,—*the robin in the
    trees!*

And *yit* it's lonesome—lonesome!—It's a *Sund'y-
    day,* to *me,*
It 'pears-like—more'n any day I nearly ever see!—
Still, with the Stars and Stripes above, a-flutterin'
    in the air,
On ev'ry soldier's grave I'd love to lay a lily thare.

TOWN AND COUNTRY

THEY'S a predjudice allus 'twixt country and
    town
  Which I wisht in my hart wasent so.
You take *city* people, jest square up and down,
  And they're mighty good people to know:
And whare's better people a-livin', to-day,
  Than us in the *country?*—Yit good
As both of us is, we're divorsed, you might say,
  And won't compermise when we could!

Now as nigh into town fer yer Pap, ef you please,
  Is what's called the sooburbs.—Fer thare
You'll at least ketch a whiff of the breeze and a sniff
  Of the breth of wild-flowrs ev'rywhare.
They's room fer the childern to play, and grow,
    too—
  And to roll in the grass, er to climb
Up a tree and rob nests, like they *ortent* to do,
  But they'll do *anyhow* ev'ry time!

My Son-in-law said, when he lived in the town,
  He jest natchurly pined, night and day,
Fer a sight of the woods, er a acre of ground
  Whare the trees wasent all cleared away!

127

And he says to me onc't, whilse a-visitin' us
    On the farm, "It's not strange, I declare,
That we can't coax you folks, without raisin' a fuss,
    To come to town, visitin' thare!"

And says I, "Then git back whare you sorto'
        belong—
    And *Madaline,* too,—and yer three
Little childern," says I, "that don't know a bird-
        song,
    Ner a hawk from a chicky-dee-dee!
Git back," I-says-I, "to the blue of the sky
    And the green of the fields, and the shine
Of the sun, with a laugh in yer voice and yer eye
    As harty as Mother's and mine!"

Well—long-and-short of it,—he's compermised
        some—
    He's moved in the sooburbs.—And now
They don't haf to coax, when they want us to come,
    'Cause we turn in and go *anyhow!*
Fer thare—well, they's room fer the songs and
        purfume
    Of the grove and the old orchurd-ground,
And they's room fer the childern out thare, and
        they's room
    Fer theyr Gran'pap to waller 'em round!

THE FIRST BLUEBIRD

JEST rain and snow! and rain again!
   And dribble! drip! and blow!
Then snow! and thaw! and slush! and then—
   Some more rain and snow!

This morning I was 'most afeard
   To *wake* up—when, I jing!
I seen the sun shine out and heerd
   The first bluebird of Spring!—
Mother she'd raised the winder some;—
And in acrost the orchurd come,
   Soft as a' angel's wing,
A breezy, treesy, beesy hum,
   Too sweet for anything!

The winter's shroud was rent apart—
   The sun bu'st forth in glee,—
And when *that bluebird* sung, my hart
   Hopped out o' bed with me!

LINES TO
PERFESSER JOHN CLARK RIDPATH
A. M., LL. D. T-Y-TY

*[Cumposed by A Old Friend of the Fambily
sence 'way back in the Forties, when they Settled
nigh Fillmore, Putnam County, this State, whare
John was borned and growed up, you might say, like
the wayside flower.]*

YOUR neghbors in the country, whare you come
 from, hain't fergot!—
We knowed you even better than your own-self, like
 as not.
We profissied your runnin'-geers 'ud stand a soggy
 load
And pull her, purty stiddy, up a mighty rocky road:
We been a-watchin' your career sence you could
 write your name—
But way you writ it *first,* I'll say, was jest a burnin'
 shame!—
Your "J. C." in the copy-book, and "Ridpath"—
 mercy-sakes!—

130

Quiled up and tide in dubble bows, lookt like a nest
　　o' snakes!—
　　But *you* could read it, I *suppose,* and kindo'
　　　　gloted on
　　A-bein' *"J. C. Ridpath"* when *we* only called you
　　　　"John."

But you'd work's well as fool, and what you had to
　　do was *done:*
We've watched you at the wood-pile—not the
　　wood-shed—wasent none,—
And snow and sleet, and haulin', too, and lookin'
　　after stock,
And milkin', nights, and feedin' pigs,—then turnin'
　　back the clock,
So's you could set up studyin' your 'Rethmatic, and
　　fool
Your Parents, whilse a-piratin' your way through
　　winter school!
And I've heerd tell—from your own folks—you've
　　set and baked your face
A-readin' Plutark Slives all night by that old fi-er-
　　place.—
　　Yit, 'bout them times, the blackboard, onc't, had
　　　　on it, I *de*-clare,
　　"Yours truly, *J. Clark* Ridpath."—And the
　　　　teacher—left it thare!

And they was other symptums, too, that pinted,
    plane as day,
To nothin' short of *College!*—and *one* was the
    lovin' way
Your mother had of cheerin' you to efforts brave
    and strong,
And puttin' more faith in you, as you needed it
    along:
She'd pat you on the shoulder, er she'd grab you by
    the hands,
And *laugh* sometimes, er *cry* sometimes.—They's
    few that understands
Jest *what* theyr mother's drivin at when they act
    thataway;—
But I'll say this fer *you,* John-Clark,—you
    answered, night and day,
    To ev'ry trust and hope of hers—and half your
      College fame
    Was battled fer and won fer her and glory of her
      name.

The likes of *you* at *College!* But you went thare.
    How you paid
Your way nobody's astin'—but you *worked,*—you
    hain't afraid,—
Your *clothes* was, more'n likely, kindo' out o' style,
    perhaps,
And not as snug and warm as some 'at hid the other
    chaps;—

But when it come to *Intullect*—they tell me yourn
 was dressed
A *leetle* mite *superber*-like than any of the rest!
And thare you *stayed*—and thare you've made your
 rickord, fare and square—
Tel *now* it's *Fame* 'at writes your name, approvin',
 ev'rywhare—
 Not *jibblets* of it, nuther,—but all John Clark
  Ridpath, set
 Plum at the dashboard of the whole-endurin'
  Alfabet!

ELIZABETH

MAY I, 1891

I

ELIZABETH! Elizabeth!
The first May-morning whispereth
Thy gentle name in every breeze
That lispeth through the young-leaved trees,
New raimented in white and green
Of bloom and leaf to crown thee queen;—
And, as in odorous chorus, all
The orchard-blossoms sweetly call
Even as a singing voice that saith,
    Elizabeth! Elizabeth!

II

Elizabeth! Lo, lily-fair,
In deep, cool shadows of thy hair,
Thy face maintaineth its repose.—
Is it, O sister of the rose,
So better, sweeter, blooming thus

134

Than in this briery world with us?—
　Where frost o'ertaketh, and the breath
　Of biting winter harrieth
With sleeted rains and blighting snows
　All fairest blooms—Elizabeth!

III

Nay, then!—So reign, Elizabeth,
Crowned, in thy May-day realm of death!
Put forth the scepter of thy love
In every star-tipped blossom of
The grassy dais of thy throne!
Sadder are we, thus left alone,
But gladder they that thrill to see
Thy mother's rapture, greeting thee.
　Bereaved are we by life—not death—
　　Elizabeth! Elizabeth!

SONGS OF A LIFE-TIME

MRS. SARAH T. BOLTON'S POEMS

SONGS of a Life-Time—with the Singer's head
   A silvery glory shining midst the green
Of laurel-leaves that bind a brow serene.
And godlike as was ever garlanded.—
So seems *her* glory who herein has wed
   Melodious Beauty to the strong of mien
   And kingly Speech—made kinglier by this queen
In lilied cadence voiced and raimented.
Songs of a Life-Time: by your own sweet stress
   Of singing were ye loved of bygone years—
      As through our day ye are, and shall be hence,
Till *fame divine* marks your melodiousness
   And on the Singer's lips, with smiles and tears,
      Seals there the kiss of love and reverence.

136

AN OLD MAN'S MEMORY

THE delights of our childhood is soon passed
    away,
  And our gloryus youth it departs,—
And yit, dead and burried, they's blossoms of May
  Ore theyr medderland graves in our harts.
So, friends of my barefooted days on the farm,
  Whether truant in city er not,
God prosper you same as He's prosperin' me,
  Whilse your past hain't despised er fergot.

Oh! they's nothin', at morn, that's as grand unto me
  As the glorys of Natchur so fare,—
With the Spring in the breeze, and the bloom in the
    trees,
  And the hum of the bees ev'rywhare!
The green in the woods, and the birds in the boughs,
  And the dew spangled over the fields;
And the bah of the sheep and the bawl of the cows
  And the call from the house to your meals!

Then ho! fer your brekfast! and ho! fer the toil
  That waiteth alike man and beast!
Oh! it's soon with my team I'll be turnin' up soil,
  Whilse the sun shoulders up in the East

Ore the tops of the ellums and beeches and oaks,
　To smile his Godspeed on the plow,
And the furry and seed, and the Man in his need,
　And the joy of the swet of his brow!

US FARMERS IN THE COUNTRY

US farmers in the country, as the seasons go
    and come,
Is purty much like other folks,—we're apt to
    grumble some!
The Spring's too back'ard fer us, er too for'ard—
    ary one—
We'll jaw about it anyhow, and have our way er
    none!
The thaw's set in too suddent; er the frost's stayed
    in the soil
Too long to give the wheat a chance, and crops is
    bound to spoil!
The weather's eether most too mild, er too out-
    rageous rough,
And altogether too much rain, er not half rain
    enugh!

Now what I'd like and what you'd like is plane
    enugh to see:
It's jest to have old Providence drop round on you
    and me
And ast us what our views is first, regardin' shine er
    rain,
And post 'em when to shet her off, er let her on
    again!

And yit I'd ruther, after all—consider'n' other
    chores
I' got on hands, a-tendin' both to my affares and
    yours—
I'd ruther miss the blame I'd git, a-rulin' things up
    thare,
And spend my extry time in praise and gratitude
    and prayer.

ON A DEAD BABE

FLY away! thou heavenly one!—
    I do hail thee on thy flight!
Sorrow? thou hath tasted none—
    Perfect joy is yourn by right.
        Fly away! and bear our love
        To thy kith and kin above!

I can tetch thy finger-tips
    Ca'mly, and bresh back the hair
From thy forr'ed with my lips,
    And not leave a tear-drop thare.—
        Weep fer *Tomps and Ruth*—and
            me—
        But I can not weep fer *thee*.

"MYLO JONES'S WIFE"

"MYLO JONES'S wife" was all
  I heerd, mighty near, last Fall—
Visitun relations down
T'other side of Morgantown!
Mylo Jones's wife she does
This and that, and "those" and "thus"!—
Can't bide babies in her sight—
Ner no childern, day and night,
Whoopin' round the premises—
Ner no nothin' else, I guess!

Mylo Jones's wife she 'lows
She's the boss of her own house!—
Mylo—consequences is—
Stays whare things seem *some* like *his,*—
Uses, mostly, with the stock—
Coaxin' "Old Kate" not to balk,
Ner kick hoss-flies' branes out, ner
Act, I s'pose, so much like *her!*
Yit the wimern-folks tells you
She's *perfection.*—Yes they do!

Mylo's wife she says she's found
Home hain't home with *men-folks* round
When they's work like *hern* to do—

Picklin' pears and *butcher'n'*, too,
And a-render'n' lard, and then
Cookin' fer a pack o' men
To come trackin' up the flore
She's scrubbed *tel* she'll scrub no *more!*—
Yit she'd keep things clean ef they
Made her scrub tel Jedgmunt Day!

Mylo Jones's wife she sews
Carpet-rags and patches clothes
Jest year *in* and *out!*—and yit
Whare's the livin' use of it?
She asts Mylo that.—And he
Gits back whare he'd ruther be,
With his team;—jest *plows*—and don't
Never sware—like some folks won't!
Think ef *he'd cut loose,* I gum!
'D he'p his heavenly chances some!

Mylo's wife don't see no use,
Ner no reason ner excuse
Fer his pore relations to
Hang round like they allus do!
Thare 'bout onc't a year—and *she*—
She jest *ga'nts* 'em, folks tells me,
On spiced pears!—Pass Mylo one,
He says "No, he don't chuse none!"
Workin' men like Mylo they
'D ort to have *meat* ev'ry day!

Dad-burn Mylo Jones's wife!
Ruther rake a blame case-knife
'Crost my wizzen than to see
Sich a womern rulin' *me!*—
Ruther take and turn in and
Raise a fool mule-colt by hand!
Mylo, though—od-rot the man!—
Jest keeps ca'm—like some folks *can*—
And 'lows such as her, I s'pose,
Is *Man's he'pmeet!*—Mercy knows!

A PEN-PICTUR' OF A CERT'IN FRIVVOLUS
OLD MAN

MOST ontimely old man yit!
　　'Pear-like sometimes he jest *tries*
His fool-self, and takes the bitt
　　In his teeth and jest de-fies
All perpryties!—Lay and swet
　　Doin' *nothin'*—only jest
Sorto' speckillatun on
Whare old summer-times is gone,
　　And 'bout things that he loved best
When a youngster! Heerd him say
Spring-times made him thataway—
　　Speshully on *Sund'ys*—when
　　Sun shines out and in again,
And the lonesome old hens they
　　Git off under the old kern-
　　Bushes, and in deep concern
Talk-like to theyrselves, and scratch
　　Kindo' absunt-minded, jest
Like theyr thoughts was fur away
In some neghbor's gyarden-patch
　　Folks has tended keerfullest!
Heerd the old man dwell on these
　　Idys time and time again!—
Heerd him claim that orchurd-trees
　　Bloomin', put the mischief in

His old hart sometimes that bad
And owdacious that he "*had*
   To break loose *some*way," says he,
   "Ornry as I ust to be!"

Heerd him say one time—when I
Was a sorto' standin' by,
   And the air so still and clear,
   Heerd the bell fer church clean here!—
Said: "Ef I could climb and set
   On the old three-cornerd rail
Old home-place, nigh Maryette',
   Swap my soul off, hide and tale!"
And-sir! blame ef tear and laugh
Didn't ketch him half and half!
   "Oh!" he says, "to wake and be
Barefoot, in the airly dawn
   In the pastur'!—thare," says he,
"Standin' whare the cow's slep' on
   The cold, dewy grass that's got
   Print of her jest steamy hot
Fer to warm a feller's heels
In a while!—How good it feels!
   Sund'y!—Country!—Morning!—Hear
Nothin' but the *silunce*—see
   Nothin' but green woods and clear
Skies and unwrit poetry
By the acre! . . . Oh!" says he,
   "What's this voice of mine?—to seek
   To speak out, and yit *can't* speak!

"Think!—the lazyest of days"—
  Takin' his contrairyest leap,
  He went on,—"git up, er sleep—
Er whilse feedin', watch the haze
  Dancin' crost the wheat,—and keep
My pipe goin' laisurely—
Puff and whiff as pleases me,—
  Er I'll leave a trail of smoke
Through *the house!*—no one'll say
'Throw that nasty thing away!'
  'Pear-like nothin' sacerd's broke,
Goin' barefoot ef I chuse!—

  I *have fiddled;*—and dug bait
And *went fishin';*—pitched hoss-shoes—
Whare they couldn't see us from
The main road.—And I've *beat* some.

  I've set round and had my joke
With the thrashers at the barn—
And I've swapped 'em yarn fer yarn!—
  Er I've he'pped the childern poke
Fer hens'-nests—agged on a match
'Twixt the boys, to watch 'em scratch
  And paw round and rip and tare,
  And bu'st buttons and pull hair
To theyr rompin' harts' content—
  And me jest a-settin' thare
Hatchin' out more devilment!

  "What you s'pose now ort to be
Done with sich a man?" says he—
  "Sich a fool-old-man as me!"

THOUGHTS ON A PORE JOKE

I LIKE fun—and I like jokes
'Bout as well as most o' folks!—
Like my joke, and like my fun;—
But a joke, I'll state right here,
'S got some p'int—er I don't keer
Fer no joke that hain't got none.—
I hain't got no use, I'll say,
Fer a *pore* joke, anyway!

F'r instunce, now, when *some* folks gits
To relyin' on theyr wits,
Ten to one they git too smart
And *spile* it all, right at the start!
Feller wants to jest go slow
And do his *thinkin'* first, you know.
'F I can't think up somepin' good,
I set still and chaw my cood!
'F you *think* nothin'—jest keep on,
But don't *say* it—er you're gone!

EVAGENE BAKER

Who Was Dyin' of Dred Consumtion as These
Lines Was Penned by a True Friend

PORE afflicted Evagene!
  Whilse the woods is fresh and green,
And the birds on ev'ry hand
Sings in rapture sweet and grand,—
Thou, of all the joyus train,
Art bedridden, and in pain
  Sich as only them can cherish
  Who, like flowrs, is first to perish!

When the neghbors brought the word
She was down, the folks inferred
It was jest a cold she'd caught,
Dressin' thinner than she'd ort
Fer the frolicks and the fun
Of the dancin' that she'd done
  'Fore the Spring was flush er ary
  Blossom on the peach er cherry.

But, last Sund'y, her request
Fer the Church's prayers was jest
Rail hart-renderin' to hear!—
Many was the silunt tear

And the tremblin' sigh, to show
She was dear to us below
   On this earth—and *dearer,* even,
   When we thought of her a-leavin'!

Sisters prayed, and coted from
Genesis to Kingdom-come
Provin' of her title clear
To the mansions.—"Even *her,*"
They claimed, "might be saved, *someway,*
Though she'd danced, and played crowkay,
   And wrought on her folks to git her
   Fancy shoes that never fit her!"

Us to pray fer *Evagene!*—
With her hart as puore and clean
As a rose is after rain
When the sun comes out again!—
What's the use to pray fer *her?*
She don't need no prayin' fer!—
   Needed, all her life, more *playin'*
   Than she ever needed prayin'!

I jest thought of all she'd been
Sence her *mother* died, and when
She turned in and done *her* part—
All *her* cares on that child-hart!—
Thought of years she'd slaved—and had
Saved the farm—danced and was glad . . .
   Mayby Him who marks the sporry
   Will smooth down her wings to-morry!

ON ANY ORDENARY MAN IN A HIGH
STATE OF LAUGHTURE AND DELIGHT

AS it's give' me to perceive,
I most cert'in'y believe
When a man's jest glad plum through,
God's pleased with him, same as you.

THE HOODOO

OWNED a pair o' skates onc't.—Traded
   Fer 'em,—stropped 'em on and waded
Up and down the crick, a-waitin'
Tel she'd freeze up fit fer skatin'.
Mildest winter I remember—
   More like Spring- than Winter-weather!—
Didn't *frost* tel 'bout December—
   Git up airly, ketch a feather
Of it, mayby, 'crost the winder—
Sunshine swinge it like a cinder!

Well—I *waited*—and *kep'* waitin'!
   Couldn't see my money's wo'th in
Them-air skates, and was no skatin'
   Ner no hint o' ice ner nothin'!
So, one day—along in airly
Spring—I swapped 'em off—and barely
Closed the dicker, 'fore the weather
   Natchurly jes' slipped the ratchet,
And crick—tail-race—all together,
   Froze so tight, cat couldn't scratch it!

CUORED O' SKEERIN'

'LISH, you rickollect that-air
    Dad-burn skittish old bay mare
Was no livin' with!—'at skeerd
'T ever'thing she seed er heerd!—
Th'owed 'Ves' Anders, and th'owed Pap,
First he straddled her—*k-slap!*—
And Izory—well!—th'owed *her*
Hain't no tellin' jest how fur!—
Broke her collar-bone—and might
Jest 'a' kilt the gyrl outright!

Course I'd heerd 'em make their boast
She th'ow any feller, 'most,
Ever topped her! S' I, "I know
One man 'at she'll never th'ow!"
So I rid her in to mill,
And, jest comin' round the hill,
Met a *traction-engine!*—Ort
Jest 'a' heerd that old mare snort,
And lay back her yeers, and see
Her a-tryin' to th'ow *me!*
Course I never said a word,
But thinks I, "My ladybird,
You'll git cuored, right here and now,
Of yer dy-does anyhow!"

So I stuck her—tel she'd jest
Done her very level best;
Then I slides off—strips the lines
Over her fool-head, and finds
Me a little saplin'-gad,
'Side the road:—And there we had
Our own fun!—jest wore her out!
Mounted her, and faced about,
And jest made her *nose* that-air
Little traction-engine there!

OLD WINTERS ON THE FARM

I HAVE jest about decided
   It'd keep a *town-boy* hoppin'
  Fer to work all winter, choppin'
Fer a' old fireplace, like *I* did!
Lawz! them old times wuz contrairy!—
   Blame' backbone o' winter, 'peared-like,
   Wouldn't break!—and I wuz skeerd-like
Clean on into *Feb'uary!*
   Nothin' ever made me madder
Than fer Pap to stomp in, layin'
On a' extry forestick, sayin',
   "Groun'-hog's out and seed his shadder!"

"COON-DOG WESS"

"COON-DOG WESS"—he allus went
 'Mongst us here by that-air name.
Moved in this-here Settlement
 From next county—he laid claim,—
Lived down in the bottoms—whare
Ust to be some coons in thare!—

In nigh Clayton's, next the crick,—
 Mind old Billy ust to say
Coons in thare was jest that thick,
 He'p him corn-plant any day!—
And, in rostneer-time, be then
Aggin' him to plant again!

Well,—In Spring o' '67,
 This-here "Coon-dog Wess" he come—
Fetchin' 'long 'bout forty-'leven
 Ornriest-lookin' hounds, I gum!
Ever mortul-man laid eyes
On sence dawn o' Christian skies!

Wife come traipsin' at the rag-
 Tag-and-bobtail of the crowd,
Dogs and childern, with a bag

156

Corn-meal and some side-meat,—*Proud*
And as *independunt—My!-*
Yit a mild look in her eye.

Well—this "Coon-dog Wess" he jest
   Moved in that-air little pen
Of a pole-shed, aidgin' west
   On "The Slues o' Death," called then.—
Otter- and mink-hunters ust
To camp thare 'fore game vam-moosd.

Abul-bodied man,—and lots
   Call fer *choppers*—and fer hands
To git *cross-ties out.*—But what's
   Work to sich as understands
Ways appinted and is hence
Under special providence?—

"Coon-dog Wess's" holts was *hounds*
   And *coon-huntin';* and he knowed
His own range, and stayed in bounds
   And left work fer them 'at showed
Talents fer it—same as his
Gifts regardin' coon-dogs is.

Hounds of ev'ry mungerl breed
   Ever whelped on earth!—Had these
Yeller kind, with punkin-seed
   Marks above theyr eyes—and fleas
Both to sell and keep!—Also
These-here *lop-yeerd* hounds, you know.—

Yes-and *brindle* hounds—and long,
    Ga'nt hounds, with them eyes they' got
So blame *sorry,* it seems wrong,
    'Most, to kick 'em as to not!
Man, though, wouldn't dast, I guess,
Kick a hound fer "Coon-dog Wess"!

'Tended to his own affairs
    Stric'ly ;—made no brags,—and yit
You could see 'at them hounds' cares
    'Peared like *his,*—and he'd 'a' fit
Fer 'em, same as wife er child!—
Them facts made folks rickonciled,

Sorto', fer to let him be
    And not pester him. And then
Word begin to spread 'at he
    Had brung in as high as ten
Coon-pelts in one night—and yit
Didn't 'pear to boast of it!

Neghborhood made some complaints
    'Bout them plague-gone hounds at night
Howlin' fit to wake the saints,
    Clean from dusk tel plum daylight!
But to "Coon-dog Wess" them-thare
Howls was "music in the air"!

Fetched his pelts to Gilson's Store—
    Newt he shipped fer him, and said,
Sence *he'd* cooned thare, he'd shipped more

Than three hundred pelts!—"By Ned!
Git shet of my *store,*" Newt says,
"I'd go in with 'Coon-dog Wess'!"

And the feller 'peared to be
  Makin' best and most he could
Of his rale prospairity:—
  Bought some household things—and *good,*—
Likewise, wagon-load onc't come
From wherever he'd moved from.

But pore feller's huntin'-days,
  'Bout them times, was glidin' past!—
Goes out onc't one night and *stays!*
  . . . Neghbors they turned out, at last,
Headed by his wife and one
Half-starved hound—and search begun.

Boys said, that blame hound, he led
  Searchin' party, 'bout a half-
Mile ahead, and bellerin', said,
  Worse'n ary yearlin' calf!—
Tel, at last, come fur-off sounds
Like the howl of other hounds.

And-sir, shore enugh, them signs
  Fetched 'em—in a' hour er two—
Whare the *pack* was;—and they finds
  "Coon-dog Wess" *right thare;*—And you
Would admitted he was right
Stayin', as he had, *all night!*

Facts is, cuttin' down a tree,
  The blame thing had sorto' fell
In a twist-like—*mercy me!*
  And had ketched him.—Couldn't tell,
Wess said, *how* he'd managed—yit
He'd got both legs under it!

Fainted and come to, I s'pose,
  'Bout a dozen times whilse they
Chopped him out!—And wife she froze
  To him!—bresh his hair away
And smile cheerful'—only when
He'd faint.—Cry and kiss him *then.*

Had *his* nerve!—And nussed him through,—
  Neghbors he'pped her—all she'd stand.—
Had a loom, and she could do
  Carpet-weavin' railly grand!—
"'Sides," she ust to laugh and say,
"She'd have Wess, now, *night* and day!"

As fer *him,* he'd say, says-ee,
  "I'm resigned to bein' lame:—
They was four coons up that tree,
  And hounds got 'em, jest the same!"
'Peared like, one er two legs less
Never worried "Coon-Dog Wess"!

GOIN' TO THE FAIR

OLD STYLE

WHEN Me an' my Ma an' Pa went to the Fair,
  Ma borried Mizz Rollins-uz rigg to go there,
'Cause *our* buggy's *new,* an' Ma says, "Mercy-sake!
It wouldn't hold *half* the folks *she's* go' to take!"
An' she took Marindy, an' Jane's twins, an' Jo,
An' Aunty Van Meters-uz girls—an' old Slo'
Magee, 'at's so fat, come a-scrougin' in there,
When me an' my Ma an' Pa went to the Fair!

The road's full o' loads-full 'ist ready to bu'st,
An' all hot, an' smokin' an' chokin' with dust;
The Wolffs an' their wagon, an' Brizentines, too—
An' horses 'ist r'ared when the toot-cars come
    through!
An' 'way from fur off we could hear the band play,
An' peoples all there 'u'd 'ist whoop an' hooray!
An' I stood on the dashboard, an' Pa boost' me there
'Most high as the fence, when we went to the Fair.

An' when we 'uz there an' inside, we could see
Wher' the flag's on a pole wher' a show's go' to be;
An' boys up in trees, an' the grea'-big balloon
'At didn't goned up a-tall, all afternoon!

161

An' a man in the crowd there gived money away—
An' Pa says *"he'd* ruther earn *his* by the day!"—
An' *he* gim-me some, an' says "ain't nothin' there
Too good fer his boy," when we went to the Fair!

Wisht The Raggedy Man wuz there, too!—but he
    says,
"Don't talk fairs to *me,* child! I went to one;—
    yes,—
An' they wuz a swing there ye rode—an' I rode,
An' a thing-um-a-jing 'at ye blowed—an' I blowed;
An' they wuz a game 'at ye played—an' I played,
An' a hitch in the same wher' ye paid—an' I paid;
An' they wuz *two* bad to one good peoples there—
Like *you* an' your *Pa* an' Ma went to the Fair!"

THE WATCHES OF THE NIGHT

O THE waiting in the watches of the night!
In the darkness, desolation, and contrition
and affright;
The awful hush that holds us shut away from all
delight:
The ever-weary memory that ever weary goes
Recounting ever over every aching loss it
knows—
The ever-weary eyelids gasping ever for repose—
In the dreary, weary watches of the night!

Dark—stifling dark—the watches of the night!
With tingling nerves at tension, how the blackness
flashes white
With spectral visitations smitten past the inner
sight!—
What shuddering sense of wrongs we've wrought
that may not be redressed—
Of tears we did not brush away—of lips we left
unpressed,
And hands that we let fall, with all their loyalty
unguessed!
Ah! the empty, empty watches of the night!

What solace in the watches of the night?—
What frailest staff of hope to stay—what faintest
    shaft of light?
Do we *dream,* and dare *believe* it, that by never
    weight of right
  Of our own poor weak deservings, we shall win
    the dawn at last—
  Our famished souls find freedom from this
    penance for the past,
  In a faith that leaps and lightens from the gloom
    that flees aghast—
    Shall we survive the watches of the night?

ONE leads us through the watches of the night—
By the ceaseless intercession of our loved ones lost
    to sight
He is with us through all trials, in His mercy and
    His might;—
  With our mothers there about Him, all our
    sorrow disappears,
  Till the silence of our sobbing is the prayer the
    Master hears,
  And His hand is laid upon us with the tenderness
    of tears
    In the waning of the watches of the night.

OSCAR C. McCULLOCH

INDIANAPOLIS, DECEMBER 12, 1891

WHAT would best please our friend, in
   token of
  The sense of our great loss?—Our sighs and
    tears?
  Nay, these he fought against through all his years,
Heroically voicing, high above
Grief's ceaseless minor, moaning like a dove,
  The pæan triumphant that the soldier hears,
  Scaling the walls of death, midst shouts and
    cheers,
The old Flag laughing in his eyes' last love.

Nay, then, to pleasure him were it not meet
  To yield him bravely, as his fate arrives?—
Drape him in radiant roses, head and feet,
  And be partakers, while his work survives,
Of his fair fame,—paying the tribute sweet
  To all humanity—our nobler lives.

WHAT CHRIS'MAS FETCHED THE
WIGGINSES

WINTER-TIME, er Summer-time,
  Of late years I notice I'm,
Kind o' like, more subjec' to
What the *weather* is. Now, *you*
Folks 'at lives in *town,* I s'pose,
Thinks it's bully when it snows;
But the chap 'at chops and hauls
Yer wood fer ye, and then stalls,
And snapps tuggs and swingletrees,
And then has to walk er freeze,
Hain't so much "stuck *on*" the snow
As stuck *in* it—Bless ye, no!—
When it's packed, and sleighin' 's good,
And *church* in the neighberhood,
Them 'at's *got* their girls, I guess,
Takes 'em, likely, more er less.
Tell the plain fac's o' the case,
No men-folks about our place
On'y me and Pap—and he
'Lows 'at young folks' company
Allus made him sick! So I

166

Jes' don't want, and jes' don't try!
Chinkypin, the dad-burn town,
'S too fur off to loaf aroun'
Eether day er night—and no
Law compellin' me to go!—
'Less'n some Old-Settlers' Day,
Er big-doin's thataway—
Then, to tell the p'inted fac',
I've went more so's to come back
By old Guthrie's still-house, where
Minors *has* got licker there—
That's pervidin' we could show 'em
Old folks sent fer it from home!
Visit roun' the neighbers some,
When the *boys* wants me to come.—
Coon-hunt with 'em; er set traps
Fer mussrats; er jes', perhaps,
Lay in roun' the stove, you know,
And parch corn, and let her snow!
Mostly, nights like these, you'll be
(Ef you' got a writ fer *me*)
Ap' to skeer me up, I guess,
In about the Wigginses'.
Nothin' roun' *our* place to keep
Me at home—with Pap asleep
'Fore it's dark; and Mother in
Mango pickles to her chin;
And the girls, all still as death,
Piecin' quilts.—Sence I drawed breath
Twenty year' ago, and heerd
Some girls whisper'n' so's it 'peared

Like they had a row o' pins
In their mouth—right there begins
My first rickollections, built
On that-air blame' old piece-quilt!

Summer-time, it's jes' the same—
'Cause I've noticed,—and I claim,
As I said afore, I'm more
Subjec' to the weather, *shore,*
'Proachin' my majority,
Than I ever ust to be!
Callin' back *last* Summer, say,—
Don't seem hardly past away—
With night closin' in, and all
S' lonesome-like in the dewfall:
Bats—ad-drat their ugly muggs!—
Flicker'n' by; and lightnin'-bugs
Huckster'n' roun' the airly night
Little sickly gasps o' light;—
Whippoorwills, like all possess'd,
Moanin' out their mournfullest;—
Frogs and katydids and things
Jes' *clubs* in and sings and sings
Their *ding-dangdest!*—Stock's all fed,
And Pap's warshed his feet fer bed;—
Mother and the girls all down
At the milk-shed, foolin' roun'—
No wunder 'at I git blue,
And lite out—and so would you!
I cain't stay aroun' no place
Whur they hain't no livin' face:—

'Crost the fields and thue the gaps
Of the hills they's friends, perhaps,
Waitin' somers, 'at kin be
Kind o' comfertin' to me!

Neighbers all is plenty good,
Scattered thue this neighberhood;
Yit, of all, I like to jes'
Drap in on the Wigginses.—
Old man, and old lady too,
'Pear-like, makes so much o' you—
Least, they've allus pampered me
Like one of the fambily.—
The boys, too, 's all thataway—
Want you jes' to come and stay;—
Price, and Chape, and Mandaville,
Poke, Chasteen, and "Catfish Bill"—
Poke's the runt of all the rest,
But he's jes' the beatin'est
Little schemer, fer fourteen,
Anybody ever seen!—
"Like his namesake," old man claims,
"Jeems K. Poke, the first o' names!
Full o' tricks and jokes—and you
Never know what *Poke's* go' do!"
Genius, too, that-air boy is,
With them awk'ard hands o' his:
Gits this blame' pokeberry-juice,
Er some stuff, fer ink—and goose-
Quill pen-p'ints: And then he'll draw
Dogdest pictures yevver saw!—

Jes' make deers and eagles good
As a writin' teacher could!
Then they's two twin boys they've riz
Of old Coonrod Wigginses
'At's deceast—and glad of it,
'Cause his widder's livin' yit!
'Course *the boys* is mostly jes'
Why I go to Wigginses'.—
Though *Melviney,* sometimes, *she*
Gits her slate and algebry
And jes' sets there cipher'n' thue
Sums old Ray hisse'f cain't do!—
Jes' sets there, and tilts her chair
Forreds tel, 'pear-like, her hair
Jes' *spills* in her lap—and then
She jes' dips it up again
With her hands, as white, I swan,
As the apern she's got on!

Talk o' hospitality!—
Go to Wigginses' with me—
Overhet, or froze plum thue,
You'll find welcome waitin' you:—
Th'ow out yer tobacker 'fore
You set foot acrost that floor,—
"Got to eat whatever's set—
Got to drink whatever's wet!"
Old man's sentimuns—them's his—
And means jes' the best they is!

Then he lights his pipe; and she,
The old lady, presen'ly
She lights hern; and Chape and Poke.—
I hain't got none, ner don't smoke,—
(In the crick afore their door—
Sort o' so's 'at I'd be shore—
Drownded mine one night and says
"I won't smoke at *Wiggenses'!*")
Price he's mostly talkin' 'bout
Politics, and "thieves turned out"—
What he's go' to be, ef he
Ever "gits there"—and "we'll see!"—
Poke he 'lows they's blame' few men
Go' to hold their breath tel then!
Then Melviney smiles, as she
Goes on with her algebry,
And the clouds clear, and the room's
Sweeter'n crabapple-blooms!
(That Melviney, she's got some
Most surprisin' ways, i gum!—
Don't 'pear-like she ever *says*
Nothin', yit you'll *listen* jes'
Like she *was* a-talkin', and
Half-way seem to understand,
But not quite,—*Poke* does, I know,
'Cause he good as told me so,—
Poke's *her* favo-rite; and he—
That is, confidentially—
He's *my* favo-rite—and I
Got my whurfore and my why!)

I hain't never be'n no hand
Much at talkin', understand,
But they's *thoughts* o' mine 'at's jes'
Jealous o' them Wigginses!—
Gift o' talkin' 's what they' got,
Whuther they want to er not.—
F'r instunce, start the old man on
Huntin'-scrapes, 'fore game was gone,
'Way back in the Forties, when
Bears stold pigs right out the pen,
Er went waltzin' 'crost the farm
With a beehive on their arm!—
And—sir, *ping!* the old man's gun
Has plumped over many a one,
Firin' at him from afore
That-air very cabin door!
Yes—and *painters,* prowlin' 'bout,
Allus darkest nights.—Lay out
Clost yer cattle.—Great, big red
Eyes a-blazin' in their head,
Glitter'n' 'long the timber-line—
Shine out some and then *un-shine,*
And shine back—Then, stiddy! *whizz!*
'N' there yer Mr. Painter is
With a hole bored spang between
Them-air eyes! . . . Er start Chasteen,
Say, on blooded racin'-stock,
Ef you want to hear him talk;
Er tobacker—how to raise,
Store, and k-yore it, so's she pays. . . .
The old lady—and she'll cote

Scriptur' tel she'll git yer vote!
Prove to you 'at wrong is right,
Jes' as plain as black is white:
Prove when you're asleep in bed
You're a-standin' on yer head,
And yer train 'at's goin' West,
'S goin' East its level best;
And when bees dies, it's their wings
Wears out—And a thousan' things!
And the boys is "chips," you know,
"Off the old block"—So I go
To the Wigginses', 'cause—jes'
'Cause I *like* the Wigginses—
Even ef Melviney *she*
Hardly 'pears to notice me!

Rid to Chinkypin this week—
Yisterd'y.—No snow to speak
Of, and didn't have no sleigh
Anyhow; so, as I say,
I rid in—and froze one ear
And both heels—and I don't keer!—
"Mother and the girls kin jes'
Bother 'bout their Chris'mases
Next time fer *theirse'v's,* i jack!"
Thinks-says-I, a-startin' back,—
Whole durn meal-bag full of things
Wropped in paper sacks, and strings
Liable to snap their holt
Jes' at any little jolt!
That in front o' me, and *wind*

With *nicks* in it, 'at jes' skinned
Me alive!—I'm here to say
Nine mile' hossback thataway
Would 'a' walked my log! But, as
Somepin' allus comes to pass,
As I topped old Guthrie's hill,
Saw a buggy, front the Still,
P'inted home'ards, and a thin
Little chap jes' climbin' in.
Six more minutes I were there
On the groun's!—And 'course it were—
It were little Poke—and he
Nearly fainted to see *me!*—
"You be'n in to Chinky, too?"
"Yes; and go' ride back with you,"
I-says-I. He he'pped me find
Room fer my things in behind—
Stript my hoss's reins down, and
Putt his mitt' on the right hand
So's to lead—"Pile in!" says he,
"But you've struck pore company!"
Noticed he was pale—looked sick,
Kind o' like, and had a quick
Way o' flickin' them-air eyes
O' his roun' 'at didn't size
Up right with his usual style—
S' I, "You *well?*" He tried to smile,
But his chin shuck and tears come.—
"I've run 'Viney 'way from home!"

Don't know jes' what all occurred
Next ten seconds—Nary word,
But my heart jes' drapt, stobbed thue,
And whirlt over and come to.—
Wrenched a big quart-bottle from
That fool-boy!—and cut my thumb
On his little fiste-teeth—helt
Him snug in one arm, and felt
That-air little heart o' his
Churn the blood o' Wigginses
Into that old bead 'at spun
Roun' her, spilt at Lexington!
His k'niptions, like enough,
He'pped us both,—though it was rough—
Rough on him, and rougher on
Me when, last his nerve was gone
And he laid there still, his face
Fishin' fer some hidin'-place
Jes' a leetle lower down
In my breast than he'd yit foun'!
Last I kind o' soothed him, so's
He could talk.—And what you s'pose
Them-air revelations of
Poke's was? . . . He'd be'n writin' love-
Letters to Melviney, and
Givin' her to understand
They was from "a young man who
Loved her," and—"the violet's blue
'N' sugar's sweet"—and Lord knows what!

Tel, 'peared-like, Melviney got
S' inter*est*ed in "the young
Man," Poke *he* says, 'at she brung
A' answer onc't fer him to take,
Statin' "she'd die fer his sake,"
And writ fifty *x*'s "fer
Love-kisses fer him from her!" . . .
I was standin' in the road
By the buggy, all I knowed
When Poke got that fur.—"That's why,"
Poke says, "I 'fessed up the lie—
Had to—'cause I see," says he,
" 'Viney was in *airnest*—she
Cried, too, when I told her.—Then
She swore me, and smiled again,
And got Pap and Mother to
Let me hitch and drive her thue
Into Chinkypin, to be
At Aunt 'Rindy's Chris'mas-tree—
That's to-night." Says I, "Poke—durn
Your lyin' soul!—'s that beau o' hern—
That—*she*—loves—Does *he* live in
That hell-hole o' Chinkypin?"
"No," says Poke, "er 'Viney would
Went some *other* neighberhood."
"Who *is* the blame' whelp?" says I.
"Promised 'Viney, hope I'd die
Ef I ever told!" says Poke,
Pittiful and jes' heartbroke'—
"'Sides that's why she left the place,—
'She cain't look him in the face

Now no more on earth!' she says."—
And the child broke down and jes'
Sobbed! . . . Says I, "Poke, I p'tend
T' be *your* friend, and your *Pap's* friend,
And your *Mother's* friend, and all
The *boys'* friend, little, large and small—
The *whole fambily's* friend—and you
Know that means *Melviney,* too.—
Now—you hursh yer troublin'!—I'm
Go' to he'p friends ever' time—
On'y in *this* case, *you* got
To he'p *me*—and, like as not,
I kin he'p *Melviney* then,
And we'll have her home again.
And now, Poke, with your consent,
I'm go' go to that-air gent
She's in love with, and confer
With *him* on his views o' *her.*—
Blast him! give the man *some* show.—
Who *is* he?—*I'm go' to know!*"
Somepin' struck the little chap
Funny, 'peared-like.—Give a slap
On his leg—laughed thue the dew
In his eyes, and says: *"It's you!"*

Yes, and—'cordin' to the last
Love-letters of ours 'at passed
Thue his hands—we was to be
Married Chris'mas.—"Gee-mun-*nee!*
Poke," says I, "it's *suddent*—yit
We *kin* make it! You're to git

Up to-morry, say, 'bout *three*—
Tell your folks you're go' with me:—
We'll hitch up, and jes' drive in
'N' *take* the town o' Chinkypin!"

THE GUDEWIFE

MY gudewife—she that is tae be—
   O she sall seeme sang-sweete tae me
As her ain croon tuned wi' the chiel's
   Or spinnin'-wheel's.
An' faire she'll be, an' saft, an' light,
   An' muslin-bright
As her spick apron, jimpy laced
   The-round her waiste.—
Yet aye as rosy sall she bloome
   Intil the roome
(The where alike baith bake an' dine)
   As a full-fine
Ripe rose, lang rinset wi' the raine,
   Sun-kist againe,
Sall seate me at her table-spread,
   White as her bread.—
Where I, sae kissen her for *grace,*
   Sall see her face
Smudged, yet aye sweeter, for the bit
   O' floure on it,
Whiles, witless, she sall sip wi' me
Luve's tapmaist-bubblin' ecstasy.

RIGHT HERE AT HOME

RIGHT here at home, boys, in old Hoosierdom,
　　Where strangers allus joke us when they come,
And brag o' *their* old States and interprize—
Yit *settle* here; and 'fore they realize,
They're "hoosier" as the rest of us, and live
Right here at home, boys, with their past fergive'!

Right here at home, boys, is the place, I guess,
Fer me and you and plain old happiness:
We hear the World's lots grander—likely so,—
We'll take the World's word fer it and not go.—
We know *its* ways ain't *our* ways—so we'll stay
Right here at home, boys, where we *know* the way.

Right here at home, boys, where a well-to-do
Man's plenty rich enough—and knows it, too,
And's got a' extry dollar, any time,
To boost a feller up 'at *wants* to climb
And's got the git-up in him to go in
And *git there,* like he purt' nigh allus kin!

Right here at home, boys, is the place fer us!—
Where folks' heart's bigger'n their money-pu's';
And where a *common* feller's jes' as good

As ary other in the neighberhood:
The World at large don't worry you and me
Right here at home, boys, where we ort to be!

Right here at home, boys—jes' right where we air!—
Birds don't sing any sweeter anywhere:
Grass don't grow any greener'n she grows
Acrost the pastur' where the old path goes,—
All things in ear-shot's purty, er in sight,
Right here at home, boys, ef we *size* 'em right.

Right here at home, boys, where the old home-place
Is sacerd to us as our mother's face,
Jes' as we rickollect her, last she smiled
And kissed us—dyin' so and rickonciled,
Seein' us all at home here—none astray—
Right here at home, boys, where she sleeps to-day.

LITTLE MARJORIE

"WHERE is little Marjorie?"
There's the robin in the tree,
With his gallant call once more
From the boughs above the door!
There's the bluebird's note, and there
Are spring-voices everywhere
Calling, calling ceaselessly—
"Where is little Marjorie?"

And her old playmate, the rain,
Calling at the window-pane
In soft syllables that win
Not her answer from within—
"Where is little Marjorie?"—
Or is it the rain, ah me!
Or wild gusts of tears that were
Calling us—not calling her!

"Where is little Marjorie?"
Oh, in high security
She is hidden from the reach
Of all voices that beseech:
She is where no troubled word,
Sob or sigh is ever heard,
Since God whispered tenderly—
"Where is little Marjorie?"

KATHLEEN MAVOURNEEN

1892

[*Frederick Nicholls Crouch, the Musical Genius and Composer of the world-known air "Kathleen Mavourneen," was, at above date, living, in helpless age, in his adopted country, America—a citizen since 1849.*]

KATHLEEN MAVOURNEEN! The song is
still ringing
As fresh and as clear as the trill of the birds;
In world-weary hearts it is throbbing and singing
In pathos too sweet for the tenderest words.
Oh, have we forgotten the one who first breathed it?
Oh, have we forgotten his rapturous art—
Our meed to the master whose genius bequeathed
it?
Oh, why art thou silent, thou Voice of the
Heart?—
*Our meed to the master whose genius bequeathed
it—*
Oh, why are we silent, Kathleen Mavourneen!

Kathleen Mavourneen! Thy lover still lingers;
  The long night is waning, the stars pale and few;
Thy sad serenader, with tremulous fingers,
  Is bowed with his tears as the lily with dew;
The old harp-strings quaver, the old voice is shaking;
  In sighs and in sobs moans the yearning refrain;
The old vision dims, and the old heart is break-
    ing . . .
Kathleen Mavourneen, inspire us again!
The old vision dims, and the old heart is breaking:
  Oh, why are we silent, Kathleen Mavourneen!

OLD JOHN HENRY

OLD John's jes' made o' the commonest stuff—
      Old John Henry—
He's tough, I reckon,—but none too tough—
Too tough though's better than not enough!
      Says old John Henry.
He does his best, and when his best's bad,
He don't fret none, ner he don't git sad—
He simply 'lows it's the best he had:
      Old John Henry!

His doctern's jes' o' the plainest brand—
      Old John Henry—
A smilin' face and a hearty hand
'S religen 'at all folks understand,
      Says old John Henry.
He's stove up some with the rhumatiz,
And they hain't no shine on them shoes o' his,
And his hair hain't cut—but his eye-teeth is:
      Old John Henry!

He feeds hisse'f when the stock's all fed—
      Old John Henry—
And sleeps like a babe when he goes to bed—
And dreams o' Heaven and home-made bread,
      Says old John Henry.

He hain't refined as he'd ort to be
To fit the statutes o' poetry,
Ner his clothes don't fit him—but *he* fits *me:*
   Old John Henry!

BEING HIS MOTHER

BEING his mother,—when he goes away
 I would not hold him overlong, and so
 Sometimes my yielding sight of him grows O
So quick of tears, I joy he did not stay
To catch the faintest rumor of them! Nay,
 Leave always his eyes clear and glad, although
 Mine own, dear Lord, do fill to overflow;
Let his remembered features, as I pray,
Smile ever on me! Ah! what stress of love
 Thou givest me to guard with Thee thiswise:
 Its fullest speech ever to be denied
Mine own—being his mother! All thereof
 Thou knowest only, looking from the skies
 As when not Christ alone was crucified.

GREEN FIELDS AND RUNNING BROOKS

HO! green fields and running brooks!
Knotted strings and fishing-hooks
Of the truant, stealing down
Weedy back-ways of the town.

Where the sunshine overlooks,
By green fields and running brooks,
All intruding guests of chance
With a golden tolerance.

Cooing doves, or pensive pair
Of picnickers, straying there—
By green fields and running brooks,
Sylvan shades and mossy nooks!

And—O Dreamer of the Days,
Murmurer of roundelays
All unsung of words or books,
Sing green fields and running brooks!

SOME SCATTERING REMARKS OF BUB'S

WUNST I tooked our pepper-box lid
    An' cut little pie-dough biscuits, I did,
An' cooked 'em on our stove one day
When our hired girl she said I may.

Honey's the *goodest* thing—Oo-*ooh!*
An' blackburry-pies is goodest, too!
But wite hot biscuits, ist soakin' wet
Wiv tree-mullasus, is goodest yet!

Miss Maimie she's my Ma's friend,—an'
She's purtiest girl in all the lan'!—
An' sweetest smile an' voice an' face—
An' eyes ist looks like p'serves tas'e'!

I *ruther* go to the Circus-show;
But, 'cause my *parunts* told me so,
I ruther go to the Sund'y-school,
'Cause there I learn the goldun rule.

Say, Pa,—what *is* the goldun rule
'At's allus at the Sund'y-school?

BY HER WHITE BED

BY her white bed I muse a little space:
    She fell asleep—not very long ago,—
  And yet the grass was here and not the snow—
The leaf, the bud, the blossom, and—her face!—
Midsummer's heaven above us, and the grace
  Of Love's own day, from dawn to afterglow;
  The fireflies' glimmering, and the sweet and low
Plaint of the whippoorwills, and every place
In thicker twilight for the roses' scent.
  Then *night*.—She slept—in such tranquillity,
    I walk atiptoe still, nor *dare* to weep,
Feeling, in all this hush, she rests content—
    That though God stood to wake her for me, she
      Would mutely plead: "Nay, Lord! Let *him* so
        sleep."

HOW JOHN QUIT THE FARM

NOBODY on the old farm here but Mother, me
    and John,
Except, of course, the extry he'p when harvest-
    time come on,—
And *then,* I want to say to you, we *needed* he'p
    about,
As you'd admit, ef you'd 'a' seen the way the crops
    turned out!

A better quarter-section ner a richer soil warn't
    found
Than this-here old-home place o' ourn fer fifty miles
    around!—
The house was small—but plenty-big we found it
    from the day
That John—our only livin' son—packed up and
    went away.

You see, we tuk sich pride in John—his mother
    more'n me—
That's natchurul; but *both* of us was proud as proud
    could be;

Fer the boy, from a little chap, was most oncommon
    bright,
And seemed in work as well as play to take the
    same delight.

He allus went a-whistlin' round the place, as glad
    at heart
As robins up at five o'clock to git an airly start;
And many a time 'fore daylight Mother's waked me
    up to say—
"Jes' listen, David!—listen!—Johnny's beat the
    birds to-day!"

High-sperited from boyhood, with a most inquirin'
    turn,—
He wanted to learn ever'thing on earth they was to
    learn:
He'd ast more plaguy questions in a mortal-minute
    here
Than his grandpap in Paradise could answer in a
    year!

And *read!* w'y, his own mother learnt him how to
    read and spell;
And "The Childern of the Abbey"—w'y, he knowed
    that book as well
At fifteen as his parents!—and "The Pilgrim's
    Progress," too—
Jes' knuckled down, the shaver did, and read 'em
    through and through!

At eighteen, Mother 'lowed the boy must have a
    better chance—
That we ort to educate him, under any circum-
    stance;
And John he j'ned his mother, and they ding-
    donged and kep' on,
Tel I sent him off to school in town, half glad that
    he was gone.

But—I missed him—w'y, of course I did!—The
    Fall and Winter through
I never built the kitchen fire, er split a stick in two,
Er fed the stock, er butchered, er swung up a
    gambrel-pin,
But what I thought o' John, and wished that he was
    home ag'in.

He'd come, sometimes—on Sund'ys most—and stay
    the Sund'y out;
And on Thanksgivin'-Day he 'peared to like to be
    about:
But a change was workin' on him—he was stiller
    than before,
And didn't joke, ner laugh, ner sing and whistle
    any more.

And his talk was all so proper; and I noticed, with
    a sigh,
He was tryin' to raise side-whiskers, and had on a
    stripèd tie,

And a standin'-collar, ironed up as stiff and slick
    as bone;
And a breastpin, and a watch and chain and plug-
    hat of his own.

But when Spring-weather opened out, and John was
    to come home
And he'p me through the season, I was glad to see
    him come;
But my happiness, that evening, with the settin'
    sun went down,
When he bragged of "a position" that was offered
    him in town.

"But," says I, "you'll not accept it?" "W'y, of
    course I will," says he.—
"This drudgin' on a farm," he says, "is not the life
    fer me;
I've set my stakes up higher," he continued, light
    and gay,
"And town's the place fer *me,* and I'm a-goin' right
    away!"

And go he did!—his mother clingin' to him at the
    gate,
A-pleadin' and a-cryin'; but it hadn't any weight.
I was tranquiller, and told her 'twarn't no use to
    worry so,
And onclapsed her arms from round his neck round
    mine—and let him go!

I felt a little bitter feelin' foolin' round about
The aidges of my conscience; but I didn't let it
  out;—
I simply retch out, trimbly-like, and tuk the boy's
  hand,
And though I didn't say a word, I knowed he'd understand.

And—well!—sence then the old home here was
  mighty lonesome, shore!
With we a-workin' in the field, and Mother at the
  door,
Her face ferever to'rds the town, and fadin' more
  and more—
Her only son nine miles away, a-clerkin' in a store!

The weeks and months dragged by us; and sometimes the boy would write
A letter to his mother, sayin' that his work was
  light,
And not to feel oneasy about his health a bit—
Though his business was confinin', he was gittin'
  used to it.

And sometimes he would write and ast how *I* was
  gittin' on,
And ef I had to pay out much fer he'p sence he was
  gone;
And how the hogs was doin', and the balance of the
  stock,
And talk on fer a page er two jes' like he used to
  talk.

And he wrote, along 'fore harvest, that he guessed
    he would git home,
Fer business would, of course, be dull in town.—
    But *didn't* come:—
We got a postal later, sayin' when they had no trade
They filled the time "invoicin' goods," and that was
    why he stayed.

And then he quit a-writin' altogether: Not a word—
Exceptin' what the neighbers brung who'd been
    to town and heard
What store John was clerkin' in, and went round
    to inquire
If they could buy their goods there less and sell
    their produce higher.

And so the Summer faded out, and Autumn wore
    away,
And a keener Winter never fetched around Thanks-
    givin'-Day!
The night before that day of thanks I'll never quite
    fergit,
The wind a-howlin' round the house—it makes me
    creepy yit!

And there set me and Mother—me a-twistin' at the
    prongs
Of a green scrub-ellum forestick with a vicious pair
    of tongs,
And Mother sayin', *"David! David!"* in a' under-
    tone,
As though she thought that I was thinkin' bad-
    words unbeknown.

"I've dressed the turkey, David, fer to-morrow,"
      Mother said,
A-tryin' to wedge some pleasant subject in my
      stubborn head,—
"And the mince-meat I'm a-mixin' is perfection
      mighty nigh;
And the pound-cake is delicious-rich—" "Who'll
      eat 'em?" I-says-I.

"The cramberries is drippin'-sweet," says Mother,
      runnin' on,
P'tendin' not to hear me;—"and somehow I thought
      of John
All the time they was a-jellin'—fer you know they
      allus was
His fav*orite*—he likes 'em so!" Says I, "Well,
      s'pose he does?"

"Oh, nothin' much!" says Mother, with a quiet sort
      o' smile—
"This gentleman behind my cheer may tell you after
      while!"
And as I turnt and looked around, some one riz up
      and leant
And putt his arms round Mother's neck, and
      laughed in low content.

"It's *me*," he says—"your fool-boy John, come back
      to shake your hand;
Set down with you, and talk with you, and make
      you understand

How dearer yit than all the world is this old home
    that we
Will spend Thanksgivin' in fer life—jes' Mother,
    you and me!"

.   .   .   .

Nobody on the old farm here but Mother, me and
    John,
Except, of course, the extry he'p when harvest-
    time comes on;
And then, I want to say to you, we *need* sich he'p
    about,
As you'd admit, ef you could see the way the crops
    turns out!

HIS MOTHER'S WAY

TOMPS 'ud allus haf to say
  Somepin' 'bout "his Mother's way."—
He lived hard-like—never j'ined
Any church of any kind.—
"It was Mother's way," says he,
"To be good enough fer *me*
And her too,—and cert'inly
  Lord has heerd *her* pray!"
Propped up on his dyin' bed,—
"Shore as Heaven's overhead,
I'm a-goin' there," he said—
  "It was Mother's way."

THE HOOSIER FOLK-CHILD

THE Hoosier Folk-Child—all unsung—
Unlettered all of mind and tongue;
Unmastered, unmolested—made
Most wholly frank and unafraid:
Untaught of any school—unvexed
Of law or creed—all unperplexed—
Unsermoned, ay, and undefiled,
An all imperfect-perfect child—
A type which (Heaven forgive us!) you
And I do tardy honor to,
And so profane the sanctities
Of our most sacred memories.
Who, growing thus from boy to man,
That dares not be American?
Go, Pride, with prudent underbuzz—
Go *whistle!* as the Folk-Child does.

The Hoosier Folk-Child's world is not
Much wider than the stable-lot
Between the house and highway fence
That bounds the home his father rents.
His playmates mostly are the ducks
And chickens, and the boy that "shucks
Corn by the shock," and talks of town,

And whether eggs are "up" or "down,"
And prophesies in boastful tone
Of "owning horses of his own,"
And "being his own man," and "when
He gets to be, what he'll do then."—
Takes out his jack-knife dreamily
And makes the Folk-Child two or three
Crude corn-stalk figures,—a wee span
Of horses and a little man.

The Hoosier Folk-Child's eyes are wise
And wide and round as brownies' eyes:
The smile they wear is ever blent
With all-expectant wonderment,—
On homeliest things they bend a look
As rapt as o'er a picture-book,
And seem to ask, whate'er befall,
The happy reason of it all:—
Why grass is all so glad a green,
And leaves—and what their lispings mean;—
Why buds grow on the boughs, and why
They burst in blossom by and by—
As though the orchard in the breeze
Had shook and popped its *pop-corn trees,*
To lure and whet, as well they might,
Some seven-league giant's appetite!

The Hoosier Folk-Child's chubby face
Has scant refinement, caste or grace,—
From crown to chin, and cheek to cheek,
It bears the grimy water-streak

Of rinsings such as some long rain
Might drool across the window-pane
Wherethrough he peers, with troubled frown,
As some lorn team drives by for town.
His brow is elfed with wispish hair,
With tangles in it here and there,
As though the warlocks snarled it so
At midmirk when the moon sagged low,
And boughs did toss and skreek and shake,
And children moaned themselves awake,
With fingers clutched, and starting sight
Blind as the blackness of the night!

The Hoosier Folk-Child!—Rich is he
In all the wealth of poverty!
He owns nor title nor estate,
Nor speech but half articulate,—
He owns nor princely robe nor crown;—
Yet, draped in patched and faded brown,
He owns the bird-songs of the hills—
The laughter of the April rills;
And his are all the diamonds set
In Morning's dewy coronet,—
And his the Dusk's first minted stars
That twinkle through the pasture-bars
And litter all the skies at night
With glittering scraps of silver light;—
The rainbow's bar, from rim to rim,
In beaten gold, belongs to him.

THEIR SWEET SORROW

THEY meet to say farewell: Their way
Of saying this is hard to say.—
He holds her hand an instant, wholly
Distressed—and she unclasps it slowly.

He bends *his* gaze evasively
Over the printed page that she
Recurs to, with a new-moon shoulder
Glimpsed from the lace-mists that infold her.

The clock, beneath its crystal cup,
Discreetly clicks—*"Quick! Act! Speak up!"*
A tension circles both her slender
Wrists—and her raised eyes flash in splendor,

Even as he feels his dazzled own.—
Then, blindingly, round either thrown,
They feel a stress of arms that ever
Strain tremblingly—and *"Never! Never!"*

Is whispered brokenly, with half
A sob, like a belated laugh,—
While cloyingly their blurred kiss closes,—
Sweet as the dew's lip to the rose's.

DAWN, NOON AND DEWFALL

I

DAWN, noon and dewfall! Bluebird and robin
  Up and at it airly, and the orchard-blossoms
    bobbin'!
Peekin' from the winder, half awake, and wishin'
I could go to sleep ag'in as well as go a-fishin'!

II

On the apern o' the dam, legs a-danglin' over,
Drowsy-like with sound o' worter and the smell o'
    clover:
Fish all out a-visitin'—'cept some dratted minnor!
Yes, and mill shet down at last and hands is gone
    to dinner.

III

Trompin' home acrost the fields: Lightnin'-bugs
    a-blinkin'
In the wheat like sparks o' things feller keeps
    a-thinkin':—
Mother waitin' supper, and the childern there to
    cherr me;
And fiddle on the kitchen wall a-jes' a-eechin' fer
    me!

LONGFELLOW

THE winds have talked with him confidingly;
　The trees have whispered to him; and the
　　night
Hath held him gently as a mother might,
And taught him all sad tones of melody:
The mountains have bowed to him; and the sea,
　In clamorous waves, and murmurs exquisite,
　Hath told him all her sorrow and delight —
Her legends fair—her darkest mystery.
　His verse blooms like a flower, night and day;
Bees cluster round his rhymes; and twitterings
　Of lark and swallow, in an endless May,
Are mingling with the tender songs he sings.—
　Nor shall he cease to sing—in every lay
　Of Nature's voice he sings—and will alway.

HIS VIGIL

CLOSE the book and dim the light,
I shall read no more to-night.
No—I am not sleepy, dear—
Do not go: sit by me here
In the darkness and the deep
Silence of the watch I keep.
Something in your presence so
Soothes me—as in long ago
I first felt your hand—as now—
In the darkness touch my brow:
I've no other wish than you
Thus should fold mine eyelids to,
Saying naught of sigh or tear—
Just as God were sitting here.

ANTHONY HOPE.

James Whitcomb Riley.   Robert J. Burdette.

THE QUARREL

THEY faced each other: Topaz-brown
  And lambent burned her eyes and shot
Sharp flame at his of amethyst.—
"I hate you! Go, and be forgot
As death forgets!" their glitter *hissed*
(So *seemed* it) in their hatred. Ho!
Da——d any mortal front her so?—
———————— is eyebrows knitted down—
Tense nostril, mouth—no muscle slack,—
And black—the suffocating black—
The stifling blackness of her frown!

Ah! but the lifted face of her!
And the twitched lip and tilted head!
Yet he did neither wince nor stir,—
Only—his hands clenched; and, instead
Of words, he answered with a stare
That stammered not in aught it said,
As might his voice if trusted there.

And what—what spake his steady gaze?—
Was there a look that harshly fell
To scoff her?—or a syllable
Of anger?—or the bitter phrase
That myrrhs the honey of love's lips,

Or curdles blood as poison-drips?
What made their breasts to heave and swell
As billows under bows of ships
In broken seas on stormy days?
We may not know—nor *they* indeed—
What mercy found them in their need.

A sudden sunlight smote the gloom;
And round about them swept a breeze,
With faint breaths as of clover-bloom;
A bird was heard, through drone of bees,—
Then, far and clear and eerily,
A child's voice from an orchard-tree—
Then laughter, sweet as the perfume
Of lilacs, could the hearing see.
And he—O Love! he fed thy name
On bruisèd kisses, while her dim
Deep eyes, with all their inner flame,
Like drowning gems were turned on him.

JOHN BROWN

WRIT in between the lines of his life-deed
  We trace the sacred service of a heart
 Answering the Divine command, in every part
Bearing on human weal: His love did feed
The loveless; and his gentle hands did lead
 The blind, and lift the weak, and balm the smart
 Of other wounds than rankled at the dart
In his own breast, that gloried thus to bleed.
He served the lowliest first—nay, then alone—
 The most despisèd that e'er wreaked vain breath
  In cries of suppliance in the reign whereat
Red Guilt sate squat upon her spattered throne.—
 For these doomed there it was he went to death.
  God! how the merest man loves one like that!

GO, WINTER!

GO, Winter! Go thy ways! We want again
The twitter of the bluebird and the wren;
Leaves ever greener growing, and the shine
    Of Summer's sun—not thine.—

Thy sun, which mocks our need of warmth and love
And all the heartening fervencies thereof,
It scarce hath heat enow to warm our thin
    Pathetic yearnings in.

So get thee from us! We are cold, God wot,
Even as *thou* art.—We remember not
How blithe we hailed thy coming.—That was O
    Too long—too long ago!

Get from us utterly! Ho! Summer then
Shall spread her grasses where thy snows have been,
And thy last icy footprint melt and mold
    In her first marigold.

THANKSGIVING

LET us be thankful—not alone because
 Since last our universal thanks were told
We have grown greater in the world's applause,
 And fortune's newer smiles surpass the old—

But thankful for all things that come as alms
 From out the open hand of Providence :—
The winter clouds and storms—the summer calms—
 The sleepless dread—the drowse of indolence.

Let us be thankful—thankful for the prayers
 Whose gracious answers were long, long delayed,
That they might fall upon us unawares,
 And bless us, as in greater need we prayed.

Let us be thankful for the loyal hand
 That love held out in welcome to our own,
When love and *only* love could understand
 The need of touches we had never known.

Let us be thankful for the longing eyes
 That gave their secret to us as they wept,
Yet in return found, with a sweet surprise,
 Love's touch upon their lids, and, smiling, slept.

And let us, too, be thankful that the tears
  Of sorrow have not all been drained away,
That through them still, for all the coming years,
  We may look on the dead face of To-day.

AUTUMN

AS a harvester, at dusk,
Faring down some wooded trail
Leading homeward through the musk
Of May-apple and papaw,
Hazel-bush and spice and haw,—
So comes Autumn, swart and hale,
Drooped of frame and slow of stride,
But withal an air of pride
Looming up in stature far
Higher than his shoulders are;
Weary both in arm and limb,
Yet the wholesome heart of him
Sheer at rest and satisfied.

Greet him as with glee of drums
And glad cymbals, as he comes!
Robe him fair, O Rain and Shine!
He the Emperor—the King—
Royal lord of everything
Sagging Plenty's granary floors
And out-bulging all her doors;
He the god of corn and wine,
Honey, milk, and fruit and oil—
Lord of feast, as lord of toil—
Jocund host of yours and mine!

Ho! the revel of his laugh!—
Half is sound of winds, and half
Roar of ruddy blazes drawn
Up the throats of chimneys wide,
Circling which, from side to side,
Faces—lit as by the Dawn,
With her highest tintings on
Tip of nose, and cheek, and chin—
Smile at some old fairy tale
Of enchanted lovers, in
Silken gown and coat of mail,
With a retinue of elves
Merry as their very selves,
Trooping ever, hand in hand,
Down the dales of Wonderland.

Then the glory of his song!—
Lifting up his dreamy eyes—
Singing haze across the skies;
Singing clouds that trail along
Towering tops of trees that seize
Tufts of them to stanch the breeze;
Singing slanted strands of rain
In between the sky and earth,
For the lyre to mate the mirth
And the might of his refrain:
Singing southward-flying birds
Down to us, and afterwards
Singing them to flight again:
Singing blushes to the cheeks
Of the leaves upon the trees—

Singing on and changing these
Into pallor, slowly wrought,
Till the little, moaning creeks
Bear them to their last farewell,
As Elaine, the lovable,
Was borne down to Lancelot.—
Singing drip of tears, and then
Drying them with smiles again.

Singing apple, peach and grape,
Into roundest, plumpest shape;
Rosy ripeness to the face
Of the pippin; and the grace
Of the dainty stamen-tip
To the huge bulk of the pear,
Pendent in the green caress
Of the leaves, and glowing through
With the tawny laziness
Of the gold that Ophir knew,—
Haply, too, within its rind
Such a cleft as bees may find,
Bungling on it half aware,
And wherein to see them sip,
Fancy lifts an oozy lip,
And the singer's falter there.

Sweet as swallows swimming through
Eddyings of dusk and dew,
Singing happy scenes of home
Back to sight of eager eyes
That have longed for them to come,

Till their coming is surprise
Uttered only by the rush
Of quick tears and prayerful hush:
Singing on, in clearer key,
Hearty palms of you and me
Into grasps that tingle still
Rapturous, and ever will!
Singing twank and twang of strings—
Trill of flute and clarinet
In a melody that rings
Like the tunes we used to play,
And our dreams are playing yet!
Singing lovers, long astray,
Each to each; and, sweeter things,—
Singing in their marriage-day,
And a banquet holding all
These delights for festival.

JOHN ALDEN AND PERCILLY

WE got up a Christmas-doin's
    Last Christmas Eve—
Kind o' dimonstration
   'At I railly believe
Give more satisfaction—
   Take it up and down—
Than airy intertainment
   Ever come to town!

Railly was a *theater*—
   That's what it was,—
But, bein' in the church, you know,
   We had a *"Santy Claus"*—
So's to git the *old folks*
   To patternize, you see,
And *back* the institootion up
   Kind o' *morally*.

School-teacher writ the thing—
   (Was a friend o' mine)
Got it out o' Longfeller's
   Pome "Evangeline"—

Er somers—'bout the *Purituns*.—
  *Any*way, the part
"*John Alden*" fell to *me*—
  And learnt it all by heart!

Claircy was "*Percilly*"—
  (School-teacher 'lowed
Me and her could act them two
  Best of all the crowd)—
Then—blame' ef he didn't
  Git her Pap, i jing!—
To take the part o' "*Santy Claus*,"
  To wind up the thing.

Law! the fun o' practisun!—
  Was a week er two
Me and Claircy didn't have
  Nothin' else to do!—
Kep' us jes' a-meetin' round,
  Kind o' here and there,
Ever' night rehearsin'-like,
  And gaddin' ever'where!

Game was wo'th the candle, though!—
  Christmas Eve at last
Rolled around.—And 'tendance jes'
  Couldn't been su'passed!—
Neighbers from the country
  Come from Clay and Rush—
Yes, and 'crost the county-line
  Clean from Puckerbrush!

Meetin'-house jes' trimbled
  As "Old Santy" went
Round amongst the childern,
  With their pepperment
'And sassafrac and wintergreen
  Candy, and "a ball
O' pop-corn," the preacher 'nounced,
  "Free fer each and all!"

School-teacher suddenly
  Whispered in my ear,—
"Guess I got you:—*Christmas-gift!—*
  Christmas is here!"
I give *him* a gold pen,
  And case to hold the thing.—
And *Claircy* whispered, *"Christmas-gift!"*
  And I give her *a ring*.

"And now," says I, "jes' watch *me*—
  Christmas-gift," says I,
"I'm a-goin' to git one—
  'Santy's' comin' by!"—
Then I rech' and grabbed him:
  And, as you'll infer,
'Course I got the old man's,
  And *he* gimme *her!*

THE RHYMES OF IRONQUILL

I'VE allus held—till jest of late—
  That *Poetry* and me
Got on best, not to 'sociate—
  That is, *most* poetry;
But t'other day my *son-in-law*,
  Milt—be'n in town to mill—
Fetched home a present-like, fer Ma,—
  The Rhymes of Ironquill.

Milt ust to teach; and, 'course, *his* views
  Ranks over *common* sense;—
That's *biased* me, till I refuse
  'Most all he rickommends.—
But Ma *she* read and read along
  And cried, like women will,
About that "Washerwoman's Song"
  In Rhymes of Ironquill.

And then she made *me* read the thing,
  And found my specs and all:
And I jest leant back there—i jing!—
  My cheer ag'inst the wall—

220

And read and *read,* and read and *read,*
    All to myse'f—ontil
I lit the lamp and went to bed
    With Rhymes of Ironquill!

I propped myse'f up there, and—*durn!*—
    I never shet an eye
Till daylight!—hogged the whole concern
    Tee-total, mighty nigh!—
I'd sigh sometimes, and cry sometimes,
    Er laugh jest fit to kill—
Clean *captured*-like with them-air rhymes
    O' that-air Ironquill!

Read that-un 'bout old "Marmaton"
    'At hain't be'n ever "sized"
In Song before—and yit's rolled on
    Jest same as 'postrophized!—
Putt me in mind o' *our* old crick
    At *Freeport*—and the *mill*—
And Hinchman's Ford—till jest *home*sick—
    Them Rhymes of Ironquill!

Read that-un, too, 'bout "Game o' Whist,"
    And likenin' Life to fun
Like *that*—and playin' out yer fist,
    However cards is run:
And them "Tobacker-Stemmers' Song"
    They sung with sich a will
Down 'mongst the misery and wrong—
    In Rhymes of Ironquill.

And old John Brown, who broke the sod
  Of freedom's faller field
And sowed his *heart* there, thankin' God
  Pore slaves would git the yield—
Rained his last tears fer them and *us*
  To irrigate and till
A crop of Song as glorious
  As Rhymes of Ironquill.

And—sergeant, died there in the War,
  'At talked, out of his head . . .
He went "back to the Violet Star,"
  I'll bet—jest like he said!—
Yer Wars kin riddle bone and flesh,
  And blow out brains, and spill
Life-blood,—but *Somepin'* lives on, fresh
  As Rhymes of Ironquill!

THE CURSE OF THE WANDERING FOOT

ALL hope of rest withdrawn me!—
     What dread command hath put
This awful curse upon me—
     The curse of the wandering foot?
Forward and backward and thither,
     And hither and yon again—
Wandering ever! And whither?
     Answer them, God! Amen.

The blue skies are far o'er me—
     The bleak fields near below:
Where the mother that bore me?—
     Where her grave in the snow?—
Glad in her trough of a coffin—
     The sad eyes frozen shut
That wept so often, often,
     The curse of the wandering foot!

Here in your marts I care not
     Whatsoever ye think.
Good folk many who dare not
     Give me to eat and drink:

Give me to sup of your pity—
  Feast me on prayers!—O ye,
Met I your Christ in the city,
  He would fare forth with me—

Forward and onward and thither,
  And hither again and yon,
With milk for our drink together
  And honey to feed upon—
Nor hope of rest withdrawn us,
  Since the one Father put
The blessèd curse upon us—
  The curse of the wandering foot.

AS MY UNCLE UST TO SAY

I'VE thought a power on men and things—
　　As my uncle ust to say,—
And ef folks don't work as they pray, i jings!
　　W'y, they ain't no use to pray!
Ef you want somepin', and jes' dead-set
A-pleadin' fer it with both eyes wet,
And *tears* won't bring it, w'y, you try *sweat,*
　　As my uncle ust to say.

They's some don't know their A, B, C's—
　　As my uncle ust to say—
And yit don't waste no candle-grease,
　　Ner whistle their lives away!
But ef they can't write no book, ner rhyme
No ringin' song fer to last all time,
They can blaze the way fer "the march
　　　　sublime,"
　　As my uncle ust to say.

Whoever's Foreman of all things here,
　　As my uncle ust to say,
He knows each job 'at we're best fit fer,
　　And our round-up, night and day:

And a-sizin' *His* work, east and west,
And north and south, and worst and best,
I ain't got nothin' to suggest,
    As my uncle ust to say.

WHITTIER—AT NEWBURYPORT

SEPTEMBER 7, 1892

HAIL to thee, with all good cheer!
Though men say thou liest here
                    Dead,
And mourn, all uncomforted.

By thy faith refining mine,
Life still lights those eyes of thine,
                    Clear
As the Autumn atmosphere.

Ever still thy smile appears
As the rainbow of thy tears
                    Bent
O'er thy love's vast firmament.

Thou endurest—shalt endure,
Purely, as thy song is pure.
                    Hear
Thus my hail: Good cheer! good cheer!

227

ROSAMOND C. BAILEY

THOU brave, good woman! Loved of every
        one;
    Not only that in singing thou didst fill
    Our thirsty hearts with sweetness, trill on trill
Even as a wild bird singing in the sun—
Not only that in all thy carols none
    But held some tincturing of tears to thrill
    Our gentler natures, and to quicken still
Our human sympathies; but thou hast won
Our equal love and reverence because
    That thou wast ever mindful of the poor,
        And thou wast ever faithful to thy friends.
So, loving, serving all, thy best applause
    Thy requiem—the vast throng at the door
        Of the old church, with mute prayers and
        amens.

TENNYSON

ENGLAND, OCTOBER 5, 1892

WE of the New World clasp hands
  with the Old
In newer fervor and with firmer hold
  And nobler fellowship!
O Master Singer, with the finger-tip
Of Death laid thus on thy melodious lip!

All ages thou hast honored with thine art,
And ages yet unborn thou wilt be part
  Of all songs pure and true!
Thine now the universal homage due
From Old and New World—ay, and still
  The New!

MRS. BENJAMIN HARRISON

WASHINGTON, OCTOBER 25, 1892

NOW utter calm and rest;
　　Hands folded o'er the breast
In peace the placidest,
　　All trials past;
All fever soothed—all pain
Annulled, in heart and brain
Never to vex again—
　　She sleeps at last.

She sleeps; but O most dear
And best beloved of her
Ye sleep not—nay, nor stir,
　　Save but to bow
The closer each to each,
With sobs and broken speech,
That all in vain beseech
　　Her answer now.

And lo! we weep with you,
One grief the wide world through,
Yet with the faith she knew
　　We see her still,

Even as here she stood—
All that was pure and good
And sweet in womanhood—
    God's will her will.

THE POEMS HERE AT HOME

THE Poems here at Home!—Who'll write 'em
  down,
Jes' as they air—in Country and in Town?—
Sowed thick as clods is 'crost the fields and lanes,
Er these-'ere little hop-toads when it rains!—
Who'll "voice" 'em? as I heerd a feller say
'At speechified on Freedom, t'other day,
And soared the Eagle tel, it 'peared to me,
She wasn't bigger'n a bumblebee!

Who'll sort 'em out and set 'em down, says I,
'At's got a stiddy hand enough to try
To do 'em jestice 'thout a-foolin' some,
And headin' facts off when they want to come?—
Who's got the lovin' eye, and heart, and brain
To reco'nize 'at nothin's made in vain—
'At the Good Bein' made the bees and birds
And brutes first choice, and us-folks afterwards?

What We want, as I sense it, in the line
O' poetry is somepin' Yours and Mine—
Somepin' with live stock in it, and out-doors,
And old crick-bottoms, snags, and sycamores:

Putt weeds in—pizen-vines, and underbresh,
As well as johnny-jump-ups, all so fresh
And sassy-like!—and groun'-squir'ls,—yes, and
    "We,"
As sayin' is,—"We, Us and Company!"

Putt in old Nature's sermonts,—them's the best,—
And 'casion'ly hang up a hornets' nest
'At boys 'at's run away from school can git
At handy-like—and let 'em tackle it!
Let us be wrought on, of a truth, to feel
Our proneness fer to hurt more than we heal,
In ministratin' to our vain delights—
Fergittin' even insec's has their rights!

No "Ladies' Amaranth," ner "Treasury" book—
Ner "Night Thoughts," nuther—ner no "Lally
    Rook"!
We want some poetry 'at's to Our taste,
Made out o' truck 'at's jes' a-goin' to waste
'Cause smart folks thinks it's altogether too
Outrageous common—'cept fer me and you!—
Which goes to argy, all sich poetry
Is 'bliged to rest its hopes on You and Me.

LITTLE COUSIN JASPER

LITTLE Cousin Jasper, he
  Don't live in this town, like me,—
He lives 'way to Rensselaer,
An' ist comes to visit here.

He says 'at our court-house square
Ain't nigh big as theirn is there!—
He says their town's big as four
Er five towns like this, an' more!

He says ef his folks moved here
He'd cry to leave Rensselaer—
'Cause they's prairies there, an' lakes,
An' wile-ducks an' rattlesnakes!

Yes, 'n' little Jasper's Pa
Shoots most things you ever saw!—
Wunst he shot a deer, one day,
'At swummed off an' got away.

Little Cousin Jasper went
An' camped out wunst in a tent
Wiv his Pa, an' helt his gun
While he kilt a turrapun.

An' when his Ma heerd o' that,
An' more things his Pa's bin at,
She says, "Yes, 'n' he'll git shot
'Fore he's man-grown, like as not!"

An' they's mussrats there, an' minks,
An' di-dippers, an' chee-winks,—
Yes, 'n' cal'mus-root you chew
All up an' 't 'on't pizen you!

An', in town, 's a flag-pole there—
Highest one 'at's anywhere
In this world!—wite in the street
Where the big mass-meetin's meet.

Yes, 'n' Jasper he says they
Got a brass band there, an' play
On it, an' march up an' down
An' all over round the town!

Wisht our town ain't like it is!—
Wisht it's ist as big as his!
Wisht 'at *his* folks they'd move *here,*
An' *we'd* move to Rensselaer!

THE DOODLE-BUGS'S CHARM

WHEN Uncle Sidney he comes here—
    An' Fred an' me an' Min,—
My Ma she says she bet you yet
    The roof'll tumble in!
Fer Uncle he ist *romps* with us:
    An' wunst, out in our shed,
He telled us 'bout the Doodle-Bugs,
    An' what they'll do, he said,
Ef you'll ist holler "Doodle-Bugs!"—
    Out by our garden-bed—
"Doodle-Bugs! Doodle-Bugs!
    Come up an' git some bread!"

Ain't Uncle Sidney funny man?—
    "He's childish 'most as me"—
My Ma sometimes she tells him that—
    "He ac's so foolishly!"
W'y, wunst, out in our garden-path,
    Wite by the pie-plant bed,
He all sprawled out there in the dirt
    An' ist scrooched down his head,
An' "Doodle! Doodle! Doodle-Bugs!"
    My Uncle Sidney said,—
"Doodle-Bugs! Doodle-Bugs!
    Come up an' git some bread!"

An' nen he showed us little holes
   All bored there in the ground,
An' little weenty heaps o' dust
   'At's piled there all around:
An' Uncle said, when he's like us,
   Er purt' nigh big as Fred,
That wuz the Doodle-Bugs's Charm—
   To call 'em up, he said:—
"Doodle! Doodle! Doodle-Bugs!"
   An' they'd poke out their head—
"Doodle-Bugs! Doodle-Bugs!
   Come up an' git some bread!"

"HOME AG'IN"

I'M a-feelin' ruther sad,
  Fer a father proud and glad
As *I* am—my only child
Home, and all so rickonciled!
Feel so strange-like, and don't know
What the mischief ails me so!
'Stid o' bad, I ort to be
Feelin' good pertickerly—
Yes, and extry thankful, too,
'Cause my nearest kith-and-kin,
My Elviry's schoolin' 's through,
And I' got her home ag'in—
        Home ag'in with me!

Same as ef her mother'd been
Livin', I have done my best
By the girl, and watchfulest;
Nussed her—keerful' as I could—

238

From a baby, day and night,—
Drawin' on the neighberhood
And the women-folks as light
As needsessity 'ud 'low—
'Cept in "teethin'," onc't, and fight
Through black-measles. Don't know now
How we ever saved the child!
Doc *he'd* give her up, and said,
As I stood there by the bed
Sort o' foolin' with her hair
On the hot, wet pillar there,
"Wuz no use!"—And at them-air
Very words she waked and smiled—
Yes, and *knowed* me.   And that's where
I broke down, and simply jes'
Bellered like a boy—I guess!—
Women claim I did, but I
Allus helt I didn't cry,
But wuz laughin',—and I *wuz,*—
Men don't cry like *women* does!
Well, right then and there I felt
'T'uz her mother's doin's, and,
Jes' like to myse'f, I knelt
Whisperin', "I understand." . . .
So I've raised her, you might say,
Stric'ly in the narrer way
'At her mother walked therein—
Not so quite religiously,

Yit still strivin'-like to do
Ever'thing a father *could*
Do he knowed the *mother* would
Ef she'd lived—And now all's through
And I' got her home ag'in—
    Home ag'in with me!

And I' been so lonesome, too,
Here o' late, especially,—
"Old Aunt Abigail," you know,
Ain't no company;—and so
Jes' the hired hand, you see—
Jonas—like a relative
More—sence he come here to live
With us, nigh ten year' ago.
Still he don't count much, you know,
In the way o' company—
Lonesome, 'peared-like, 'most as me!
So, as *I* say, I' been so
Special lonesome-like and blue,
With Elviry, like she's been,
'Way so much, last two or three
Year'—But now she's home ag'in—
    Home ag'in with me!

Driv in fer her yisterday,
Me and Jonas—gay and spry,—
We jes' cut up, all the way!—
Yes, and sung!—tel, blame it! I
Keyed my voice up 'bout as high

As when—days 'at I wuz young—
"Buckwheat-notes" wuz all they sung.
Jonas bantered me, and 'greed
To sing one 'at town-folks sing
Down at Split Stump 'er High-Low—
Some new "ballet," said, 'at he'd
Learnt—about "The Grape-vine Swing."
And when *he* quit, *I* begun
To chune up my voice and run
Through the what's-called "scales" and "do-
Sol-me-fa's" I *ust* to know—
Then let loose old favor*ite* one,
"Hunters o' Kentucky!" *My!*
Tel I thought the boy would *die!*
And we *both* laughed—Yes, and still
Heerd more laughin', top the hill;
Fer we'd missed Elviry's train,
And she'd lit out 'crost the fields,—
Dewdrops dancin' at her heels,
And cut up old Smoots's lane
So's to meet us. And there in
Shadder o' the chinkypin,
With a danglin' dogwood-bough
Bloomin' 'bove her—See her now!—
Sunshine sort o' flickerin' down
And a kind o' laughin' all
Round her new red parasol,
Tryin' to git at *her!*—well—like
I jumped out and showed 'em how—
Yes, and jes' the place to strike

That-air mouth o' hern—as sweet
As the blossoms breshed her brow
Er sweet-williams round her feet—
White and blushy, too, as she
"Howdied" up to Jonas, and
Jieuked her head, and waved her hand.
"Hey!" says I, as she bounced in
The spring-wagon, reachin' back
To give *me* a lift, "whoop-ee!"
I-says-ee, "you're home ag'in—
  Home ag'in with me!"

Lord! how *wild* she wuz, and glad,
Gittin' home!—and things she had
To inquire about, and talk—
Plowin', plantin', and the stock—
News o' neighborhood; and how
Wuz the Deem-girls doin' now,
Sence that-air young chicken-hawk
They was "tamin'" soared away
With their settin'-hen, one day?—
'(Said she'd got Mame's postal-card
'Bout it, very day 'at she
Started home from Bethany.)
How wuz produce—eggs, and lard?—
Er wuz stores still claimin' "hard
Times," as usual? And, says she,
Troubled-like, "How's Deedie—say?
Sence pore child e-loped away
And got back, and goin' to 'ply
Fer school-license by and by—

And where's 'Lijy workin' at?
And how's 'Aunt' and 'Uncle Jake'?
How wuz 'Old Maje'—and the cat?
And wuz Marthy's baby fat
As his 'Humpty-Dumpty' ma?—
Sweetest thing she ever saw!—
Must run 'crost and see her, too,
Soon as she turned in and got
Supper fer us—smokin'-hot—
And the 'dishes' all wuz through.—"
Sich a supper! W'y, I set
There and et, and et, and et!—
Jes' et on, tel Jonas he
Pushed his chair back, laughed, and says,
"I could walk *his* log!" and we
All laughed then, tel 'Viry she
Lit the lamp—and I give in!—
Riz and kissed her: "Heaven bless
You!" says I—"you're home ag'in—
Same old dimple in your chin,
Same white apern," I-says-ee,
"Same sweet girl, and good to see
As your *mother* ust to be,—
And I' got you home ag'in—
        Home ag'in with me!"

I turns then to go on by her
Through the door—and see her eyes
Both wuz swimmin', and she tries
To say somepin'—can't—and so
Grabs and hugs and lets me go.

Noticed Aunty'd made a fire
In the settin'-room and gone
Back where her p'serves wuz on
Bilin' in the kitchen. I
Went out on the porch and set,
Thinkin'-like. And by and by
Heerd Elviry, soft and low,
At the organ, kind o' go
A mi-anderin' up and down
With her fingers 'mongst the keys—
"Vacant Chair" and "Old Camp-
     Groun'." . .
Dusk was moist-like, with a breeze
Lazin' round the locus' trees—
Heerd the hosses champin', and
Jonas feedin', and the hogs—
Yes, and katydids and frogs—
And a tree-toad, somers. Heerd
Also whipperwills.—*My land!*—
All so mournful ever'where—
Them out here, and her in there,—
'Most like 'tendin' *services!*
Anyway, I must 'a' jes'
Kind o' drapped asleep, I guess;
'Cause when Jonas must 'a' passed
Me, a-comin' in, I knowed
Nothin' of it—yit it seemed
Sort o' like I kind o' dreamed
'Bout him, too, a-slippin' in,
And a-watchin' back to see
Ef I *wuz* asleep, and then

Passin' in where 'Viry wuz;
And where I declare it does
'Pear to me I heerd him say,
Wild and glad and whisperin'—
'Peared-like heerd him say, says-ee,
"Ah! I' got you home ag'in—
    Home ag'in with me!"

THE SPOILED CHILD

'CAUSE Herbert Graham's a' only child—
  "Wuz I there, Ma?"
His parunts uz got him purt' nigh spiled—
  "Wuz I there, Ma?"
Allus ever'where his Ma tells
Where *she's* bin at, little Herbert yells,
  "Wuz I there, Ma?"
An' when she telled us wunst when she
Wuz ist 'bout big as him an' me,
  W'y, little Herbert he says, says-ee,
  "Wuz I there, Ma?"
Foolishest young-un you ever saw.—
"Wuz I there, Ma? Wuz I there, Ma?"

THE BEE-BAG

WHEN I was ist a Brownie—a weenty-
teenty Brownie—
Long afore I got to be like Childerns is to-day,—
My good old Brownie granny gimme sweeter thing
'an can'y—
'An' 'at's my little bee-bag the Fairies stold away!
O my little bee-bag—
My little funny bee-bag—
My little honey bee-bag
The Fairies stold away!

One time when I bin swung in wiv annuver Brownie
young-un
An' lef' sleepin' in a pea-pod while our parunts
went to play,
I waked up ist a-cryin' an' a-sobbin' an' a-sighin'
Fer my little funny bee-bag the Fairies stold
away!
O my little bee-bag—
My little funny bee-bag—
My little honey bee-bag
The Fairies stold away!

It's awful much bewilder'n', but 'at's why I'm *a
      Childern,*
  Ner goin' to git to be no more a Brownie sence
    that day!
My parunts, so imprudent, lef' me sleepin' when
    they shouldn't!
  An' I want my little bee-bag the Fairies stold
    away!
          O my little bee-bag—
          My little funny bee-bag—
          My little honey bee-bag
            The Fairies stold away!

THE TRULY MARVELOUS

GIUNTS is the biggest mens they air
In all this world er anywhere!—
An' Tom Thumb he's the most little-est man,
'Cause wunst he lived in a oyshture-can!

OLD CHUMS

"IF I die first," my old chum paused to say,
    "Mind! not a whimper of regret:—instead,
    Laugh and be glad, as I shall.—Being dead,
I shall not lodge so very far away
But that our mirth shall mingle.—So, the day
    The word comes, joy with me." "I'll try," I said,
    Though, even speaking, sighed and shook my head
And turned, with misted eyes. His roundelay
Rang gaily on the stair; and then the door
    Opened and—closed. . . . Yet something of the
        clear,
    Hale hope, and force of wholesome faith he had
Abided with me—strengthened more and more.—
    Then—then they brought his broken body here:
    And I laughed—whisperingly—and we were
        glad.

"THIS DEAR CHILD-HEARTED WOMAN
THAT IS DEAD"

I

THIS woman, with the dear child-heart,
   Ye mourn as dead, is—where and what?
With faith as artless as her Art,
           I question not,—

But dare divine, and feel, and know
   Her blessedness—as hath been writ
In allegory.—Even so
           I fashion it:—

II

A stately figure, rapt and awed
   In her new guise of Angelhood,
Still lingered, wistful—knowing God
           Was very good.—

Her thought's fine whisper filled the pause;
   And, listening, the Master smiled,
And lo! the stately angel was
         —A little child.

251

"HOW DID YOU REST, LAST NIGHT?"

"HOW did you rest, last night?"—
 I've heard my gran'pap say
Them words a thousand times—that's right—
 Jes' them words thataway!
As punctchul-like as morning dast
 To ever heave in sight
Gran'pap 'ud allus haf to ast—
 "How did you rest, last night?"

Us young-uns used to grin,
 At breakfast, on the sly,
And mock the wobble of his chin
 And eyebrows helt so high
And kind: *"How did you rest, last night?"*
 We'd mumble and let on
Our voices trimbled, and our sight
 Wuz dim, and hearin' gone.

.   .   .   .

Bad as I ust to be,
 All I'm a-wantin' is
As puore and ca'm a sleep fer me
 And sweet a sleep as his!

252

And so I pray, on Jedgment Day
  To wake, and with its light
See *his* face dawn, and hear him say—
  "How did you rest, last night?"

TO—"THE J. W. R. LITERARY CLUB"

WELL, it's enough to turn his head to have a
    feller's name
Swiped with a *Literary* Club!—But *you're* the ones
    to blame!—
I call the World to witness that I never *agged* ye
    to it
By ever writin' *Classic-like—because I couldn't*
    do it.
I never run to "Hellicon," ner writ about "Per-nas-
    sus,"
Ner ever tried to rack er ride around on old
    "P-*gass*us"!
When "Tuneful Nines" has cross'd my lines, the
    ink 'ud blot and blur it,
And pen 'ud jest putt back fer home, and take the
    short-way fer it!
And so, as I'm a-sayin',—when you name your
    Literary
In honor o' this name o' mine, it's railly nesses-
    sary—
Whilse I'm *a-thankin'* you and all—to *warn* you, ef
    you do it,
I'll haf to jine the thing myse'f 'fore I can live up
    to it!

OUT OF THE DARK AND THE DEARTH

HO! but the darkness was densely black!
  And young feet faltered and groped their
    way,
With never the gleam of a star, alack!
  Nor a moonbeam's lamest ray!—
    Blind of light as the blind of sight.—
    And that was the night—the night!

And out of the blackness, vague and vast,
  And out of the dark and the dearth, behold!—
A great ripe radiance grew at last
  And burst like a bubble of gold,
    Gilding the way that the feet danced on.—
    And that was the dawn—The Dawn!

LITTLE DAVID

THE mother of the little boy that sleeps
Has blest assurance, even as she weeps:
She knows her little boy has now no pain—
No further ache, in body, heart or brain;
All sorrow is lulled for him—all distress
Passed into utter peace and restfulness.—
All health that heretofore has been denied—
All happiness, all hope, and all beside
Of childish longing, now he clasps and keeps
In voiceless joy—the little boy that sleeps.

HOME AGAIN

I'M bin a-visitun 'bout a week
To my little Cousin's at Nameless Creek;
An' I'm got the hives an' a new straw hat,
An' I'm come back home where my beau lives at.

A SEA-SONG FROM THE SHORE

HAIL! Ho!
Sail! Ho!
Ahoy! Ahoy! Ahoy!
Who calls to me,
So far at sea?
Only a little boy!

Sail! Ho!
Hail! Ho!
The sailor he sails the sea:
I wish he would capture
A little sea-horse
And send him home to me.

I wish, as he sails
Through the tropical gales,
He would catch me a sea-bird, too,
With its silver wings
And the song it sings,
And its breast of down and dew!

I wish he would catch me a
Little mermaid,
Some island where he lands,
With her dripping curls,
And her crown of pearls,
And the looking-glass in her hands!

Hail! Ho!
Sail! Ho!
Sail far o'er the fabulous main!
And if I were a sailor,
I'd sail with you,
Though I never sailed back again.

THE DEAD WIFE

ALWAYS I see her in a saintly guise
   Of lilied raiment, white as her own brow
When first I kissed the tear-drops to the eyes
    That smile forever now.

Those gentle eyes! They seem the same to me,
   As, looking through the warm dews of mine
     own,
I see them gazing downward patiently
    Where, lost and all alone

In the great emptiness of night, I bow
   And sob aloud for one returning touch
Of the dear hands that, Heaven having now,
    I need so much—so much!

TO ELIZABETH

OBIT JULY 8, 1893

O NOBLE, true and pure and lovable
    As thine own blessed name, ELIZA-
        BETH !—
    Aye, even as its cadence lingereth
Upon the lips that speak it, so the spell
Of thy sweet memory shall ever dwell
    As music in our hearts. Smiling at Death
    As on some later guest that tarrieth,
Too gratefully o'erjoyed to say farewell,
Thou hast turned from us but a little space—
    We miss thy presence but a little while,
        Thy voice of sympathy, thy word of cheer,
The radiant glory of thine eyes and face,
    The glad midsummer morning of thy smile,—
        For still we feel and know that thou art
        here.

ARMAZINDY

ARMAZINDY;—fambily name
   Ballenger,—you'll find the same,
As her Daddy answered it,
In the old War-rickords yit,—
And, like him, she's airnt the good
Will o' all the neighberhood.—
Name ain't down in *History,*—
But, i jucks! it *ort* to be!
Folks is got respec' fer *her*—
Armazindy Ballenger!—
'Specially the ones 'at knows
Fac's o' how her story goes
From the start:—Her father blowed
Up—eternally furloughed—
When the old "Sultana" bu'st,
And sich men wuz needed wusst.—
Armazindy, 'bout fourteen-
Year-old then—and thin and lean
As a killdee,—but—*my la!*—
Blamedest nerve you ever saw!
The girl's mother'd *allus* be'n
Sickly—wuz consumpted when
Word came 'bout her husband.—So

Folks perdicted *she'd* soon go—
(Kind o' grief *I* understand,
Losin' *my* companion,—and
Still a widower—and still
Hinted at, like neighbers will!)
So, app'inted, as folks said,
Ballenger a-bein' dead,
Widder, 'peared-like, gradjully,
Jes' grieved after him tel *she*
Died, nex' Aprile wuz a year,—
And in Armazindy's keer
Leavin' the two twins, as well
As her pore old miz'able
Old-maid aunty 'at had be'n
Struck with palsy, and wuz then
Jes' a he'pless charge on *her*—
Armazindy Ballenger.

Jevver watch a primrose 'bout
Minute 'fore it blossoms out—
Kind o' loosen-like, and blow
Up its muscles, don't you know,
And, all suddent, bu'st and bloom
Out life-size?—Well, I persume
'At's the only measure I
Kin size Armazindy by!—
Jes' a *child, one* minute,—nex',
Woman-grown, in all respec's
And intents and purposuz—
'At's what Armazindy wuz!

Jes' a *child,* I tell ye! Yit
She made things git up and git
Round that little farm o' hern!—
Shouldered all the whole concern;—
Feed the stock, and milk the cows—
Run the *farm* and run the *house!*—
Only thing she didn't do
Wuz to plough and harvest too—
But the house and childern took
Lots o' keer—and had to look
After her old fittified
Grand-aunt.—Lord! ye could 'a' cried,
Seein' Armazindy smile,
'Peared-like, sweeter all the while!
And I've heerd her laugh and say:—
"Jes' afore Pap marched away,
He says, 'I depend on *you,*
Armazindy, come what may—
You must be a Soldier, too!'"

Neighbers, from the fust, 'ud come—
And she'd *let* 'em help her *some,*—
"Thanky, ma'am!" and "Thanky, sir!"
But no charity fer *her!*—
"*She* could raise the means to pay
Fer her farm-hands ever' day
Sich wuz needed!"—And she *could*—
In cash-money jes' as good
As farm-produc's ever brung
Their perducer, *old* er young!

So folks humored her and smiled,
And at last wuz rickonciled
Fer to let her have her own
Way about it.—But a-goin'
Past to town, they'd stop and see
"Armazindy's fambily,"
As they'd allus laugh and say,
And look sorry right away,
Thinkin' of her Pap, and how
He'd indorse his "Soldier" now!

'Course *she* couldn't never be
Much in *young-folks'* company—
Plenty of *in*-vites to go,
But das't leave the house, you know—
'Less'n *Sund'ys* sometimes, when
Some old *Granny*'d come and 'ten'
Things, while Armazindy *has*
Got away fer Church er "Class."
Most the youngsters *liked* her—and
'Twuzn't hard to understand,—
Fer, by time she wuz sixteen,
Purtier girl you never seen—
'Ceptin' she lacked schoolin', ner
Couldn't rag out stylisher—
Like some *neighber*-girls, ner thumb
On their blame' melodium,
Whilse their pore old mothers sloshed
Round the old back-porch and washed
Their clothes fer 'em—rubbed and scrubbed
Fer girls'd ort to jes' be'n clubbed!

—And jes' sich a girl wuz Jule
Reddinhouse.—*She'd* be'n to school
At *New Thessaly,* i gum!—
Fool before, but that he'pped *some*—
'Stablished-like more confidence
'At she *never* had no sense.
But she wuz a cunnin', sly,
Meek and lowly sort o' lie,
'At men-folks like me and you
B'lieves jes' 'cause we ortn't to.—
Jes' as purty as a snake,
And as *pizen*—mercy sake!
Well, about them times it wuz,
Young Sol Stephens th'ashed fer us;
And we sent him over to
Armazindy's place to do
Her work fer her.—And-sir!   Well—
Mighty little else to tell,—
Sol he fell in love with her—
Armazindy Ballenger!

Bless ye!—'Ll, of all the love
'At I've ever yit knowed of,
That-air case o' theirn beat all!
W'y, she *worshiped* him!—And Sol,
'Peared-like, could 'a' kissed the sod
(Sayin' is) where that girl trod!
Went to town, she did, and bought
Lot o' things 'at neighbers thought
Mighty strange fer *her* to buy,—
Raal chintz dress-goods—and 'way high!—

Cut long in the skyrt,—also
Gaiter-pair o' shoes, you know;
And lace collar;—yes, and fine
Stylish hat, with ivy-vine
And red ribbons, and these-'ere
Artificial flowers and queer
Little beads and spangles, and
Oysturch-feathers round the band!
Wore 'em, Sund'ys, fer a while—
Kind o' went to Church in style,
Sol and Armazindy!—Tel
It was noised round purty well
They wuz *promised.*—And they wuz—
Sich news travels—well it does!—
Pity 'at *that* did!—Fer jes'
That-air fac' and nothin' less
Must 'a' putt it in the mind
O' Jule Reddinhouse to find
Out some dratted way to hatch
Out *some* plan to break the match—
'Cause she *done* it!—*How?* they's none
Knows adzac'ly *what* she done;
Some claims she writ letters to
Sol's folks, up nigh Pleasant View
Somers—and described, you see,
"Armazindy's fambily"—
Hintin' "ef Sol married *her,*
He'd jes' be pervidin' fer
Them-air twins o' hern, and old
Palsied aunt 'at couldn't hold
Spoon to mouth, and layin' near

Bedrid' on to eighteen year',
And still likely, 'pearantly,
To live out the century !"
Well—whatever plan Jule laid
Out to reach the p'int she made,
It wuz *desper't*.—And she won,
Finully, by marryun
Sol herse'f—*e-lopin'*, too,
With him, like she *had* to do,—
'Cause her folks 'ud allus swore
"Jule should never marry pore !"

This-here part the story I
Allus haf to hurry by,—
Way 'at Armazindy jes'
Drapped back in her linsey dress,
And grabbed holt her loom, and shet
Her jaws square.—And ef she fret
Any 'bout it—never 'peared
Sign 'at *neighbers* seed er heerd ;—
Most folks liked her all the more—
I know *I* did—certain-shore !—
('Course *I'd* knowed her *Pap,* and what
Stock she come of.—Yes, and thought,
And think *yit,* no man on earth
'S worth as much as that girl's worth !)

As fer Jule and Sol, they had
Their sheer !—less o' good than bad !—
Her folks let her go.—They said,
"Spite o' them she'd made her bed

And must sleep in it!"—But she,
'Peared-like, didn't sleep so free
As she ust to—ner so *late,*
Ner so *fine,* I'm here to state!—
Sol wuz pore, of course, and she
Wuzn't ust to poverty—
Ner she didn't 'pear to jes'
'Filiate with lonesomeness,—
'Cause Sol *he* wuz off and out
With his th'asher nigh about
Half the time; er, season done,
He'd be off mi-anderun
Round the country, here and there,
Swappin' hosses. Well, that-air
Kind o' livin' didn't suit
Jule a bit!—and then, to boot,
She had now the keer o' two
Her own childern—and to do
Her own work and cookin'—yes,
And sometimes fer *hands,* I guess,
Well as fambily of her own.—
Cut her pride clean to the bone!
So how *could* the whole thing end?—
She set down, one night, and penned
A short note, like—'at she sewed
On the childern's blanket—blowed
Out the candle—pulled the door
To close after her—and, shore-
Footed as a cat is, clumb
In a rigg there and left home,

With a man a-drivin' who
"Loved her ever fond and true,"
As her note went on to say,
When Sol read the thing next day.

Raaly didn't 'pear to be
Extry waste o' sympathy
Over Sol—pore feller!—Yit,
Sake o' them-air little bit
O' two *orphants*—as you might
Call 'em *then,* by law and right,—
Sol's old friends wuz sorry, and
Tried to hold him out their hand
Same as allus: But he'd flinch—
Tel, jes' 'peared-like, inch by inch,
He let *all* holts go; and so
Took to drinkin', don't you know,—
Tel, to make a long tale short,
He wuz fuller than he ort
To 'a' be'n, at work one day
'Bout his th'asher, and give way,
Kind o' like and fell and ketched
In the beltin'.
                    . . . Rid and fetched
Armazindy to him.—He
Begged me to.—But time 'at she
Reached his side, he smiled and *tried*
To speak:—Couldn't. So he died. . . .
Hands all turned and left her there
And went somers else—*some*where.

Last, she called us back—in clear
Voice as man'll ever hear—
Clear and stiddy, 'peared to me,
As her old Pap's ust to be.—
Give us orders what to do
'Bout the body—he'pped us, too.
So it wuz, Sol Stephens passed
In Armazindy's hands at last.
More'n that, she claimed 'at she
Had consent from him to be
Mother to his childern—now
'Thout no parents anyhow.

Yes-sir! and she's *got* 'em, too,—
Folks saw nothin' else 'ud do—
So they let her have *her way*—
Like she's doin' yit to-day!
Years now, I've be'n coaxin' her—
Armazindy Ballenger—
To in-large her fambily
Jes' *one* more by takin' *me*—
Which I'm feared she never will,
Though I'm 'lectioneerin' still.

THREE SINGING FRIENDS

I

LEE O. HARRIS

SCHOOLMASTER and Songmaster! Memory
    Enshrines thee with an equal love, for thy
    Duality of gifts,—thy pure and high
Endowments—Learning rare, and Poesy.
These were as mutual handmaids, serving thee,
    Throughout all seasons of the years gone by,
    With all enduring joys 'twixt earth and sky—
In turn shared nobly with thy friends and me.
Thus is it that thy clear song, ringing on,
    Is endless inspiration, fresh and free
        As the old Mays at verge of June sunshine;
And musical as then, at dewy dawn,
    The robin hailed us, and all twinklingly
        Our one path wandered under wood and vine.

II

BENJ. S. PARKER

Thy rapt song makes of Earth a realm of light
    And shadow mystical as some dreamland
    Arched with unfathomed azure—vast and
        grand

With splendor of the morn; or dazzling bright
With orient noon; or strewn with stars of night
　　Thick as the daisies blown in grasses fanned
　　By odorous midsummer breezes and
Showered over by all bird-songs exquisite.
This is thy voice's beatific art—
　　To make melodious all things below,
　　　　Calling through them, from far, diviner
　　　　　　space,
Thy clearer hail to us.—The faltering heart
　　Thou cheerest; and thy fellow mortal so
　　　　Fares onward under Heaven with lifted face.

III

JAMES NEWTON MATTHEWS

Bard of our Western world!—its prairies wide,
　　With edging woods, lost creeks and hidden
　　　　ways;
　　Its isolated farms, with roundelays
Of orchard warblers heard on every side;
Its cross-road schoolhouse, wherein still abide
　　Thy fondest memories,—since there thy gaze
　　First fell on classic verse; and thou, in praise
Of that, didst find thine own song glorified.
So singing, smite the strings and counterchange
　　The lucently melodious drippings of
　　　　Thy happy harp, from airs of "Tempe Vale,"
To chirp and trill of lowliest flight and range,
　　In praise of our To-day and home and love—
　　　　Thou meadow-lark no less than nightingale.

AT HIS WINTRY TENT

SAMUEL RICHARDS—ARTIST—DENVER, COLORADO

NOT only master of his art was he,
　But master of his spirit—winged indeed
　For lordliest height, yet poised for lowliest need
Of those, alas! upheld less buoyantly.
He gloried even in adversity,
　And won his country's plaudits, and the meed
　Of Old World praise, as one loath to succeed
While others were denied like victory.
Though passed, I count him still my master-friend,
　Invincible as through his mortal fight,—
　　The laughing light of faith still in his eye
As, at his wintry tent, pitched at the end
　Of life, he gaily called to me "Good night,
　　Old friend, good night—for there is no
　　good-by."

UP AND DOWN OLD BRANDYWINE

UP and down old Brandywine,
    In the days 'at's past and gone—
With a dad-burn hook-and-line
    And a saplin'-pole—i swawn!
        I've had more fun, to the square
        Inch, than ever *any*where!
        Heaven to come can't discount *mine,*
        Up and down old Brandywine!

Hain't no sense in *wishin'*—yit
    Wisht to goodness I *could* jes'
"Gee" the blame' world round and git
    Back to that old happiness!—
        Kind o' drive back in the shade
        "The old Covered Bridge" there laid
        'Crosst the crick, and sort o' soak
        My soul over, hub and spoke!

Honest, now!—it hain't no *dream*
    'At I'm wantin',—but *the fac's*
As they wuz; the same old stream,
    And the same old times, i jacks!—

Gimme back my bare feet—and
Stonebruise too!—And scratched and tanned!—
And let hottest dog-days shine
Up and down old Brandywine!

In and on betwixt the trees
  'Long the banks, pour down yer noon,
Kind o' curdled with the breeze
  And the yallerhammer's tune;
    And the smokin', chokin' dust
    O' the turnpike at its wusst—
    Saturd'ys, say, when it seems
    Road's jes' jammed with country teams!

Whilse the old town, fur away
  'Crosst the hazy pastur'-land,
Dozed-like in the heat o' day
  Peaceful' as a hired hand.
    Jolt the gravel th'ough the floor
    O' the old bridge!—grind and roar
    With yer blame' percession-line—
    Up and down old Brandywine!

Souse me and my new straw hat
  Off the foot-log!—what *I* care?—
Fist shoved in the crown o' that—
  Like the old Clown ust to wear.—
    Wouldn't swap it fer a' old
    Gin-u-wine raal crown o' gold!—
    Keep yer *King* ef you'll gim-me
    Jes' the boy I ust to be!

Spill my fishin'-worms! er steal
  My best "goggle-eye!"—but you
Can't lay hands on joys I feel
  Nibblin' like they ust to do!
    So, in memory, to-day
    Same old ripple lips away
    At my "cork" and saggin' line,
    Up and down old Brandywine!

There the logs is, round the hill,
  Where "Old Irvin" ust to lift
Out sunfish from daylight till
  Dewfall—'fore he'd leave "The Drift"
    And give *us* a chance—and then
    Kind o' fish back home again,
    Ketchin' 'em jes' left and right
    Where *we* hadn't got "a bite"!

Er, 'way windin' out and in,—
  Old path th'ough the iurnweeds
And dog-fennel to yer chin—
  Then come suddent, th'ough the reeds
    And cattails, smack into where
    Them-air woods-hogs ust to scare
    Us clean 'crosst the County-line,
    Up and down old Brandywine!

But the dim roar o' the dam
  It 'ud coax us furder still
To'rds the old race, slow and ca'm,
  Slidin' on to Huston's mill—

Where, I 'spect, "the Freeport crowd"
Never *warmed* to us er 'lowed
We wuz quite so overly
Welcome as we aimed to be.

Still it 'peared-like ever'thing—
   Fur away from home as *there*—
Had more *relish*-like, i jing!—
   Fish in stream, er bird in air!
      O them rich old bottom-lands,
      Past where Cowden's Schoolhouse stands!
      Wortermelons—*master-mine!*
      Up and down old Brandywine!

And sich pop-paws!—Lumps o' raw
   Gold and green,—jes' oozy th'ough
With ripe yaller—like you've saw
   Custard-pie with no crust to:
      And jes' *gorges* o' wild plums,
      Till a feller'd suck his thumbs
      Clean up to his elbows! *My!*—
      Me some more er lem me die!

Up and down old Brandywine!
   Stripe me with pokeberry-juice!—
Flick me with a pizen-vine
   And yell *"Yip!"* and lem me loose!
      —Old now as I then wuz young,
      'F I could sing as I *have* sung,
      Song 'ud shorely ring *dee-vine*
      Up and down old Brandywine!

WRITIN' BACK TO THE HOME-FOLKS

M Y dear old friends—It jes' beats all,
    The way you write a letter
So's ever' *last* line beats the *first*,
    And ever' *next*-un's better!—
W'y, ever' fool-thing you putt down
    You make so inter*est*in',
A feller, readin' of 'em all,
    Can't tell which is the *best*-un.

It's all so comfortin' and good,
    'Pears-like I almost *hear* ye
And git more sociabler, you know,
    And hitch my cheer up near ye
And jes' smile on ye like the sun
    Acrosst the whole per-rairies
In Aprile when the thaw's begun
    And country couples marries.

It's all so good-old-fashioned like
    To *talk* jes' like we're *thinkin'*,
Without no hidin' back o' fans
    And giggle-un and winkin';

279

Ner sizin' how each other's dressed—
  Like some is allus doin',—
"*Is* Marthy Ellen's basque be'n *turned*
  Er shore-enough a new-un!"—

Er "ef Steve's city-friend hain't jes'
  'A *lee*tle kind o' sort o' ' "—
Er "wears them-air blame' eye-glasses
  Jes' 'cause he hadn't ort to?"—
And so straight on, *dad-libitum,*
  Tel all of us feels, *some*way,
Jes' like our "comp'ny" wuz the best
  When we git up to come 'way!

That's why I like *old* friends like *you,*—
  Jes' 'cause you're so *abidin'.*—
Ef I wuz built to live *"fer keeps,"*
  My principul residin'
Would be amongst the folks 'at kep'
  Me allus *thinkin'* of 'em,
And sort o' eechin' all the time
  To tell 'em how I love 'em.—

Sich folks, you know, I jes' love so
  I wouldn't live without 'em,
Er couldn't even drap asleep
  But what I *dreamp'* about 'em,—
And ef we minded God, I guess
  We'd *all* love one another
Jes' like one famb'ly,—me and Pap
  And Madaline and Mother.

WE DEFER THINGS

WE say and we say and we say,
  We promise, engage and declare,
Till a year from to-morrow is yesterday,
  And yesterday is—Where?

FOR THIS CHRISTMAS

YE old-time stave that pealeth out
 To Christmas revelers all,
At tavern-tap and wassail bout,
 And in ye banquet hall,—
Whiles ye old burden rings again,
 Add yet ye verse, as due:
"God bless you, merry gentlemen"—
 And gentlewomen, too!

TO A POET-CRITIC

YES,—the bee sings—I confess it—
  Sweet as honey—Heaven bless it!—
Yit he'd be a *sweeter* singer
Ef he didn't have no stinger.

A NOON LULL

'POSSUM in de 'tater-patch;
   Chicken-hawk a-hangin'
Stiddy 'bove de stable-lot,
   An' cyarpet-loom a-bangin'!
Hi! Mr. Hoppergrass, chawin' yo' terbacker,
Flick ye wid er buggy-whirp yer spit er little
      blacker!

Niggah in de roas'in'-yeers,
   Whiskers in de shuckin';
Weasel croppin' mighty shy,
   But ole hen a-cluckin'!
—What's got de matter er de mule-colt now?
Drapt in de turnip-hole, chasin' f'um de cow!

RABBIT IN THE CROSS-TIES

RABBIT in the cross-ties.—
 Punch him out—quick!
Git a twister on him
 With a long prong stick.
Watch him on the south side—
 Watch him on the—Hi!—
There he goes! Sic him, Tige!
 Yi! Yi!! Yi!!!

WHEN LIDE MARRIED *HIM*

WHEN Lide married *him*—w'y, she had to jes'
    dee-fy
The whole popilation!—But she never bat' an eye!
Her parents begged, and *threatened*—she must give
    him up—that *he*
Wuz jes' "a common drunkard!"—And he *wuz,*
    appearantly.—
        Swore they'd chase him off the place
        Ef he ever showed his face—
Long after she'd *eloped* with him and *married* him
    fer shore!—
When Lide married *him,* it wuz *"Katy, bar the
    door!"*

When Lide married *him*—Well! she had to go
    and be
A *hired girl* in town somewheres—while he tromped
    round to see
What *he* could git that *he* could do,—you might say,
    jes' sawed wood
From door to door!—that's what he done—'cause
    that wuz best he could!
        And the strangest thing, i jing!
        Wuz, he didn't *drink* a thing,—

But jes' got down to bizness, like he someway
    wanted to,
When Lide married *him*, like they warned her *not*
    to do!

When Lide married *him*—er, ruther, *had* be'n mar-
    ried
A little up'ards of a year—some feller come and
    carried
That *hired girl* away with him—a ruther *stylish*
    feller
In a bran-new green spring-wagon, with the wheels
    striped red and yeller:
        And he whispered, as they driv
        To'rds the country, *"Now we'll live!"*—
And *somepin' else* she *laughed* to hear, though both
    her eyes wuz dim,
'Bout *"trustin' Love and Heav'n above,* sence Lide
    married *him!"*

"RINGWORM FRANK"

JEST Frank Reed's his *real* name—though
   Boys all calls him "Ringworm Frank,"
'Cause he allus *runs round* so.—
   No man can't tell where to bank
      Frank'll be,
      Next you see
Er *hear* of him!—Drat his melts!—
That man's allus *somers else!*

We're old pards.—But Frank he jest
   Can't stay still!—Wuz *prosper'n'* here,
But lit out on furder West
   Somers on a ranch, last year:
      Never heard
      Nary a word
How he liked it, tel to-day,
Got this card, reads thisaway:—

"Dad-burn climate out here makes
   Me homesick all Winter long,
And when Spring-time *comes,* it takes
   Two pee-wees to sing one song,—
      One sings '*pee,*'
      And the other one '*wee!*'
Stay right where you air, old pard.—
Wisht *I* wuz this postal card!"

THE YOUTHFUL PATRIOT

O WHAT did the little boy do
    'At nobody wanted him to?
Didn't do nothin' but romp an' run,
An' whoop an' holler an' bang his gun
An' bu'st fire-crackers, an' ist have fun—
    An' 'at's all the little boy done!

PONCHUS PILUT

PONCHUS PILUT *ust* to be
Ist a *Slave,* an' now he's *free.*
Slaves wuz on'y ist before
The War wuz—an' *ain't* no more.

He works on our place fer us,—
An' comes here—*sometimes* he does.
He shocks corn an' shucks it.—An'
He makes hominy "by han' "!—

Wunst he bringed us some, one trip,
Tied up in a piller-slip:
Pa says, when Ma cooked it, "MY!
This-here's gooder'n you *buy!*"

Ponchus *pats* fer me an' sings;
An' he says most *funny* things!
Ponchus calls a dish a *"deesh"*—
Yes, an' *he* calls fishes *"feesh"!*

When Ma want him eat wiv us
He says, " 'Skuse me—'deed you mus'!
Ponchus know' good manners, Miss.—
He ain' eat wher' White-folks is!"

'Lindy takes *his* dinner out
Wher' he's workin'—roun' about.—
Wunst he et his dinner spread
In our ole wheelborry-bed.

Ponchus Pilut says " '*at's* not
His *right* name,—an' done fergot
What his *sho'-'nuff* name is now—
An' don' matter none *nohow!*"

Yes, an' Ponchus he'ps Pa, too,
When our *butcherin'* '*s* to do,
An' scalds hogs—an' says, "Take care
'Bout it, er you'll *set the hair!*"

Yes, an' out in our back yard
He he'ps 'Lindy rendur lard;
An', wite in the fire there, he
Roast' a pigtail wunst fer me.—

An' ist nen th'ole tavurn bell
Rung, down-town, an' he says, "Well!—
Hear dat! *Lan' o' Caanan,* Son,
Ain't dat bell say '*Pigtail done!*'

> —'*Pigtail done!*
> *Go call Son!*—
> *Tell dat*
> *Chile dat*
> *Pigtail done!*' "

SLUMBER-SONG

SLEEP, little one! The Twilight folds her
       gloom
  Full tenderly about the drowsy Day,
And all his tinseled hours of light and bloom
      Like toys are laid away.

Sleep! sleep! The noon-sky's airy cloud of white
  Has deepened wide o'er all the azure plain;
And, trailing through the leaves, the skirts of Night
      Are wet with dews as rain.

But rest thou sweetly, smiling in thy dreams,
  With round fists tossed like roses o'er thy head,
And thy tranc'd lips and eyelids kissed with gleams
      Of rapture perfected.

THE CIRCUS PARADE

THE Circus!—The Circus!—The throb of the
    drums,
And the blare of the horns, as the Band-wagon
    comes;
The clash and the clang of the cymbals that beat,
As the glittering pageant winds down the long
    street!

In the Circus parade there is glory clean down
From the first spangled horse to the mule of the
    Clown,
With the gleam and the glint and the glamour and
    glare
Of the days of enchantment all glimmering there!

And there are the banners of silvery fold
Caressing the winds with their fringes of gold,
And their high-lifted standards, with spear-tips
    aglow,
And the helmeted knights that go riding below.

There's the Chariot, wrought of some marvelous
    shell
The Sea gave to Neptune, first washing it well
With its fabulous waters of gold, till it gleams
Like the galleon rare of an Argonaut's dreams.

And the Elephant, too, (with his undulant stride
That rocks the high throne of a king in his pride),
That in jungles of India shook from his flanks
The tigers that leapt from the Jujubee-banks.

Here's the long, ever-changing, mysterious line
Of the Cages, with hints of their glories divine
From the barred little windows, cut high in the rear
Where the close-hidden animals' noses appear.

Here's the Pyramid-car, with its splendor and flash,
And the Goddess on high, in a hot-scarlet sash
And a pen-wiper skirt!—O the rarest of sights
Is this "Queen of the Air" in cerulean tights!

Then the far-away clash of the cymbals, and then
The swoon of the tune ere it wakens again
With the capering tones of the gallant cornet
That go dancing away in a mad minuet.

The Circus!—The Circus!—The throb of the
    drums,
And the blare of the horns, as the Band-wagon
    comes;
The clash and the clang of the cymbals that beat,
As the glittering pageant winds down the long
    street.

FOLKS AT LONESOMEVILLE

PORE-FOLKS lives at Lonesome-
     ville—
  Lawzy! but they're pore
Houses with no winders in,
  And hardly any door:
Chimbly all tore down, and no
  Smoke in that at all—
Ist a stovepipe through a hole
  In the kitchen wall!

Pump 'at's got no handle on;
  And no wood-shed—And, *wooh!*—
Mighty cold there, choppin' wood,
  Like pore-folks has to do!—
Winter-time, and snow and sleet
  Ist fairly fit to kill!—
Hope to goodness *Santy Claus*
  Goes to Lonesomeville!

THE THREE JOLLY HUNTERS

O THERE were three jolly hunters;
And a-hunting they did go,
With a spaniel-dog, and a pointer-dog,
And a setter-dog also.
                    Looky there!

And they hunted and they hal-looed;
And the first thing they did find
Was a dingling-dangling hornet's-nest
A-swinging in the wind.
                    Looky there!

And the first one said—"What is it?"
Said the next, "We'll punch and see":
And the next one said, a mile from there,
"I wish we'd let it be!"
                    Looky there!

And they hunted and they hal-looed;
And the next thing they did raise
Was a bobbin' bunny cottontail
That vanished from their gaze.
                    Looky there!

One said it was a hot baseball,
  Zipped through the brambly thatch,
But the others said 'twas a note by post,
  Or a telegraph-despatch.
              Looky there!

So they hunted and they hal-looed;
  And the next thing they did sight
Was a great big bulldog chasing them,
  And a farmer, hollerin' "Skite!"
              Looky there!

And the first one said, "Hi-jinktum!"
  And the next, "Hi-jinktum-jee!"
And the last one said, "Them very words
  Had just occurred to me!"
              Looky there!

THE LITTLE DOG-WOGGY

A LITTLE Dog-Woggy
Once walked round the World:
So he shut up his house; and, forgetting
His two puppy-children
Locked in there, he curled
Up his tail in pink bombazine netting,
And set out
To walk round
The World.

He walked to Chicago,
And heard of the Fair—
Walked on to New York, where he *never,*—
In fact, he discovered
That many folks there
Thought less of Chicago than ever,
As he musing-
Ly walked round
The World.

He walked on to Boston,
And round Bunker Hill,
Bow-wowed, but no citizen heerd him—
Till he ordered his baggage
And called for his bill,

And then, bless their souls! how they cheered
            him,
        As he gladly
        Walked on round
            The World.

    He walked and walked on
    For a year and a day—
Dropped down at his own door and panted,
    Till a teamster came driving
    Along the highway
And told him that house there was ha'nted
        By the two starve-
        Dest pups in
            The World.

CHARMS

I

PRUNE your corn in the gray of the morn
  With a blade that's shaved the dead,
And barefoot go and hide it so
  The rain will rust it red:
Dip your foot in the dew and put
  A print of it on the floor,
And stew the fat of a brindle cat,
  And say this o'er and o'er :—
    Corny! morny! blady! dead!
    Gory! sory! rusty! red!
    Footsy! putsy! floory! stew!
    Fatsy! catsy!
          Mew!
          Mew!
      Come grease my corn
      In the gray of the morn!
        Mew! Mew! Mew!

300

II

TO REMOVE FRECKLES—SCOTCH ONES

Gae the mirkest night an' stan'
'Twixt twa graves, ane either han';
Wi' the right han' fumblin' ken
Wha the deid mon's name's ance be'n,—
Wi' the ither han' sae read
Wha's neist neebor o' the deid;
An it be or wife or lass,
Smoor tha twa han's i' the grass,
Weshin' either wi' the ither,
Then tha faice wi baith thegither;
Syne ye'll seeket at cockcraw—
Ilka freckle's gang awa!

A FEW OF THE BIRD-FAMILY

THE Old Bob-white and Chipbird;
   The Flicker, and Chewink,
And little hopty-skip bird
   Along the river-brink.

The Blackbird, and Snowbird,
   The Chicken-hawk, and Crane;
The glossy old black Crow-bird,
   And Buzzard down the lane.

The Yellowbird, and Redbird,
   The Tomtit, and the Cat;
The Thrush, and that Red*head*-bird
   The rest's all pickin' at!

The Jay-bird, and the Bluebird,
   The Sapsuck, and the Wren—
The Cockadoodle-doo-bird,
   And our old Settin'-hen!

302

THROUGH SLEEPY-LAND

WHERE do you go when you go to sleep,
  Little Boy! Little Boy! where?
'Way—'way in where's Little Bo-Peep,
And Little Boy Blue, and the Cows and Sheep
  A-wandering 'way in there—in there—
    A-wandering 'way in there!

And what do you see when lost in dreams,
  Little Boy, 'way in there?
Firefly-glimmers and glowworm gleams,
And silvery, low, slow-sliding streams,
  And mermaids, smiling out—'way in where
    They're a-hiding—'way in there!

Where do you go when the Fairies call,
  Little Boy! Little Boy! where?
Wade through the dews of the grasses tall,
Hearing the weir and the waterfall
  And the Wee Folk—'way in there—in
      there—
    And the Kelpies—'way in there!

And what do you do when you wake at **dawn,**
  Little Boy! Little Boy! what?
Hug my Mommy and kiss her on
Her smiling eyelids, sweet and wan,
  And tell her everything I've forgot,
    A-wandering 'way in there—in there—
    Through the blind-world 'way in there!

THE TRESTLE AND THE BUCK-SAW

THE Trestle and the Buck-Saw
    Went out a-walking once,
And stayed away and stayed away
    For days and weeks and months:
And when they got back home again,
    Of all that had occurred,
The neighbors said the gossips said
    They never said a word.

THE KING OF OO-RINKTUM-JING

DAINTY Baby Austin!
Your Daddy's gone to Boston
    To see the King
    Of Oo-Rinktum-Jing
And the whale he rode acrost on!

Boston Town's a city:
But O it's such a pity!—
    They'll greet the King
    Of Oo-Rinktum-Jing
With never a nursery ditty!

But me and you and Mother
Can stay with Baby-brother,
    And sing of the King
    Of Oo-Rinktum-Jing
And laugh at one another!

So what cares Baby Austin
If Daddy *has* gone to Boston
    To see the King
    Of Oo-Rinktum-Jing
And the whale he rode acrost on?

THE TOY PENNY-DOG

MA put my Penny-Dog
    Safe on the shelf,
An' left no one home but him,
    Me an' myself;
So I clumbed a big chair
    I pushed to the wall—
But the Toy Penny-Dog
    Ain't there at all!
I went back to Dolly—
    An' *she* 'uz gone too,
An' little Switch 'uz layin' there;—
    An' Ma says *"Boo!"*—
An' there she wuz a-peepin'
    Through the front-room door:
An' I ain't goin' to be a bad
    Little girl no more!

JARGON-JINGLE

TAWDERY!—faddery! Feathers and fuss!
   Mummery!—flummery! Wusser and wuss!
All o' Humanity—Vanity Fair!—
Heaven for nothin', and—nobody there!

THE GREAT EXPLORER

H E sailed o'er the weltery watery miles
   For a tabular year-and-a-day,
To the kindless, kinkable Cannibal Isles
   He sailed and he sailed away!
He captured a loon in a wild lagoon,
   And a yak that weeps and smiles,
And a bustard-bird, and a blue baboon,
   In the kindless Cannibal Isles
     And wilds
       Of the kinkable Cannibal Isles.

He swiped in bats with his butterfly-net,
   In the kindless Cannibal Isles
And got short-waisted and over-het
   In the haunts of the crocodiles;
And nine or ten little Pigmy Men
   Of the quaintest shapes and styles
He shipped back home to his old Aunt Jenn,
   From the kindless Cannibal Isles
     And wilds
       Of the kinkable Cannibal Isles.

THE SCHOOLBOY'S FAVORITE

Over the river and through the wood
  Now Grandmother's cap I spy:
Hurrah for the fun!—Is the pudding done?
  Hurrah for the pumpkin-pie!
                    —School Reader

FER any boy 'at's little as me,
  Er any little girl,
That-un's the goodest poetry piece
  In any book in the worl'!
An' ef grown-peoples wuz little ag'in
  I bet they'd say so, too,
Ef *they'd* go see *their* ole Gran'ma,
  Like our Pa lets *us* do!

Over the river an' through the wood
  Now Gran'mother's cap I spy:
Hurrah fer the fun!—Is the puddin' done?—
  Hurrah fer the punkin-pie!

An' 'll tell *you* why 'at's the goodest piece:—
  'Cause it's ist like *we* go
To *our* Gran'ma's, a-visitun there,
  When our Pa he says so;

310

An' Ma she fixes my little cape-coat
    An' little fuzz-cap ; an' Pa
He tucks me away—an' yells *"Hoo-ray!"*—
An' whacks Ole Gray, an' drives the sleigh
    Fastest you ever saw !

Over the river an' through the wood
    Now Gran'mother's cap I spy:
Hurrah fer the fun!—Is the puddin' done?—
    Hurrah fer the punkin-pie!

An' Pa ist snuggles me 'tween his knees—
    An' I he'p hold the lines,
An' peek out over the buffalo-robe ;—
An' the wind ist *blows!*—an' the snow ist
    snows!—
    An' the sun ist shines! an' shines !—
An' th' ole horse tosses his head an' coughs
    The frost back in our face.—
An' I' ruther go to my Gran'ma's
    Than any other place !

Over the river an' through the wood
    Now Gran'mother's cap I spy:
Hurrah fer the fun!—Is the puddin' done?—
    Hurrah fer the punkin-pie!

An' all the peoples they is in town
    Watches us whizzin' past
To go a-visitun *our* Gran'ma's,
    Like we all went there last ;—

But *they* can't go, like ist *our* folks
An' Johnny an' Lotty, and three
Er four neighber-childerns, an' Rober-ut
    Volney,
An' Charley an' Maggy an' me!

Over the river an' through the wood
   Now Gran'mother's cap I spy:
Hurrah fer the fun!—Is the puddin' done?—
   Hurrah fer the punkin-pie!

From a photograph taken when forty-six years old

ALBUMANIA

Some certain misty yet tenable signs
Of the oracular Raggedy Man,
Happily found in these fugitive lines
Culled from the Album of 'Lizabuth Ann.

FRIENDSHIP

O FRIENDSHIP, when I muse on you,
  As thoughtful minds, O Friendship, do,
I muse, O Friendship, o'er and o'er,
O Friendship—as I said before.

LIFE

"What is Life?" If the *Dead* might say,
  'Spect they'd answer, under breath,
Sorry-like yet a-laughin':—A
  Poor pale yesterday of Death!

LIFE'S HAPPIEST HOURS

  Best, I guess,
    Was the old *"Recess."*—
'Way back there's where I'd love to be—

Shet of each lesson and hateful rule,
    When the whole round World was as sweet to me
As the big ripe apple I brung to School.

MARION-COUNTY MAN HOMESICK ABROAD

I, who had hobnobbed with the shades of kings,
    And canvassed grasses from old masters' graves,
And in cathedrals stood and looked at things
    In niches, crypts and naves;—
My heavy heart was sagging with its woe,
    Nor Hope to prop it up, nor Promise, nor
One woman's hands—and O I wanted so
    To be felt sorry for!

BIRDY! BIRDY!

The Redbreast loves the blooming bough—
    The Bluebird loves it same as he;—
And as they sit and sing there now,
    So do I sing to thee—
Only, dear heart, unlike the birds,
    I do not climb a tree
        To sing—
    I do not climb a tree.

When o'er this page, in happy years to come,
    Thou jokest on these lines and on my name,
Doubt not my love and say, "Though he lies dumb,
    He's lying, just the same!"

THE LITTLE MOCK-MAN

THE Little Mock-man on the Stairs—
He mocks the lady's horse 'at rares
    At bi-sickles an' things,—
He mocks the mens 'at rides 'em, too;
An' mocks the Movers, drivin' through,
An' hollers, "Here's the way *you* do
    With them-air hitchin'-strings!"
        "Ho! ho!" he'll say,
        Ole Settlers' Day,
    When they're all jogglin' by,—
        "You look like *this*,"
        He'll say, an' twis'
    His mouth an' squint his eye
An' 'tend-like *he* wuz beat the bass
    Drum at both ends—an' toots an' blares
Ole dinner-horn an' puffs his face—
    The Little Mock-man on the Stairs!

The Little Mock-man on the Stairs
Mocks all the peoples all he cares
    'At passes up an' down!
He mocks the chickens round the door,
An' mocks the girl 'at scrubs the floor,

An' mocks the rich, an' mocks the pore,
 An' ever'thing in town!
  "Ho! ho!" says he,
  To you er me;
 An' ef we turns an' looks,
  He's all cross-eyed
  An' mouth all wide
 Like Giunts is, in books.—
"Ho! ho!" he yells, "look here at *me*,"
 An' rolls his fat eyes roun' an' glares,—
"*You* look like *this!*" he says, says he—
 The Little Mock-man on the Stairs!

The Little Mock—
 The Little Mock—
  The Little Mock-man on the Stairs,
He mocks the music-box an' clock,
 An' roller-sofy an' the chairs;
 He mocks his Pa, an' specs he wears;
 He mocks the man 'at picks the pears
 An' plums an' peaches on the shares;
 He mocks the monkeys an' the bears
 On picture-bills, an' rips an' tears
 'Em down,—an' mocks ist all he cares,
 An' EVER'*body* EVER'*wheres!*

SUMMER-TIME AND WINTER-TIME

IN the golden noon-shine,
　Or in the pink of dawn;
In the silver moonshine,
　Or when the moon is gone;
Open eyes, or drowsy lids,
　'Wake or 'most asleep,
I can hear the katydids,—
　"Cheep! Cheep! Cheep!"

Only in the winter-time
　Do they ever stop,
In the chip-and-splinter-time,
　When the backlogs pop,—
Then it is, the kettle-lids,
　While the sparkles leap,
Lisp like the katydids,—
　"Cheep! Cheep! Cheep!"

HOME-MADE RIDDLES

ALL BUT THE ANSWERS

I

NO one ever saw it
Till I dug it from the ground;
I found it when I lost it,
And lost it when I found:
I washed it, and dressed it,
And buried it once more—
Dug it up, and loved it then
Better than before.
I was paid for finding it—
I don't know why or how,—
But I lost, found, and kept it,
And haven't got it now.

II

Sometimes it's all alone—
Sometimes in a crowd;
It says a thousand bright things,
But never talks aloud.
Everybody loves it,
And likes to have it call.

318

But if you shouldn't happen to,
   It wouldn't care at all.
First you see or hear of it,
   It's a-singing,—then
You may look and listen,
   But it never sings again.

THE LOVELY CHILD

LILIES are both pure and fair,
  Growing 'midst the roses there—
Roses, too, both red and pink,
Are quite beautiful, I think.

But of all bright blossoms—best—
Purest—fairest—loveliest,—
Could there be a sweeter thing
Than a primrose, blossoming?

THE YELLOWBIRD

HEY! my little Yellowbird,
    What you doing there?
Like a flashing sun-ray,
    Flitting everywhere:
Dangling down the tall weeds
    And the hollyhocks,
And the lordly sunflowers
    Along the garden-walks.

Ho! my gallant Golden-bill,
    Pecking 'mongst the weeds,
You must have for breakfast
    Golden flower-seeds:
Won't you tell a little fellow
    What you have for *tea?*—
'Spect a peck o' yellow, mellow
    Pippin on the tree.

SAD PERVERSITY

WHEN but a little boy, it seemed
    My dearest rapture ran
In fancy ever, when I dreamed
    I was a man—a man!

Now—sad perversity!—my theme
    Of rarest, purest joy
Is when, in fancy blest, I dream
    I am a little boy.

A FEEL IN THE CHRIS'MAS-AIR

THEY'S a kind o' *feel* in the air, to me,
    When the Chris'mas-times sets in,
That's about as much of a mystery
    As ever I've run ag'in'!—
Fer instunce, now, whilse I gain in weight
    And gineral health, I swear
They's a *goneness* somers I can't quite state—
    A kind o' *feel* in the air!

They's a feel in the Chris'mas-air goes right
    To the spot where a man *lives* at!—
It gives a feller a' appetite—
    They ain't no doubt about *that!*—
And yit they's *somepin'*—I don't know what—
    That follers me, here and there,
And ha'nts and worries and spares me not—
    A kind o' feel in the air!

They's a *feel,* as I say, in the air that's jest
    As blame-don sad as sweet!—
In the same ra-sho as I feel the best
    And am spryest on my feet,

They's allus a kind o' sort of a *ache*
  That I can't lo-cate no-where;—
But it comes with *Chris'mas,* and no mistake!—
  A kind o' feel in the air.

Is it the racket the childern raise?—
  W'y, *no!*—God bless 'em!—*no!*—
Is it the eyes and the cheeks ablaze—
  Like my *own* wuz, long ago?—
Is it the bleat o' the whistle and beat
  O' the little toy-drum and blare
O' the horn?—*No! no!*—it is jest the sweet—
  The sad-sweet feel in the air.

MISTER HOP-TOAD

Howdy, Mister Hop-Toad! Glad to see you
out!
Bin a month o' Sund'ys sense I seen you hereabout.
Kind o' bin a-layin' in, from the frost and snow?
Good to see you out ag'in, it's bin so long ago!
Plow's like slicin' cheese, and sod's loppin' over
even;
Loam's like gingerbread, and clods's softer'n de-
ceivin'—
Mister Hop-Toad, honest-true—Spring-time—don't
you love it?
You old rusty rascal you, at the bottom of it!

Oh! oh! oh!
I grabs up my old hoe;
But I sees *you,*
And s' I, "Ooh-ooh!
Howdy, Mister Hop-Toad! How-dee-do!"

Make yourse'f more comfo'bler—square 'round at
your ease—
Don't set saggin' slanchwise, with your nose below
your knees.

Swell that fat old throat o' yourn and lemme see
    you swaller;
Straighten up and h'ist your head!—*You* don't owe
    a dollar!—
Hain't no mor'gage on your land—ner no taxes,
    nuther;
You don't haf to work no roads, even ef you'd
    ruther.
'F I was you, and *fixed* like you, I railly wouldn't
    keer
To swap fer life and hop right in the presidential
    cheer!

          Oh! oh! oh!
          I hauls back my old hoe;
          But I sees *you,*
          And s' I, "Ooh-ooh!
      Howdy, Mister Hop-Toad! How-dee-do!"

'Long about next Aprile, hoppin' down the furry,
Won't you mind I ast you what 'peared to be the
    hurry?—
Won't you mind I hooked my hoe and hauled you
    back and smiled?—
W'y, bless you, Mister Hop-Toad, I love you like
    a child!
S'pose I'd want to 'flict you any more'n what you
    air?—
S'pose I think you got no rights 'cept the warts you
    wear?
Hulk, sulk, and blink away, you old bloat-eyed
    rowdy!—

Hain't you got a word to say?—Won't you tell me
"Howdy"?

> Oh! oh! oh!
> I swish round my old hoe;
> But I sees *you,*
> And s' I, "Ooh-ooh!
> Howdy, Mister Hop-Toad! How-dee-do!"

THE SILENT SINGER

MRS. D. M. JORDAN, APRIL 29, 1895

ALL sudden she hath ceased to sing,
Hushed in eternal slumbering,
And we make moan that she is dead.—
Nay; peace! be comforted.

Between her singing and her tears
She pauses, listening—and she hears
The Song we can not hear.—And thus
She mutely pities us.

Could she speak out, we doubt not she
Would turn to us full tenderly,
And in the old melodious voice
Say: "Weep not, but rejoice."

Ay, musical as waters run
In woodland rills through shade and sun,
The sweet voice would flow on and say,—
"Be glad with me to-day.—

"Your Earth was very dear and fair
To me—the groves and grasses there;
   The bursting buds and blossoms—O
     I always loved them so!—

"The very dews within them seemed
Reflected by mine eyes and gleamed
   Adown my cheeks in what you knew
     As 'tears,' and not as dew.

"Your birds, too, in the orchard-boughs—
I could not hear them from the house,
   But I must leave my work and stray
     Out in the open day

"And the illimitable range
Of their vast freedom—always strange
   And new to me—It pierced my heart
     With sweetness as a dart!—

"The singing! singing! singing!—All
The trees bloomed blossoms musical
   That chirped and trilled in colors till
     My whole soul seemed to fill

"To overflow with music, so
That I have found me kneeling low
   Midst the lush grass, with murmurous words
     Thanking the flowers and birds.

"So with the ones to me most dear—
I loved them, as I love them Here:
  Bear with my memory, therefore,
    As when in days of yore,

"O friends of mine, ye praised the note
Of some song, quavering from my throat
  Out of the overstress of love
    And all the pain thereof.

"And ye, too, do I love with this
Same love—and Heaven knows all it is,—
  The birds' song in it—bud and bloom—
    The turf, but not the tomb."

Between her singing and her tears
She pauses, listening—and she hears
  The Song we can not hear.—And thus
    She mutely pities us.

THE GREEN GRASS OF OLD IRELAND

THE green grass av owld Ireland!
  Whilst I be far away,
All fresh an' clean an' jewel-green
  It's growin' there to-day.
Oh, it's cleaner, greener growin'—
  All the grassy worrld around,
It's greener yet nor any grass
  That grows on top o' ground!

The green grass av owld Ireland,
  Indade, an' balm 't'ud be
To eyes like mine that drip wid brine
  As salty as the sea!
For still the more I'm stoppin' here,
  The more I'm sore to see
The glory av the green grass av owld Ireland.

Ten years ye've paid my airnin's—
  I've the l'avin's on the shelf,
Though I be here widout a queen
  An' own meself meself:

331

I'm comin' over steerage,
　But I'm goin' back firrst-class,
Patrollin' av the foremost deck
　For firrst sight av the grass.

God bless yez, free Ameriky!
　I love yez, dock an' shore!
I kem to yez in poverty
　That's worstin' me no more
But most I'm lovin' Erin yet,
　Wid all her graves, d'ye see,
By reason av the green grass av owld Ireland.

A PEACE-HYMN OF THE REPUBLIC

LOUISVILLE, KENTUCKY, SEPTEMBER 12, 1895:
TWENTY-NINTH ENCAMPMENT, G. A. R.

THERE'S a Voice across the Nation like a
    mighty ocean-hail,
Borne up from out the Southward as the seas before
    the gale;
Its breath is in the streaming Flag and in the flying
    sail—
        As we go sailing on.

'Tis a Voice that we remember—ere its summons
    soothed as now—
When it rang in battle-challenge, and we answered
    vow with vow,—
With roar of gun and hiss of sword and crash of
    prow and prow,
        As we went sailing on.

Our hope sank, even as we saw the sun sink faint
    and far,—
The Ship of State went groping through the blind-
    ing smoke of War—
Through blackest midnight lurching, all uncheered
    of moon or star,
        Yet sailing—sailing on.

333

As One who spake the dead awake, with life-blood
    leaping warm—
Who walked the troubled waters, all unscathed, in
    mortal form,—
We felt our Pilot's presence with His hand upon the
    storm,
        As we went sailing on.

O Voice of passion lulled to peace, this dawning of
    To-day—
O Voices twain now blent as one, ye sing all fears
    away,
Since foe and foe are friends, and lo! the Lord, as
    glad as they.—
        He sends us sailing on.

MY DANCIN'-DAYS IS OVER

WHAT is it in old fiddle-chunes 'at makes me
    ketch my breath
And ripples up my backbone tel I'm tickled most to
      death?—
  Kind o' like that sweet-sick feelin', in the long
      sweep of a swing,
  The first you ever swung in, with yer first sweet-
      heart, i jing!—
  Yer first picnic—yer first ice-cream—yer first o'
    ever'thing
    'At happened 'fore yer dancin'-days wuz over!

I never understood it—and I s'pose I never can,—
But right in town here, yisterd'y I heard a pore
      blind man
  A-fiddlin' old "Gray Eagle"—*And*-sir! I jes'
      stopped my load
  O' hay and listened at him—yes, and watched the
      way he "bow'd,"—
  And back I went, plum forty year', with boys and
      girls I knowed
    And loved, long 'fore my dancin'-days wuz
      over!—

At high noon in yer city,—with yer blame' Mag-
 netic-Cars
A-hummin' and a-screetchin' past—and bands and
 G. A. R.'s
 A-marchin'—and fire-ingines.—*All* the noise, the
  whole street through,
 Wuz lost on me!—I only heard a whipperwill er
  two,
 It 'peared-like, kind o' callin' 'crost the darkness
  and the dew,
  Them nights afore my dancin'-days wuz over.

'T'uz Chused'y-night at Wetherell's, er We'n'sd'y-
 night at Strawn's,
Er Fourth-o'-July-night at uther Tomps's house er
 John's!—
 With old Lew Church from Sugar Crick, with
  that old fiddle he
 Had sawed clean through the Army, from Atlanty
  to the sea—
 And yit he'd fetched her home ag'in, so's he
  could play fer me
  Onc't more afore my dancin'-days wuz over!

The woods 'at's all be'n cut away wuz growin' same
 as then;
The youngsters all wuz boys ag'in 'at's now all
 oldish men;
 And all the girls 'at *then* wuz girls—I saw 'em,
  one and all,

As *plain* as then—the middle-sized, the short-and-
    fat, and tall—
And 'peared-like, I danced "Tucker" fer 'em up
    and down the wall
    Jes' like afore my dancin'-days wuz over!

   .   .   .   .

The facts is, I wuz *dazed* so 'at I clean fergot jes'
    where
I railly wuz,—a-blockin' streets, and still a-standin'
    there:
  I heard the *po*-leece yellin', but my ears wuz kind
    o' *blurred*—
  My *eyes,* too, fer the odds o' that,—bekase I
    thought I heard
  My wife 'at's dead a-laughin'-like, and jokin',
    word-fer-word
    Jes' like afore her dancin'-days wuz over.

EUGENE FIELD

WITH gentlest tears, no less than jubilee
    Of blithest joy, we heard him, and still hear
  Him singing on, with full voice, pure and clear,
Uplifted, as some classic melody
In sweetest legends of old minstrelsy;
    Or, swarming Elfin-like upon the ear,
    His airy notes make all the atmosphere
One blur of bird and bee and lullaby.
His tribute:—Luster in the faded bloom
    Of cheeks of old, old mothers; and the fall
      Of gracious dews in eyes long dry and dim;
And hope in lover's pathways midst perfume
    Of woodland haunts; and—meed exceeding all,—
    The love of little children laurels him.

DREAM-MARCH

WASN'T it a funny dream!—perfectly be-
   wild'rin'!—
   Last night, and night before, and night before
      that,
Seemed like I saw the march o' regiments o' chil-
      dren,
   Marching to the robin's fife and cricket's rat-ta-
      tat!
Lily-banners overhead, with the dew upon 'em,
   On flashed the little army, as with sword and
      flame;
Like the buzz o' bumble-wings, with the honey on
      'em,
   Came an eery, cheery chant, chiming as it
      came:—

Where go the children? Traveling! Traveling!
   Where go the children, traveling ahead?
Some go to kindergarten; some go to day-school;
   Some go to night-school; and some go to bed!

Smooth roads or rough roads, warm or winter
      weather,
   On go the children, towhead and brown,
Brave boys and brave girls, rank and file together,
   Marching out of Morning-Land, over dale and
      down:

Some go a-gipsying out in country places—
  Out through the orchards, with blossoms on the
      boughs
Wild, sweet, and pink and white as their own glad
      faces;
  And some go, at evening, calling home the cows.

Where go the children? Traveling! Traveling!
  Where go the children, traveling ahead?
Some go to foreign wars, and camps by the fire-
      light—
  Some go to glory so; and some go to bed!

Some go through grassy lanes leading to the city—
  Thinner grow the green trees and thicker grows
      the dust;
Ever, though, to little people any path is pretty
  So it leads to newer lands, as they know it must.
Some go to singing less; some go to list'ning;
  Some go to thinking over ever-nobler themes;
Some go anhungered, but ever bravely whistling,
  Turning never home again only in their dreams.

Where go the children? Traveling! Traveling!
  Where go the children, traveling ahead?
Some go to conquer things; some go to try them;
  Some go to dream them; and some go to bed!

A CHRISTMAS MEMORY

PA he bringed me here to stay
    'Til my Ma she's well.—An' nen
He's go' hitch up, Chris'mus-day,
    An' come take me back again
Wher' my Ma's at! Won't I be
Tickled when he comes fer me!

My Ma an' my A'nty they
    'Uz each-uvver's sisters. Pa—
A'nty telled me, th' other day,—
    He comed here an' married Ma. . . .
A'nty said nen, "Go run play,
    I must work now!" . . . An' I saw,
When she turn' her face away,
    She 'uz cryin'.—An' nen I
    'Tend-like I "run play"—an' cry.

This-here house o' A'nty's wher'
They 'uz borned—my Ma an' her!—
An' her Ma 'uz my Ma's Ma,
An' her Pa 'uz my Ma's Pa—
Ain't that funny?—An' they're dead:

An' this-here's "th' ole Homestead."—
An' my A'nty said, an' cried,
It's mine, too, ef my Ma died—
Don't know what she mean—'cause my
Ma she's nuvver go' to die!

When Pa bringed me here 't'uz night—
 'Way dark night! An' A'nty spread
Me a piece—an' light the light
 An' say I must go to bed.—
 I cry not to—but Pa said,
"Be good boy now, like you telled
 Mommy 'at you're go' to be!"
 An', when he 'uz kissin' me
 My good night, his cheek's all wet
An' taste salty.—An' he held
 Wite close to me an' rocked some
 An' laughed-like—'til A'nty come
 Git me while he's rockin' yet.

A'nty he'p me, 'til I be
Purt' nigh strip-pud—nen hug me
In bofe arms an' lif' me 'way
Up in her high bed—an' pray
 Wiv me,—'bout my Ma—an' Pa—
An' ole Santy Claus—an' Sleigh—
 An' Reindeers an' little Drum—
 Yes, an' Picture-books, "Tom Thumb,"
An' "Three Bears," an' ole "Fee-Faw"—
 Yes, an' "Tweedle-Dee" an' "Dum,"

An' "White Knight" an' "Squidjicum,"
An' most things you ever saw!—
 An' when A'nty kissed me, she
 'Uz all cryin' over me!

Don't want Santy Claus—ner things
Any kind he ever brings!—
Don't want A'nty!—Don't want Pa!—
I ist only want my Ma!

TO ALMON KEEFER

INSCRIBED IN "TALES OF THE OCEAN"

THIS first book that I ever knew
  Was read aloud to me by you—
Friend of my boyhood, therefore take
It back from me, for old times' sake—
The selfsame "Tales" first read to me,
Under "the old sweet apple tree,"
Ere I myself could read such great
Big words,—but listening all elate,
At your interpreting, until
Brain, heart and soul were all athrill
With wonder, awe, and sheer excess
Of wildest childish happiness.

So take the book again—forget
All else,—long years, lost hopes, regret;
Sighs for the joys we ne'er attain,
Prayers we have lifted all in vain;
Tears for the faces seen no more,
Once as the roses at the door!

Take the enchanted book—And lo,
On grassy swards of long ago,
Sprawl out again, beneath the shade
The breezy old-home orchard made,
The veriest barefoot boy indeed—
And I will listen as you read.

LITTLE MAID-O'-DREAMS

LITTLE Maid-o'-Dreams, with your
        Eery eyes so clear and pure
Gazing, where we fain would see
Into far futurity,—
Tell us what you there behold,
In your visions manifold!
What is on beyond our sight,
Bidding till the morrow's light,
Fairer than we see to-day,
As our dull eyes only may?

Little Maid-o'-Dreams, with face
Like as in some woodland place
Lifts a lily, chaste and white,
From the shadow to the light;—
Tell us, by your subtler glance,
What strange sorcery enchants
You as now,—here, yet afar
As the realms of moon and star?—
Have you magic lamp and ring,
And genii for vassaling?

Little Maid-o'-Dreams, confess
You're divine and nothing less,—
For with mortal palms, we fear,
Yet must pet you, dreaming here—
Yearning, too, to lift the tips
Of your fingers to our lips;
Fearful still you may rebel,
High and heav'nly oracle!
Thus, though all unmeet our kiss,
Pardon this!—and this!—and this!

Little Maid-o'-Dreams, we call
Truce and favor, knowing all!—
All your magic is, in truth,
Pure foresight and faith of youth—
You're a child, yet even so,
You're a sage, in embryo—
Prescient poet—artist—great
As your dreams anticipate.—
Trusting God and Man, you do
Just as Heaven inspires you to.

EDGAR WILSON NYE

FEBRUARY 22, 1896

THE saddest silence falls when Laughter lays
   Finger on lip, and falteringly breaks
The glad voice into dying minor shakes
And quavers, lorn as airs the wind-harp plays
At urge of drearest Winter's bleakest days:
   A troubled hush, in which all hope forsakes
   Us, and the yearning upstrained vision aches
With tears that drown e'en heaven from our gaze.
Such silence—after such glad merriment!
   O prince of halest humor, wit and cheer!
   Could you yet speak to us, I doubt not we
Should catch your voice, still blithely eloquent
   Above all murmurings of sorrow here,
     Calling your love back to us laughingly.

CASSANDER

"CASSANDER! *O* Cassander!"—her mother's
        voice seems cle'r
As ever, from the old back-porch, a-hollerin' fer
        her—
    Especially in airly Spring—like May, two year'
        ago—
Last time she hollered fer her,—and Cassander
        didn't hear!

Cassander was so chirpy-like and sociable and free,
And good to ever'body, and wuz even good to me
    Though *I* wuz jes' a common—well, a farm-hand,
        don't you know,
A-workin' on her father's place, as pore as pore
        could be!

Her bein' jes' a' only child, Cassander had her way
A good-'eal more'n other girls; and neighbors ust
        to say
    She looked most like her Mother, but wuz turned
        most like her Pap,—
Except *he* had no use fer *town*-folks then—ner *yit
        to-day!*

349

I can't claim she incouraged *me:* She'd let me drive
　　　her in
To town sometimes, on Saturd'ys, and fetch her
　　　home ag'in,
　　Tel onc't she 'scused "Old Moll" and me,—and
　　　some blame' city-chap,
He driv her home, two-forty style, in face o' kith-
　　　and-kin.

She even tried to make him stay fer supper, but I
　　　'low
He must 'a' kind o' 'spicioned some objections.—
　　　Anyhow,
　　Her mother callin' at her, whilst her father stood
　　　and shook
His fist,—the town-chap turnt his team and made
　　　his partin' bow.

"Cassander! *You,* Cassander!"—hear her mother
　　　jes' as plain,
And see Cassander blushin' like the peach tree
　　　down the lane,
　　Whilse I sneaked on apast her, with a sort o'
　　　hang-dog look,
A-feelin' cheap as sorghum and as green as sugar-
　　　cane!

(You see, I'd *skooted* when she met her *town*-beau
　　　—when, in fact,
Ef I'd had sense I'd *stayed* fer her.—But sense wuz
　　　what I lacked!

So I'd cut home ahead o' her, so's I could tell 'em
    what
Wuz keepin' her. And—*you* know how a jealous
    fool'll act!)

I past her, I wuz sayin',—but she never turnt her
    head;
I swallered-like and cle'red my th'oat—but that wuz
    all I said;
  And whilse I hoped fer some word back, it wuzn't
    what I got.—
That girl'll not stay stiller on the day she's layin'
    dead!

Well, that-air silence *lasted!*—Ust to listen ever'
    day
I'd be at work and hear her mother callin' thataway;
  I'd *sight* Cassander, mayby, cuttin' home acrost
    the blue
And drizzly fields; but nary answer—nary word
    to say!

Putt in about two weeks o' that—two weeks o' rain
    and mud,
Er mostly so: I couldn't plow. The old crick like
    a flood:
  And, lonesome as a borried dog, I'd wade them
    old woods through—
The dogwood blossoms white as snow, and redbuds
    red as blood.

Last time her mother called her—sich a morning
   like as now:
The robins and the bluebirds, and the blossoms on
   the bough—
   And this wuz yit 'fore brekfust, with the sun out
      at his best,
And hosses kickin' in the barn—and dry enough to
   plow.

"Cassander! *O* Cassander!" . . . And her only
      answer—What?—
A letter, twisted round the cook-stove damper,
      smokin'-hot,
   A-statin': "I wuz married on that day of all the
      rest,
The day my husband fetched me home—ef you ain't
   all fergot!"

"Cassander! *O* Cassander!" seems, allus, 'long in
      May,
I hear her mother callin' her—a-callin', night and
   day—
   "Cassander! *O* Cassander!" allus callin', as I say,
"Cassander; *O* Cassander!" jes' a-callin' thataway.

A CHILD-WORLD

PROEM

The Child-World—long and long since lost to
        view—
        A Fairy Paradise!—
How always fair it was and fresh and new—
    How every affluent hour heaped heart and eyes
        With treasures of surprise!

Enchantments tangible: The under-brink
        Of dawns that launched the sight
Up seas of gold: The dewdrop on the pink,
    With all the green earth in it and blue height
        Of heavens infinite:

The liquid, dripping songs of orchard-birds—
        The wee bass of the bees,—
With lucent deeps of silence afterwards;
    The gay, clandestine whisperings of the breeze
        And glad leaves of the trees.

.   .   .   .

O Child-World: After this world—just as when
        I found you first sufficed
My soulmost need—if I found you again,
    With all my childish dream so realized,
        I should not be surprised.

The Child-World — long and long since lost to view —
  / A Fairy Paradise! —
How always fair it was and fresh and new —
  How every affluent hour heaped heart and eyes
    With treasures of surprise!

Enchantments tangible: The under-brink
    Of dawns that launched the sight
Up seas of gold: The dewdrop on the pink,
  With all the green earth in it and blue height
    Of heavens infinite:

The liquid, dripping songs of orchard birds —
    The wee bass of the bees, —
With lucent deeps of silence afterwards;
  The gay, clandestine whisperings of the breeze
    And glad leaves of the trees.

. . . .
Ⓞ Child-World: — After this world — just as when
    I found you first sufficed
My soul's most need — if I found you again,
  With all my childish dream so realized,
    I should not be surprised.

<u>A Child=World</u> — Yet a wondrous world no less
To those, who knew its boundless happiness.
A simple old frame house — eight rooms in all —
Set just one side the center of a small
But very hopeful Indiana town, —
The upper=story looking squarely down
Upon the main street — and the main highway,
From East to West, — historic in its day;
Known as The National Road — old=timers, all
Who linger yet, will happily recall
It as the scheme and handiwork, as well
As property, of "Uncle Sam", and tell
Of its importance "long and long afore
Railroads wuz ever dreamp' of!" — Furthermore,
The reminiscent old inhabitants
Will make that old road blossom with romance.

THE CHILD-WORLD

A CHILD-WORLD, yet a wondrous world no
    less,
To those who knew its boundless happiness.
A simple old frame house—eight rooms in all—
Set just one side the center of a small
But very hopeful Indiana town,—
The upper story looking squarely down
Upon the main street, and the main highway
From East to West,—historic in its day,
Known as The National Road—old-timers, all
Who linger yet, will happily recall
It as the scheme and handiwork, as well
As property, of "Uncle Sam," and tell
Of its importance, "long and long afore
*Rail*roads wuz ever *dreamp'* of !"—Furthermore,
The reminiscent first inhabitants
Will make that old road blossom with romance
Of snowy caravans, in long parade
Of covered vehicles, of every grade
From ox-cart of most primitive design,
To Conestoga wagons, with their fine
Deep-chested six-horse teams, in heavy gear,
High hames and chiming bells—to childish ear

355

And eye entrancing as the glittering train
Of some sun-smitten pageant of old Spain.
And, in like spirit, haply they will tell
You of the roadside forests, and the yell
Of "wolfs" and "painters," in the long night-ride,
And "screechin' catamounts" on every side.—
Of stage-coach days, highwaymen, and strange
　　　crimes,
And yet unriddled mysteries of the times
Called "Good Old." "And why 'Good Old'?" once
　　　a rare
Old chronicler was asked, who brushed the hair
Out of his twinkling eyes and said,—"Well, John,
They're 'good old times' because they're dead and
　　　gone!"

The old home site was portioned into three
Distinctive lots. The front one—natively
Facing to southward, broad and gaudy-fine
With lilac, dahlia, rose, and flowering vine—
The dwelling stood in; and behind that, and
Upon the alley north and south, left hand,
The old woodhouse,—half, trimly stacked with
　　　wood,
And half, a workshop, where a work-bench stood
Steadfastly through all seasons.—Over it,
Along the wall, hung compass, brace-and-bit,
And square, and drawing-knife, and smoothing-
　　　plane—
And a little jack-plane, too—the children's vain
Possession by pretense—in fancy they

Manipulating it in endless play,
Turning out countless curls and loops of bright,
Fine satin shavings—Rapture infinite!
Shelved quilting-frames; the tool-chest; the old box
Of refuse nails and screws; a rough gun-stock's
Outline in "curly maple"; and a pair
Of clamps and old kraut-cutter hanging there.
Some "patterns," in thin wood, of shield and scroll,
Hung higher, with a neat "cane fishing-pole"
And careful tackle—all securely out
Of reach of children, rummaging about,

Beside the woodhouse, with broad branches free
Yet close above the roof, an apple tree
Known as "The Prince's Harvest"—Magic phrase!
That was *a boy's own tree,* in many ways!—
Its girth and height meet both for the caress
Of his bare legs and his ambitiousness:
And then its apples, humoring his whim,
Seemed just to fairly *hurry* ripe for him—
Even in June, impetuous as he,
They dropped to meet him, half-way up the tree.
And O their bruised sweet faces where they fell!—
And ho! the lips that feigned to "kiss them *well*"!

"The Old Sweet-Apple Tree," a stalwart, stood
In fairly sympathetic neighborhood
Of this wild princeling with his early gold
To toss about so lavishly nor hold
In bounteous hoard to overbrim at once

All Nature's lap when came the Autumn months.
Under the spacious shade of this the eyes
Of swinging children saw swift-changing skies
Of blue and green, with sunshine shot between,
And when "the old cat died" they saw but green.

And, then, there was a cherry tree.—We all
And severally will yet recall
From our lost youth, in gentlest memory,
The blessed fact—There was a cherry tree.

There was a cherry tree. Its bloomy snows
Cool even now the fevered sight that knows
No more its airy visions of pure joy—
    As when you were a boy.

There was a cherry tree. The Bluejay set
His blue against its white—O blue as jet
He seemed there then!—But *now*—Whoever knew
    He was so pale a blue!

There was a cherry tree—Our child-eyes saw
The miracle:—Its pure-white snows did thaw
Into a crimson fruitage, far too sweet
    But for a boy to eat.

There was a cherry tree, give thanks and joy!—
There was a bloom of snow—There was a boy—
There was a Bluejay of the realest blue—
    And fruit for both of you.

Then the old garden, with the apple trees
Grouped round the margin, and "a stand of bees"
By the "white-winter-pearmain"; and a row

Of currant-bushes; and a quince or so.
The old grape-arbor in the center, by
The pathway to the stable, with the sty
Behind it, and *upon* it, cootering flocks
Of pigeons,—and the cutest "martin-box"!—
Made like a sure-enough house—with roof, and
    doors
And windows in it, and veranda-floors
And balusters all round it—yes, and at
Each end a chimney—painted red at that
And penciled white, to look like little bricks;
And, to cap all the builder's cunning tricks,
Two tiny little lightning-rods were run
Straight up their sides, and twinkled in the sun.
Who built it? Nay, no answer but a smile.—
It *may* be you can guess who, after while.

Home in his stall, "Old Sorrel" munched his hay
And oats and corn, and switched the flies away,
In a repose of patience good to see,
And earnest of the gentlest pedigree.
With half-pathetic eye sometimes he gazed
Upon the gambols of a colt that grazed
Around the edges of the lot outside,
And kicked at nothing suddenly, and tried
To act grown-up and graceful and high-bred,
But dropped, *k'whop!* and scraped the buggy-shed,
Leaving a tuft of woolly, foxy hair
Under the sharp end of a gate-hinge there.
Then, all ignobly scrambling to his feet
And whinnying a whinny like a bleat,

He would pursue himself around the lot
And—do the whole thing over, like as not! . . .
Ah! what a life of constant fear and dread
And flop and squawk and flight the chickens led!

Above the fences, either side, were seen
The neighbor-houses, set in plots of green
Dooryards and greener gardens, tree and wall
Alike whitewashed, an order in it all:
The scythe hooked in the tree-fork; and the spade
And hoe and rake and shovel all, when laid
Aside, were in their places, ready for
The hand of either the possessor or
Of any neighbor, welcome to the loan
Of any tool he might not chance to own.

THE OLD HOME-FOLKS

SUCH was the Child-World of the long ago—
The little world these children used to
know:—
Johnty, the oldest, and the best, perhaps,
Of the five happy little Hoosier chaps
Inhabiting this wee world all their own.—
Johnty, the leader, with his native tone
Of grave command—a general on parade
Whose each punctilious order was obeyed
By his proud followers.

But Johnty yet—
After all serious duties—could forget
The gravity of life to the extent,
At times, of kindling much astonishment
About him: With a quick, observant eye,
And mind and memory, he could supply
The tamest incident with liveliest mirth;
And at the most unlooked-for times on earth

Was wont to break into some travesty
On those around him—feats of mimicry
Of this one's trick of gesture—that one's walk—
Or this one's laugh—or that one's funny talk,—
The way "the watermelon-man" would try
His humor on town-folks that wouldn't buy;—
How he drove into town at morning—then
At dusk (alas!) how he drove out again.

Though these divertisements of Johnty's were
Hailed with a hearty glee and relish, there
Appeared a sense, on his part, of regret—
A spirit of remorse that would not let
Him rest for days thereafter.—Such times he,
As some boy said, "jist got too overly
Blame' good fer common boys like us, you know
To 'sociate with—'less'n we 'ud go
And jine his church!"

                    Next after Johnty came
His little towhead brother, Bud by name.—
And O how white his hair was—and how thick
His face with freckles,—and his ears, how quick
And curious and intrusive!—And how pale
The blue of his big eyes;—and how a tale
Of Giants, Trolls or Fairies, bulged them still
Bigger and bigger!—And when "Jack" would kill
The old "Four-headed Giant," Bud's big eyes
Were swollen truly into giant-size.
And Bud was apt in make-believes—would hear
His Grandma talk or read, with such an ear

And memory of both subject and big words,
That he would take the book up afterwards
And feign to "read aloud," with such success
As caused his truthful elders real distress.
But he *must* have *big words*—they seemed to give
Extremer range to the superlative—
That was his passion. "My Gran'ma," he said,
One evening, after listening as she read
Some heavy old historical review—
With copious explanations thereunto
Drawn out by his inquiring turn of mind,—
"My Gran'ma she's read *all* books—ever' kind
They is, 'at tells all 'bout the land an' sea
An' Nations of the Earth!—An' she is the
Historicul-est woman ever wuz!"
(Forgive the verse's chuckling as it does
In its erratic current.—Oftentimes
The little willowy water-brook of rhymes
Must falter in its music, listening to
The children laughing as they used to do.)

Who shall sing a simple ditty all about the Willow,
   Dainty-fine and delicate as any bending spray
That dandles high the happy bird that flutters there to
      trill a
   Tremulously tender song of greeting to the May.

Bravest, too, of all the trees!—none to match your dar-
      ing,—
   First of greens to greet the Spring and lead in leafy
      sheen;—
Ay, and you're the last—almost into winter wearing
   Still the leaf of loyalty—still the badge of green.

Ah, my lovely Willow!—Let the Waters lilt your
        graces,—
    They alone with limpid kisses lave your leaves above,
Flashing back your sylvan beauty, and in shady places
    Peering up with glimmering pebbles, like the eyes of
        love.

Next, Maymie, with her hazy cloud of hair,
And the blue skies of eyes beneath it there.
Her dignified and "little lady" airs
Of never either romping up the stairs
Or falling down them; thoughtful every way
Of others first—The kind of child at play
That "gave up," for the rest, the ripest pear
Or peach or apple in the garden there
Beneath the trees where swooped the airy swing—
She pushing it, too glad for anything!
Or, in the character of hostess, she
Would entertain her friends delightfully
In her playhouse,—with strips of carpet laid
Along the garden-fence within the shade
Of the old apple trees—where from next yard
Came the two dearest friends in her regard,
The little Crawford girls, Ella and Lu—
As shy and lovely as the lilies grew
In their idyllic home,—yet sometimes they
Admitted Bud and Alex to their play,
Who did their heavier work and helped them fix
To have a "Festibul"—and brought the bricks
And built the "stove," with a real fire and all,
And stovepipe-joint for chimney, looming tall

And wonderfully smoky—even to
Their childish aspirations, as it blew
And swooped and swirled about them till their sight
Was feverish even as their high delight.

Then Alex, with his freckles, and his freaks
Of temper, and the peach-bloom of his cheeks,
And *"amber-colored* hair"—his mother said
'Twas that, when others laughed and called it *"red"*
And Alex threw things at them—till they'd call
A truce, agreeing "'t'uzn't red *ut-tall!"*
But Alex was affectionate beyond
The average child, and was extremely fond
Of the paternal relatives of his,
Of whom he once made estimate like this:—
"I'm only got *two* brothers,—but my *Pa*
He's got most brothers'n you ever saw!—
He's got *seben* brothers!—Yes, an' they're all my
Seben Uncles!—Uncle John, an' Jim,—an' I
Got Uncle George, an' Uncle Andy, too,
An' Uncle Frank, an' Uncle Joe.—An' you
Know Uncle *Mart.*—An', all but *him,* they're great
Big mens!—An' nen's Aunt Sarah—she makes
        eight!—
I'm got *eight* uncles!—'cept Aunt Sarah *can't*
Be ist my *uncle* 'cause she's ist my *a'nt!"*

Then, next to Alex—and the last indeed
Of these five little ones of whom you read—
Was baby Lizzie, with her velvet lisp,—
As though her elfin lips had caught some wisp

Of floss between them as they strove with speech,
Which ever seemed just in, yet out of, reach—
Though what her lips missed, her dark eyes could
    say
With looks that made her meaning clear as day.
And, knowing now the children, you must know
The father and the mother they loved so :—
The father was a swarthy man, black-eyed,
Black-haired, and high of forehead ; and, beside
The slender little mother, seemed in truth
A very king of men—since, from his youth,
To his hale manhood *now*—(worthy as then,—
A lawyer and a leading citizen
Of the proud little town and county-seat—
His hopes his neighbors', and their fealty sweet)—
He had known outdoor labor—rain and shine—
Bleak Winter, and bland Summer—foul and fine.
So Nature had ennobled him and set
Her symbol on him like a coronet:
His lifted brow, and frank, reliant face—
Superior of stature as of grace,—
Even the children by the spell were wrought
Up to heroics of their simple thought,
And saw him, trim of build, and lithe and straight
And tall, almost, as at the pasture-gate
The towering ironweed the scythe had spared
For their sakes, when The Hired Man declared
It would grow on till it became a *tree,*
With cocoanuts and monkeys in—maybe !

Yet, though the children, in their pride and awe
And admiration of the father, saw
A being so exalted—even more
Like adoration was the love they bore
The gentle mother.—Her mild, plaintive face
Was purely fair, and haloed with a grace
And sweetness luminous when joy made glad
Her features with a smile; or saintly sad
As twilight, fell the sympathetic gloom
Of any childish grief, or as a room
Were darkened suddenly, the curtain drawn
Across the window and the sunshine gone.
Her brow, below her fair hair's glimmering strands,
Seemed meetest resting-place for blessing hands
Or holiest touches of soft finger-tips
And little rose-leaf cheeks and dewy lips.

Though heavy household tasks were pitiless,
No little waist or coat or checkered dress
But knew her needle's deftness; and no skill
Matched hers in shaping plait or flounce or frill;
Or fashioning, in complicate design,
All rich embroideries of leaf and vine,
With tiniest twining tendril,—bud and bloom
And fruit, so like, one's fancy caught perfume
And dainty touch and taste of them, to see
Their semblance wrought in such rare verity.

Shrined in her sanctity of home and love,
And love's fond service and reward thereof,

Restore her thus, O blessed Memory!—
Throned in her rocking-chair, and on her knee
Her sewing—her work-basket on the floor
Beside her,—Spring-time through the open door
Balmily stealing in and all about
The room; the bees' dim hum, and the far shout
And laughter of the children at their play,
And neighbor children from across the way
Calling in gleeful challenge—save alone
One boy whose voice sends back no answering
          tone—
The boy, prone on the floor, above a book
Of pictures, with a rapt, ecstatic look—
Even as the mother's, by the selfsame spell,
Is lifted, with a light ineffable—
As though her senses caught no mortal cry,
But heard, instead, some poem going by.

> The Child-heart is so strange a little thing—
>   So mild—so timorously shy and small,—
> When *grown-up* hearts throb, it goes scampering
>   Behind the wall, nor dares peer out at all!—
>   It is the veriest mouse
>   That hides in any house—
> So wild a little thing is any Child-heart!

>   *Child-heart!—mild heart!—*
>   *Ho, my little wild heart!—*
>   *Come up here to me out o' the dark,*
>   *Or let me come to you!*

So lorn at times the Child-heart needs must be,
    With never one maturer heart for friend
And comrade, whose tear-ripened sympathy

And love might lend it comfort to the end,—
    Whose yearnings, aches and stings,
    Over poor little things
Were pitiful as ever any Child-heart.

    Child-heart!—mild heart!—
    Ho, my little wild heart!—
  Come up here to me out o' the dark,
    Or let me come to you!

Times, too, the little Child-heart must be glad—
  Being so young, nor knowing, as *we* know,
The fact from fantasy, the good from bad,
  The joy from woe, the—*all* that hurts us so!
    What wonder then that thus
    It hides away from us?—
So weak a little thing is any Child-heart!

    Child-heart!—mild heart!—
    Ho, my little wild heart!—
  Come up here to me out o' the dark,
    Or let me come to you!

Nay, little Child-heart, you have never need
  To fear *us*;—we are weaker far than you—
'Tis *we* who should be fearful—we indeed
  Should hide us, too, as darkly as you do,—
    Safe, as yourself, withdrawn,
    Hearing the World roar on
Too wilful, woeful, awful for the Child-heart!

    Child-heart!—mild heart!—
    Ho, my little wild heart!—
  Come up here to me out o' the dark,
    Or let me come to you!

The clock chats on confidingly; a rose
Taps at the window, as the sunlight throws
A brilliant, jostling checkerwork of shine
And shadow, like a Persian-loom design,
Across the home-made carpet—fades,—and then
The dear old colors are themselves again.
Sounds drop in visiting from everywhere—
The bluebird's and the robin's trill are there,
Their sweet liquidity diluted some
By dewy orchard-spaces they have come:
Sounds of the town, too, and the great highway—
The Mover-wagons' rumble, and the neigh
Of over-traveled horses, and the bleat
Of sheep and low of cattle through the street—
A Nation's thoroughfare of hopes and fears,
First blazed by the heroic pioneers
Who gave up old-home idols and set face
Toward the unbroken West, to found a race
And tame a wilderness now mightier than
All peoples and all tracts American.

Blent with all outer sounds, the sounds within:—
In mild remoteness falls the household din
Of porch and kitchen: the dull jar and thump
Of churning; and the "glung-glung" of the pump,
With sudden pad and skurry of bare feet
Of little outlaws, in from field or street:
The clang of kettle,—rasp of damper-ring
And bang of cook-stove door—and everything
That jingles in a busy kitchen lifts

Its individual wrangling voice and drifts
In sweetest tinny, coppery, pewtery tone
Of music hungry ear has ever known
In wildest famished yearning and conceit
Of youth, to just cut loose and eat and eat!—
The zest of hunger still incited on
To childish desperation by long-drawn
Breaths of hot, steaming, wholesome things that
    stew
And blubber, and uptilt the pot-lids, too,
Filling the sense with zestful rumors of
The dear old-fashioned dinners children love:
Redolent savorings of home-cured meats,
Potatoes, beans and cabbage; turnips, beets
And parsnips—rarest composite entire
That ever pushed a mortal child's desire
To madness by new-grated fresh, keen, sharp
Horseradish—tang that sets the lips awarp
And watery, anticipating all
The cloyed sweets of the glorious festival.—
Still add the cinnamony, spicy scents
Of clove, nutmeg, and myriad condiments
In like-alluring whiffs that prophesy
Of sweltering pudding, cake, and custard-pie—
The swooning-sweet aroma haunting all
The house—up-stairs and down—porch, parlor, hall
And sitting-room—invading even where
The Hired Man sniffs it in the orchard-air,
And pauses in his pruning of the trees
To note the sun minutely and to—sneeze.

Then Cousin Rufus comes—the children hear
His hale voice in the old hall, ringing clear
As any bell.   Always he came with song
Upon his lips and all the happy throng
Of echoes following him, even as the crowd
Of his admiring little kinsmen—proud
To have a cousin *grown*—and yet as young
Of soul and cheery as the songs he sung.

He was a student of the law—intent
Soundly to win success, with all it meant;
And so he studied—even as he played,—
With all his heart: And so it was he made
His gallant fight for fortune—through all stress
Of battle bearing him with cheeriness
And wholesome valor.

                    And the children had
Another relative who kept them glad
And joyous by his very merry ways—
As blithe and sunny as the summer days,—
Their father's youngest brother—Uncle Mart.
The old "Arabian Nights" he knew by heart—
"Baron Munchausen," too; and likewise "The
Swiss Family Robinson."—And when these three
Gave out, as he rehearsed them, he could go
Straight on in the same line—a steady flow
Of arabesque invention that his good
Old mother never clearly understood.
He *was* to be a *printer*—wanted, though,

To be an *actor*.—But the world was "show"
Enough for *him,*—theatric, airy, gay,—
Each day to him was jolly as a play.
And some poetic symptoms, too, in sooth,
Were certain.—And, from his apprentice youth,
He joyed in verse-quotations—which he took
Out of the old "Type Foundry Specimen Book."
He craved and courted most the favor of
The children.—They were foremost in his love;
And pleasing *them,* he pleased his own boy-heart
And kept it young and fresh in every part.
So was it he devised for them and wrought
To life his quaintest, most romantic thought:—
Like some lone castaway in alien seas,
He built a house up in the apple trees,
Out in the corner of the garden, where
No man-devouring native, prowling there,
Might pounce upon them in the dead o' night—
For lo, their little ladder, slim and light,
They drew up after them. And it was known
That Uncle Mart slipped up sometimes alone
And drew the ladder in, to lie and moon
Over some novel all the afternoon.
And one time Johnty, from the crowd below,—
Outraged to find themselves deserted so—
Threw bodily their old black cat up in
The airy fastness, with much yowl and din
Resulting, while a wild periphery
Of cat went circling to another tree,
And, in impassioned outburst, Uncle Mart
Loomed up, and thus relieved his tragic heart:

" *'Hence, long-tailed, ebon-eyed, nocturnal ranger!*
*   What led thee hither 'mongst the types and cases?*
*   Didst thou not know that running midnight races*
O'er standing types was fraught with imminent
*   danger?*
Did hunger lead thee—didst thou think to find
*   Some rich old cheese to fill thy hungry maw?*
*   Vain hope! for none but literary jaw*
Can masticate our cookery for the mind!' "

So likewise when, with lordly air and grace,
He strode to dinner, with a tragic face
With ink-spots on it from the office, he
Would aptly quote more "Specimen-poetry"—
Perchance like " 'Labor's bread is sweet to eat,
(*Ahem!*) And toothsome is the toiler's meat.' "

Ah, could you see them *all,* at lull of noon!—
A sort of *boisterous* lull, with clink of spoon
And clatter of deflecting knife, and plate
Dropped saggingly, with its all-bounteous weight,
And dragged in place voraciously; and then
Pent exclamations, and the lull again.—
The garland of glad faces round the board—
Each member of the family restored
To his or her place, with an extra chair
Or two for the chance guests so often there.—
The father's farmer-client, brought home from
The court room, though he "didn't *want* to come
Tel he jist saw he *hat* to!" he'd explain,
Invariably, time and time again,

To the pleased wife and hostess, as she pressed
Another cup of coffee on the guest.—
Or there was Johnty's special chum, perchance,
Or Bud's, or both—each childish countenance
Lit with a higher glow of youthful glee,
To be together thus unbrokenly,—
Jim Offutt, or Eck Skinner, or George Carr—
The very nearest chums of Bud's these are,—
So, very probably, *one* of the three,
At least, is there with Bud, or *ought* to be.
Like interchange the town-boys each had
     known—
His playmate's dinner better than his own—
Yet blest that he was ever made to stay
At *Almon Keefer's, any* blessed day,
For *any* meal! . . . Visions of biscuits, hot
And flaky-perfect, with the golden blot
Of molten butter for the center, clear,
Through pools of clover-honey—*dear-o-dear!*—
With creamy milk for its divine "farewell":
And then, if any one delectable
Might yet exceed in sweetness, O restore
The cherry-cobbler of the days of yore
Made only by Al Keefer's mother!—Why,
The very thought of it ignites the eye
Of memory with rapture—cloys the lip
Of longing, till it seems to ooze and drip
With veriest juice and stain and overwaste
Of that most sweet delirium of taste
That ever visited the childish tongue,
Or proved, as now, the sweetest thing unsung.

Ah, Almon Keefer! what a boy you were,
With your back-tilted hat and careless hair,
And open, honest, fresh, fair face and eyes
With their all-varying looks of pleased surprise
And joyous interest in flower and tree,
And poising humming-bird, and maundering bee.

The fields and woods he knew; the tireless tramp
With gun and dog; and the night-fisher's camp—
No other boy, save Bee Lineback, had won
Such brilliant mastery of rod and gun.
Even in his earliest childhood had he shown
These traits that marked him as his father's own.
Dogs all paid Almon honor and bow-wowed
Allegiance, let him come in any crowd
Of rabbit-hunting town-boys, even though
His own dog "Sleuth" rebuked their acting so
With jealous snarls and growlings.

                                But the best
Of Almon's virtues—leading all the rest—
Was his great love of books, and skill as well
In reading them aloud, and by the spell
Thereof enthralling his mute listeners, as
They grouped about him in the orchard-grass,
Hinging their bare shins in the mottled shine
And shade, as they lay prone, or stretched supine
Beneath their favorite tree, with dreamy eyes
And Argo-fancies voyaging the skies.
"Tales of the Ocean" was the name of one
Old dog's-eared book that was surpassed by none

Of all the glorious list.—Its back was gone,
But its vitality went bravely on
In such delicious tales of land and sea
As may not ever perish utterly.
Of still more dubious caste, "Jack Sheppard"
    drew
Full admiration; and "Dick Turpin," too.
And, painful as the fact is to convey,
In certain lurid tales of their own day,
These boys found thieving heroes and outlaws
They hailed with equal fervor of applause:
"The League of the Miami"—why, the name
Alone was fascinating—is the same,
In memory, this venerable hour
Of moral wisdom shorn of all its power,
As it unblushingly reverts to when
The old barn was "the Cave," and hears again
The signal blown, outside the buggy-shed—
The drowsy guard within uplifts his head,
And *" 'Who goes there?' "* is called, in bated
    breath—
The challenge answered in a hush of death,—
"Sh!—*'Barney Gray!'* " And then *" 'What do you
    seek?' "*
" 'Stables of The League!' " the voice comes spent
    and weak,
For, ha! the *Law* is on the "Chieftain's" trail—
Tracked to his very lair!—Well, what avail?
The "secret entrance" opens—closes.—So
The "Robber-Captain" thus outwits his foe;
And, safe once more within his "cavern-halls,"

He shakes his clenched fist at the warped plank-
　　walls
And mutters his defiance through the cracks
At the balked Enemy's retreating backs
As the loud horde flees pell-mell down the lane,
And—*Almon Keefer* is himself again!

Excepting few, they were not books indeed
Of deep import that Almon chose to read;—
Less fact than fiction.—Much he favored those—
If not in poetry, in hectic prose—
That made our native Indian a wild,
Feathered and fine-preened hero that a child
Could recommend as just about the thing
To make a god of, or at least a king.

Aside from Almon's own books—two or three—
His store of lore The Township Library
Supplied him weekly: All the books with "or's"
Subtitled—lured him—after "Indian Wars,"
And "Life of Daniel Boone," —not to include
Some few books spiced with humor,—"Robin
　　Hood"
And rare "Don Quixote."—And one time he took
"Dadd's Cattle Doctor." . . . How he hugged the
　　book
And hurried homeward, with internal glee
And humorous spasms of expectancy!—
All this confession—as he promptly made
It, the day later, writhing in the shade
Of the old apple tree with Johnty and

Bud, Noey Bixler, and The Hired Hand—
Was quite as funny as the book was not. . . .
O Wonderland of wayward Childhood! what
An easy, breezy realm of summer calm
And dreamy gleam and gloom and bloom and balm
Thou art!—The Lotus-Land the poet sung,
It is the Child-World while the heart beats
    young. . . .

While the heart beats young!—O the splendor of the
    Spring,
With all her dewy jewels on, is not so fair a thing!
The fairest, rarest morning of the blossom-time of May
Is not so sweet a season as the season of to-day
While Youth's diviner climate folds and holds us, close
    caressed
As we feel our mothers with us by the touch of face and
    breast;—
Our bare feet in the meadows, and our fancies up among
The airy clouds of morning—while the heart beats young.

While the heart beats young and our pulses leap and dance,
With every day a holiday and life a glad romance,—
We hear the birds with wonder, and with wonder watch
    their flight—
Standing still the more enchanted, both of hearing and
    of sight,
When they have vanished wholly,—for, in fancy, wing-to-
    wing
We fly to Heaven with them; and, returning, still we sing
The praises of this *lower* Heaven with tireless voice and
    tongue,
Even as the Master sanctions—while the heart beats young.

While the heart beats young!—While the heart beats
    young!
O green and gold old Earth of ours, with azure overhung
And looped with rainbows!—grant us yet this grassy lap
    of thine—
We would be still thy children, through the shower and
    the shine!
So pray we, lisping, whispering, in childish love and trust,
With our beseeching hands and faces lifted from the dust
By fervor of the poem, all unwritten and unsung,
Thou givest us in answer, while the heart beats young.

Another hero of those youthful years
Returns, as Noey Bixler's name appears.
And Noey—if in any special way—
Was notably good-natured.—Work or play
He entered into with selfsame delight—
A wholesome interest that made him quite
As many friends among the old as young,—
So everywhere were Noey's praises sung.

And he was awkward, fat and overgrown,
With a round full-moon face, that fairly shone
As though to meet the simile's demand.
And, cumbrous though he seemed, both eye and
    hand
Were dowered with the discernment and deft skill
Of the true artisan: He shaped at will,
In his old father's shop, on rainy days,
Little toy-wagons, and curved-runner sleighs;
The trimmest bows and arrows—fashioned, too,
Of "seasoned timber," such as Noey knew

How to select, prepare, and then complete,
And call his little friends in from the street.
"The very *best* bow," Noey used to say,
"Hain't made o' ash ner hick'ry thataway!—
But you git *mulberry*—the *bearin'*-tree,
Now mind ye! and you fetch the piece to me,
And lemme git it *seasoned;* then, i gum!
I'll make a bow 'at you kin brag on some!
Er—ef you can't git *mulberry*,—you bring
Me a' old *locus'* hitch-post, and, i jing!
I'll make a bow o' *that* 'at *common* bows
Won't dast to pick on ner turn up their nose!"

And Noey knew the woods, and all the trees
And thickets, plants and myriad mysteries
Of swamp and bottom-land.   And he knew where
The ground-hog hid, and why located there.—
He knew all animals that burrowed, swam,
Or lived in tree-tops: And, by race and dam,
He knew the choicest, safest deeps wherein
Fish-traps might flourish nor provoke the sin
Of theft in some chance peeking, prying sneak,
Or town-boy, prowling up and down the creek.
All four-pawed creatures tamable—he knew
Their outer and their inner natures too;
While they, in turn, were drawn to him as by
Some subtle recognition of a tie
Of love, as true as truth from end to end,
Between themselves and this strange human friend.
The same with birds—he knew them every one

And he could "name them, too, without a gun."
No wonder *Johnty* loved him, even to
The verge of worship.—Noey led him through
The art of trapping redbirds—yes, and taught
Him how to keep them when he had them caught—
What food they needed, and just where to swing
The cage, if he expected them to *sing*.

And *Bud* loved Noey, for the little pair
Of stilts he made him; or the stout old hair
Trunk Noey put on wheels, and laid a track
Of scantling-railroad for it in the back
Part of the barn-lot; or the crossbow, made
Just like a gun, which deadly weapon laid
Against his shoulder as he aimed, and—"*Sping!*"
He'd hear the rusty old nail zoon and sing—
And *zip!* your Mr. Bluejay's wing would drop
A farewell-feather from the old tree-top!

And *Maymie* loved him, for the very small
But perfect carriage for her favorite doll—
A *lady's* carriage—not a *baby*-cab,—
But oil-cloth top, and two seats, lined with drab
And trimmed with white lace-paper from a case
Of shaving-soap his uncle bought some place
At auction once.

                    And *Alex* loved him yet
The best, when Noey brought him, for a pet,
A little flying-squirrel, with great eyes—

Big as a child's : And, childlike otherwise,
It was at first a timid, tremulous, coy,
Retiring little thing that dodged the boy
And tried to keep in Noey's pocket ;—till,
In time responsive to his patient will,
It became wholly docile, and content
With its new master, as he came and went,—
The squirrel clinging flatly to his breast,
Or sometimes scampering its craziest
Around his body spirally, and then
Down to his very heels and up again.

And *Little Lizzie* loved him, as a bee
Loves a great ripe red apple—utterly.
For Noey's ruddy morning-face she drew
The window-blind, and tapped the window, too ;
Afar she hailed his coming, as she heard
His tuneless whistling—sweet as any bird
It seemed to her, the one lame bar or so
Of old "Wait for the Wagon"—hoarse and low
The sound was,—so that, all about the place,
Folks joked and said that Noey "whistled bass"—
The light remark originally made
By Cousin Rufus, who knew notes, and played
The flute with nimble skill, and taste as well,
And, critical as he was musical,
Regarded Noey's constant whistling thus
"Phenomenally unmelodious."
Likewise when Uncle Mart, who shared the love
Of jest with Cousin Rufus hand-in-glove,

Said "Noey couldn't whistle *'Bonny Doon'*
Even! and, *he'd* bet, couldn't carry a tune
If it had handles to it!"

                            —But forgive
The deviations here so fugitive,
And turn again to Little Lizzie, whose
High estimate of Noey we shall choose
Above all others.—And to her he was
Particularly lovable because
He laid the woodland's harvest at her feet.—
He brought her wild strawberries, honey-sweet
And dewy-cool, in mats of greenest moss
And leaves, all woven over and across
With tender, biting "tongue-grass," and "sheep-
      sour,"
And twin-leaved beech-mast, pranked with bud and
      flower
Of every gipsy-blossom of the wild,
Dark, tangled forest, dear to any child.—
All these in season. Nor could barren, drear,
White and stark-featured Winter interfere
With Noey's rare resources: Still the same
He blithely whistled through the snow and came
Beneath the window with a Fairy sled;
And Little Lizzie, bundled heels-and-head,
He took on such excursions of delight
As even "Old Santy" with his reindeer might
Have envied her! And, later, when the snow
Was softening toward Spring-time and the glow

Of steady sunshine smote upon it,—then
Came the magician Noey yet again—
While all the children were away a day
Or two at Grandma's!—and behold when they
Got home once more;—there, towering taller than
The doorway—stood a mighty, old Snow-Man!

A thing of peerless art—a masterpiece
Doubtless unmatched by even classic Greece
In heyday of Praxiteles.—Alone
It loomed in lordly grandeur all its own.
And steadfast, too, for weeks and weeks it stood,
The admiration of the neighborhood
As well as of the children Noey sought
Only to honor in the work he wrought.
The traveler paid it tribute, as he passed
Along the highway—paused and, turning, cast
A lingering, last look—as though to take
A vivid print of it, for memory's sake,
To lighten all the empty, aching miles
Beyond with brighter fancies, hopes and smiles.
The cynic put aside his biting wit
And tacitly declared in praise of it;
And even the apprentice-poet of the town
Rose to impassioned heights, and then sat down
And penned a panegyric scroll of rhyme
That made the Snow-Man famous for all time.

And though, as now, the ever warmer sun
Of summer had so melted and undone
The perishable figure that—alas!—

Not even in dwindled white against the grass
Was left its latest and minutest ghost,
The children yet—*materially,* almost—
Beheld it—circled round it hand-in-hand—
(Or rather round the place it used to stand)—
With "Ring-a-round-a-rosy! Bottle full
O' posy!" and, with shriek and laugh, would pull
From seeming contact with it—just as when
It was the *real-est* of old Snow-Men!

Even in such a scene of senseless play
The children were surprised one summer day
By a strange man who called across the fence,
Inquiring for their father's residence;
And, being answered that this was the place,
Opened the gate, and, with a radiant face,
Came in and sat down with them in the shade
And waited—till the absent father made
His noon appearance, with a warmth and zest
That told he had no ordinary guest
In this man whose low-spoken name he knew
At once, demurring as the stranger drew
A stuffy note-book out, and turned and set
A big fat finger on a page, and let
The writing thereon testify instead
Of further speech. And as the father read
All silently, the curious children took
Exacting inventory both of book
And man:—He wore a long-napped white fur hat
Pulled firmly on his head, and under that
Rather long silvery hair, or iron-gray—

For he was not an old man,—anyway,
Not beyond sixty. And he wore a pair
Of square-framed spectacles—or rather there
Were two more than a pair,—the extra two
Flared at the corners, at the eyes' side-view,
In as redundant vision as the eyes
Of grasshoppers or bees or dragon-flies.
Later the children heard the father say
He was "A Noted Traveler," and would stay
Some days with them.—In which time host and
    guest
Discussed, alone, in deepest interest,
Some vague, mysterious matter that defied
The wistful children, loitering outside
The spare-room door. There Bud acquired a quite
New list of big words—such as "Disunite,"
And "Shibboleth," and "Aristocracy,"
And "Juggernaut," and "Squatter Sovereignty,"
And "Antislavery," "Emancipate,"
"Irrepressible Conflict," and "The Great
Battle of Armageddon"—obviously
A pamphlet brought from Washington, D. C.,
And spread among such friends as might occur
Of like views with "The Noted Traveler."

A PROSPECTIVE VISIT

WHILE *any* day was notable and dear
That gave the children Noey, history here
Records his advent emphasized indeed
With sharp italics, as he came to feed
The stock one special morning, fair and bright,
When Johnty and Bud met him, with delight
Unusual even as their extra dress—
Garbed as for holiday, with much excess
Of proud self-consciousness and vain conceit
In their new finery.—Far up the street
They called to Noey, as he came, that they,
As promised, both were going back that day
To *his* house with him!

                    And by time that each
Had one of Noey's hands—ceasing their speech
And coyly anxious, in their new attire,
To wake the comment of their mute desire,—
Noey seemed rendered voiceless. Quite a while
They watched him furtively.—He seemed to smile
As though he would conceal it ; and they saw
Him look away, and his lips purse and draw
In curious, twitching spasms, as though he might

Be whispering,—while in his eye the white
Predominated strangely.—Then the spell
Gave way, and his pent speech burst audible:
"They wuz two stylish little boys,
       and they wuz mighty bold ones,
Had two new pairs o' britches made
       out o' their Daddy's old ones!"
And at the inspirational outbreak,
Both joker and his victims seemed to take
An equal share of laughter,—and all through
Their morning visit kept recurring to
The funny words and jingle of the rhyme
That just kept getting funnier all the time.

AT NOEY'S HOUSE

AT Noey's house—when they arrived with him—
　　How snug seemed everything, and neat and
　　　　trim:
The little picket-fence, and little gate—
Its little pulley, and its little weight,—
All glib as clockwork, as it clicked behind
Them, on the little red-brick pathway, lined
With little paint-keg vases and tea-pots
Of wee moss-blossoms and forget-me-nots:
And in the windows, either side the door,
Were ranged as many little boxes more
Of like old-fashioned larkspurs, pinks and moss
And fern and phlox; while up and down across
Them rioted the morning-glory vines
On taut-set cotton strings, whose snowy lines
Whipped in and out and under the bright green
Like basting-threads; and, here and there between
A showy, shiny hollyhock would flare
Its pink among the white and purple there.—
And still behind the vines, the children saw
A strange, bleached, wistful face that seemed to
　　draw

A vague, indefinite sympathy. A face
It was of some newcomer to the place.—
In explanation, Noey, briefly, said
That it was "Jason," as he turned and led
The little fellows round the house to show
Them his menagerie of pets. And so
For quite a time the face of the strange guest
Was partially forgotten, as they pressed
About the squirrel-cage and rousted both
The lazy inmates out, though wholly loath
To whirl the wheel for them.—And then with awe
They walked round Noey's big pet owl, and saw
Him film his great, clear, liquid eyes and stare
And turn and turn and turn his head round there
The same way they kept circling—as though he
Could turn it one way thus eternally.

Behind the kitchen, then, with special pride
Noey stirred up a terrapin inside
The rain-barrel where he lived, with three or four
Little mud-turtles of a size not more
In neat circumference than the tiny toy
Dumb-watches worn by every little boy.

Then, back of the old shop, beneath the tree
Of "rusty-coats," as Noey called them, he
Next took the boys, to show his favorite new
Pet coon—pulled rather coyly into view
Up through a square hole in the bottom of
An old inverted tub he bent above,

Yanking a little chain, with "Hey! you, sir!
Here's *comp'ny* come to see you, Bolivur!"
Explanatory, he went on to say,
"I named him *Bolivur* jes' thisaway,—
He looks so *round* and *ovalish* and *fat,*
'Peared-like no other name 'ud fit but that."

Here Noey's father called and sent him on
Some errand. "Wait," he said—"I won't be gone
A half a' hour.—Take Bud, and go on in
Where Jason is, tel I git back ag'in."

Whoever *Jason* was, they found him there
Still at the front-room window.—By his chair
Leaned a new pair of crutches; and from one
Knee down, a leg was bandaged.—"Jason done
That-air with one o' these-'ere tools *we* call
A *'shin-hoe'*—but a *foot-adze* mostly all
Hardware-store-keepers calls 'em."—(*Noey* made
This explanation later.)
                              Jason paid
But little notice to the boys as they
Came in the room:—An idle volume lay
Upon his lap—the only book in sight—
And Johnty read the title,—"Light, More Light,
There's Danger in the Dark,"—though *first* and
        best—
In fact, the *whole* of Jason's interest
Seemed centered on a little *dog*—one pet
Of Noey's all uncelebrated yet—

Though *Jason,* certainly, avowed his worth,
And niched him over all the pets on earth—
As the observant Johnty would relate
The *Jason*-episode, and imitate
The all-enthusiastic speech and air
Of Noey's kinsman and his tribute there:—

"That little dog 'ud scratch at that door
And go on a-whinin' two hours before
He'd ever let up! *There!*—Jane: Let him in.—
(Hah, there, you little rat!) Look at him grin!
     Come down off o' that!—
     W'y, look at him! (*Drat
You! you-rascal-you!*)—bring me that hat!
Look *out!*—He'll snap *you!*—*He* wouldn't let
You take it away from him, now you kin bet!
That little rascal's jist natchurly mean.—
I tell you, I *never* (*Git out!!*), never seen
A *spunkier* little rip! (*Scratch to git in,
And now yer a-scratchin' to git out* ag'in!
Jane: Let him out.)   Now, watch him from here
Out through the winder!—You notice one ear
Kind o' *in*side-*out,* like he holds it?—Well,
He's got a *tick* in it—*I* kin tell!
     Yes, and he's cunnin'—
     Jist watch him a-runnin',
Sidelin'—see!—like he ain't *'plum'd true'*
And legs don't 'track' as they'd ort to do!—
Ploughin' his nose through the weeds—i jing!
Ain't he jist cuter'n anything!

"W'y, that little dog's got *grown*-people's sense;—
See how he gits out under the fence?—
And watch him a-whettin' his hind legs 'fore
His dead square run of a mile'd er more—
'Cause *Noey's* a-comin', and Trip allus knows
When *Noey's* a-comin'—and off he goes!—
Putts out to meet him and—*There they come now!*
Well-sir! it's raially singalar how
          That dog kin *tell*,—
          But he knows as well
When Noey's a-comin' home!—Reckon his *smell*
'Ud carry two mile'd?—You needn't to *smile*—
He runs to meet *him*, ever'-once-'n-a-while,
Two mile'd and over—when he's slipped away
And left him at home here, as he's done to-day—
'Thout ever knowin' where Noey wuz goin'—
But that little dog allus hits the right way!
Hear him a-whinin' and scratchin' ag'in?—
(*Little tormentin' fice!*) Jane: Let him in.

"—You say he ain't *there?*—
          Well now, I declare!—
Lem*me* limp out and look! . . . I wunder where—
Heuh, Trip!—*Heuh,* Trip!—*Heuh,* Trip! . . .
          There—
There he is!—Little sneak!—What-a'-you-'bout?—
There he is—quiled up as meek as a mouse,
His tail turnt up like a tea-kittle spout,
A-sunnin' hiss'f at the side o' the house!
Next time you scratch, sir, you'll half to git in,

My fine little feller, the best way you kin!
—Noey *he* learns him sich capers!—And they—
Both of 'em's ornrier every day!—
Both tantalizin' and meaner'n sin—
'Allus a—(*Listen there!*)—Jane: Let him in.

"—Oh! yer so *innocent!* hangin' yer head!—
(Drat ye! you'd *better* git under the bed!)
          . . . Listen at that!—
          He's tackled the cat!—
Hah, there! you little rip! come out o' that!—
Git yer blame' little eyes scratched out
'Fore you know what yer talkin' about!—
Here! come away from there!—(Let him alone—
He'll snap *you,* I tell ye, as quick as a bone!)
Hi, Trip!—*Hey,* here!—What-a'-you-'bout!—
Oo! ouch! 'Ll, I'll be blamed!—*Blast ye!* GIT OUT!
 . . . Oh, it ain't nothin'—jist *scratched* me, you
     see.—
Hadn't no idy he'd try to bite *me!*
Plague take him!—Bet he'll not try *that* ag'in!—
Hear him yelp.—(*Pore feller!*) Jane: Let him in."

THE LOEHRS AND THE HAMMONDS

"HEY, Bud! *O* Bud!" rang out a gleeful call,—
　　"The Loehrs is come to your house!"　And
　　　　　a small
But very much elated little chap,
In snowy linen suit and tasseled cap,
Leaped from the back fence just across the street
From Bixlers', and came galloping to meet
His equally delighted little pair
Of playmates, hurrying out to join him there—
"The Loehrs is come!—The Loehrs is come!" his
　　glee
Augmented to a pitch of ecstasy
Communicated wildly, till the cry
"The Loehrs is come!" in chorus quavered high
And thrilling as some pæan of challenge or
Soul-stirring chant of armied conqueror.
And who this *avant-courier* of "the Loehrs"?—
This happiest of all boys out o' doors—
Who but Will Pierson, with his heart's excess
Of summer warmth and light and breeziness!
"From our front winder I 'uz first to see
'Em all a-drivin' into town!" bragged he—
"An' seen 'em turnin' up the alley where

Your folks lives at. An' John an' Jake wuz there
Both in the wagon;—yes, an' Willy, too;
An' Mary—yes, an' Edith—with bran-new
An' purtiest-trimmed hats 'at ever wuz!—
An' Susan, an' Janey.—An' the *Hammond-uz*
In their fine buggy 'at they're ridin' roun'
So much, all over an' aroun' the town
An' *ever'*wheres,—them *city* people who's
A-visutin' at Loehrs-uz!"

              Glorious news!—
Even more glorious when verified
In the boys' welcoming eyes of love and pride,
As one by one they greeted their old friends
And neighbors.—Nor until their earth-life ends
Will that bright memory become less bright
Or dimmed indeed.

         . . . Again, at candle-light,
The faces all are gathered. And how glad
The Mother's features, knowing that she had
Her dear, sweet Mary Loehr back again.—
She always was so proud of her; and then
The dear girl, in return, was happy, too,
And with a heart as loving, kind and true
As that maturer one which seemed to blend
As one the love of mother and of friend.
From time to time, as hand in hand they sat,
The fair girl whispered something low, whereat
A tender, wistful look would gather in
The mother-eyes; and then there would begin
A sudden cheerier talk, directed to

The stranger guests—the man and woman who,
It was explained, were coming now to make
Their temporary home in town for sake
Of the wife's somewhat failing health. Yes, they
Were city people, seeking rest this way,
The man said, answering a query made
By some well-meaning neighbor—with a shade
Of apprehension in the answer. . . . No,—
They had no *children*. As he answered so,
The man's arm went about his wife, and she
Leaned toward him, with her eyes lit prayerfully:
Then she arose—he following—and bent
Above the little sleeping innocent
Within the cradle at the mother's side—
He patting her, all silent, as she cried.—
Though, haply, in the silence that ensued,
His musings made melodious interlude.

In the warm, health-giving weather
  My poor pale wife and I
Drive up and down the little town
  And the pleasant roads thereby:
Out in the wholesome country
  We wind, from the main highway,
In through the wood's green solitudes—
  Fair as the Lord's own Day.

We have lived so long together,
  And joyed and mourned as one,
That each with each, with a look for speech,
  Or a touch, may talk as none
But Love's elect may comprehend—
  Why, the touch of her hand on mine
Speaks volume-wise, and the smile of her eyes,
  To me, is a song divine.

There are many places that lure us :—
  "The Old Wood Bridge" just west
Of town we know—and the creek below,
  And the banks the boys love best :
And "Beech Grove," too, on the hilltop;
  And "The Haunted House" beyond,
With its roof half off, and its old pump-trough
  Adrift in the roadside pond.

We find our way to "The Marshes"—
  At least where they used to be;
And "The Old Camp Grounds"; and "The Indian
    Mounds,"
  And the trunk of "The Council Tree":
We have crunched and splashed through "Flint-bed
    Ford";
  And at "Old Big Bee-gum Spring"
We have stayed the cup, half lifted up,
  Hearing the redbird sing.

And then, there is "Wesley Chapel,"
  With its little graveyard, lone
At the crossroads there, though the sun sets fair
  On wild rose, mound and stone. . . .
A wee bed under the willows—
  My wife's hand on my own—
And our horse stops, too. . . . And we hear the coo
  Of a dove in undertone.

The dusk, the dew, and the silence!
  "Old Charley" turns his head
Homeward then by the pike again,
  Though never a word is said—
One more stop, and a lingering one—
  After the fields and farms,—
At the old Toll-Gate, with the woman await
  With a little girl in her arms.

The silence sank—Floretty came to call
The children in the kitchen, where they all
Went helter-skeltering with shout and din
Enough to drown most sanguine silence in,—
For well indeed they knew that summons meant
Taffy and pop-corn—so with cheers they went.

THE HIRED MAN AND FLORETTY

THE Hired Man's supper, which he sat before,
In near reach of the wood-box, the stove-door
And one leaf of the kitchen-table, was
Somewhat belated, and in lifted pause
His dexterous knife was balancing a bit
Of fried mush near the port awaiting it.

At the glad children's advent—gladder still
To find *him* there—"Jest tickled fit to kill
To see ye all!" he said, with unctuous cheer.—
"I'm tryin'-like to he'p Floretty here
To git things cleared away and give ye room
Accordin' to yer stren'th.   But I p'sume
It's a pore boarder, as the poet says,
That quarrels with his victuals, so I guess
I'll take another wedge o' that-air cake,
Florett', that you're a-*learnin'* how to bake."
He winked and feigned to swallow painfully.—
"Jest 'fore ye all come in, Floretty she
Was boastin' 'bout her *biscuits*—and they *air*
As good—sometimes—as you'll find anywhere.—

But, women gits to braggin' on their *bread,*
I'm s'picious 'bout their *pie*—as Danty said."
This raillery Floretty strangely seemed
To take as compliment, and fairly beamed
With pleasure at it all.

                —"Speakin' o' *bread*—
When she come here to live," The Hired Man
     said,—
"Never be'n out o' *Freeport* 'fore she come
Up here,—of course she needed *'sperience* some.—
So, one day, when yer Ma was goin' to set
The risin' fer some bread, she sent Florett'
To borry *leaven,* 'crost at Ryans'.—So,
She went and asked fer *twelve.*—She didn't *know,*
But thought, *whatever* 'twuz, that she could keep
One fer *herse'f* she said.   O she wuz deep!"

Some little evidence of favor hailed
The Hired Man's humor ; but it wholly failed
To touch the serious Susan Loehr, whose air
And thought rebuked them all to listening there
To her brief history of the *city* man
And his pale wife—"A sweeter woman than
She ever saw !"—So Susan testified,—
And so attested all the Loehrs beside.—
So entertaining was the history, that
The Hired Man, in the corner where he sat
In quiet sequestration, shelling corn,
Ceased wholly, listening, with a face forlorn
As Sorrow's own, while Susan, John and Jake
Told of these strangers who had come to make

Some weeks' stay in the town, in hopes to gain
Once more the health the wife had sought in vain:
Their doctor, in the city, used to know
The Loehrs—Dan and Rachel—years ago,—
And so had sent a letter and request
For them to take a kindly interest
In favoring the couple all they could—
To find some home-place for them, if they would,
Among their friends in town. He ended by
A dozen further lines, explaining why
His patient must have change of scene and air—
New faces, and the simple friendships there
With *them,* which might, in time, make her forget
A grief that kept her ever brooding yet
And wholly melancholy and depressed,—
Nor yet could she find sleep by night nor rest
By day, for thinking—thinking—thinking still
Upon a grief beyond the doctor's skill,—
The death of her one little girl.

                                   "Pore thing!"
Floretty sighed, and with the turkey-wing
Brushed off the stove-hearth softly, and peered in
The kettle of molasses, with her thin
Voice wandering into song unconsciously—
In purest, if most witless, sympathy.—

> " 'Then sleep no more:
>   Around thy heart
> Some ten-der dream may i-dlee play,
>   But mid-night song,
>   With mad-jick art,
> Will chase that dree muh-way!' "

"That-air besetment of Floretty's," said
The Hired Man,—*"singin'*—she *inhairited,*—
Her *father* wuz addicted—same as her—
To singin'—yes, and played the dulcimer!
But—gittin' back,—I s'pose yer talkin' 'bout
Them *Hammondses.* Well, Hammond he gits out
Pattents on things—inventions-like, I'm told—
And's got more money'n a house could hold!
And yit he can't git up no pattent-right
To do away with *dyin'.*—And he might
Be worth a *million,* but he couldn't find
Nobody sellin' *health* of any kind! . . .
But they's no thing onhandier fer *me*
To use than other people's misery.—
Floretty, hand me that-air skillet there
And lemme git 'er het up, so's them-air
Childern kin have their pop-corn."

                                    It was good
To hear him now, and so the children stood
Closer about him, waiting.

                        "Things to *eat,"*
The Hired Man went on, " 'smighty hard to beat!
Now, when *I* wuz a boy, we wuz so pore,
My parunts couldn't 'ford pop-corn no more
To pamper *me* with;—so, I hat to go
Without pop-corn—sometimes a *year* er so!—
And *suffer'n' saints!* how hungry I would git
Fer jest one other chance—like this—at it!
Many and many a time I've *dreamp',* at night,
About pop-corn,—all bu'sted open white,
And hot, you know—and jest enough o' salt

And butter on it fer to find no fault—
Oomh!—Well! as I was goin' on to say,—
After a-*dreamin'* of it thataway,
Then havin' to wake up and find it's all
A *dream,* and hain't got no pop-corn at-tall,
Ner hain't *had* none—I'd think, *'Well, where's the
    use!'*
And jest lay back and sob the plaster'n' loose!
And I have *prayed,* what*ever* happened, it
'Ud eether be pop-corn er death! . . . And yit
I've noticed—more'n likely so have you—
That things don't happen when you *want* 'em to."

And thus he ran on artlessly, with speech
And work in equal exercise, till each
Tureen and bowl brimmed white. And then he
    greased
The saucers ready for the wax, and seized
The fragrant-steaming kettle, at a sign
Made by Floretty; and, each child in line,
He led out to the pump—where, in the dim
New coolness of the night, quite near to him
He felt Floretty's presence, fresh and sweet
As . . . dewy night-air after kitchen-heat.

There, still, with loud delight of laugh and jest,
They plied their subtle alchemy with zest—
Till, sudden, high above their tumult, welled
Out of the sitting-room a song which held
Them stilled in some strange rapture, listening
To the sweet blur of voices chorusing:—

> " 'When twilight approaches the season
>   That ever is sacred to song,
> Does some one repeat my name over,
>   And sigh that I tarry so long?
> And is there a chord in the music
>   That's missed when my voice is away?—
> And a chord in each heart that awakens
>   Regret at my wearisome stay-ay—
>   Regret at my wearisome stay.' "

All to himself, The Hired Man thought—"Of
    course
They'll sing *Floretty* homesick!"

                          . . . O strange source
Of ecstasy! O mystery of Song!—
To hear the dear old utterance flow along:—

> " 'Do they set me a chair near the table
>   When evening's home-pleasures are nigh?—
> When the candles are lit in the parlor,
>   And the stars in the calm azure sky.' " . . .

Just then the moonlight sliced the porch slantwise,
And flashed in misty spangles in the eyes
Floretty clenched, while through the dark—
    "I jing!"
A voice asked, "Where's that song *'you'd* learn to
    sing
Ef I sent you the *ballat?'*—which I done
Last I was home at Freeport.—S'pose you run
And git it—and we'll all go in to where
They'll know the notes and sing it fer ye there."
And up the darkness of the old stairway

Floretty fled, without a word to say—
Save to herself some whisper muffled by
Her apron, as she wiped her lashes dry.

Returning, with a letter, which she laid
Upon the kitchen-table while she made
A hasty crock of "float,"—poured thence into
A deep glass dish of iridescent hue
And glint and sparkle, with an overflow
Of froth to crown it, foaming white as snow.—
And then—pound-cake, and jelly-cake as rare,
For its delicious complement,—with air
Of Hebe mortalized, she led her van
Of votaries, rounded by The Hired Man.

THE EVENING COMPANY

WITHIN the sitting-room, the company
    Had been increased in number. Two or three
Young couples had been added: Emma King,
Ella and Mary Mathers—all could sing
Like veritable angels—Lydia Martin, too,
And Nelly Millikan.—What songs they knew!—

> *"'Ever of thee—wherever I may be,*
> *Fondly I'm drea-m-ing ever of thee!'"*

And with their gracious voices blend the grace
Of Warsaw Barnett's tenor; and the bass
Unfathomed of Wick Chapman—Fancy still
Can *feel,* as well as *hear* it, thrill on thrill,
Vibrating plainly down the backs of chairs
And through the wall and up the old hall-stairs.—
Indeed, young Chapman's voice especially
Attracted *Mr. Hammond.*—For, said he,
Waiving the most Elysian sweetness of
The *ladies'* voices—altitudes above
The *man's* for sweetness;—*but*—as *contrast,* would
Not Mr. Chapman be so very good

As, just now, to oblige *all* with—in fact,
Some sort of *jolly* song,—to counteract
In part, at least, the sad, pathetic trend
Of music *generally*. Which wish our friend
"The Noted Traveler" made second to
With heartiness—and so each, in review,
Joined in—until the radiant *basso* cleared
His wholly unobstructed throat and peered
Intently at the ceiling—voice and eye
As opposite indeed as earth and sky.—
Thus he uplifted his vast bass and let
It roam at large the memories booming yet:

> " 'Old Simon the Cellarer keeps a rare store
>   Of Malmsey and Malvoi-sie,
>   Of Cyprus, and who can say how many more?—
>   But a chary old soul is he-e-ee—
>   A chary old so-u-l is he!
>   Of hock and Canary he never doth fail;
>   And all the year round, there is brewing of ale;—
>   Yet he never aileth, he quaintly doth say,
>   While he keeps to his sober six flagons a day.' "

. . . And then the chorus—the men's voices all
Warred in it—like a German Carnival.—
Even *Mrs*. Hammond smiled, as in her youth,
Hearing her husband.—And in veriest truth
"The Noted Traveler's" ever-present hat
Seemed just relaxed a little, after that,
As at conclusion of the Bacchic song
He stirred his "float" vehemently and long.

Then Cousin Rufus with his flute, and art
Blown blithely through it from both soul and
     heart—
Inspired to heights of mastery by the glad,
Enthusiastic audience he had
In the young ladies of a town that knew
No other flutist,—nay, nor *wanted* to,
Since they had heard *his* "Polly Hopkins Waltz,"
Or "Rickett's Hornpipe," with its faultless faults,
As rendered solely, he explained, "by ear,"
Having but heard it once, Commencement Year,
At "Old Ann Arbor."

            Little Maymie now
Seemed "friends" with *Mr. Hammond*—anyhow,
Was lifted to his lap—where settled, she,
Enthroned thus, in her dainty majesty,
Gained *universal* audience—although
Addressing him alone:—"I'm come to show
You my new Red-blue pencil; and *she* says"—
(Pointing to *Mrs.* Hammond)—"that she guess'
You'll make a *picture* fer me."

                "And what *kind*
Of picture?" Mr. Hammond asked, inclined
To serve the child as bidden, folding square
The piece of paper she had brought him there,—
"I don't know," Maymie said—"only ist make
A *little dirl,* like me!"

             He paused to take
A sharp view of the child, and then he drew—
A while with red, and then a while with blue—

The outline of a little girl that stood
In converse with a wolf in a great wood;
And she had on a hood and cloak of red—
As Maymie watched—*"Red Riding-Hood!"* she
    said.
"And who's *'Red Riding-Hood'?"*

                  "W'y, don't *you* know?"
Asked little Maymie—

              But the man looked so
All uninformed, that little Maymie could
But tell him *all about* Red Riding-Hood.

MAYMIE'S STORY OF RED RIDING-HOOD

W'Y, one time wuz a little-weenty dirl,
 An' she wuz named Red Riding-Hood, 'cause
  her—
Her *Ma* she maked a little red cloak fer her
'At turnt up over her head.—An' it 'uz all
Ist one piece o' red cardinul 'at's like
The drate-long stockin's the storekeepers has.—
Oh! it 'uz purtiest cloak in all the world
An' *all* this town er anywheres they is!
An' so, one day, her Ma she put it on
Red Riding-Hood, she did—one day, she did—
An' it 'uz *Sund'y*—'cause the little cloak
It 'uz too nice to wear ist *ever'* day
An' *all* the time!—An' so her Ma, she put
It on Red Riding-Hood—an' telled her not
To dit no dirt on it ner dit it mussed
Ner nothin'! An'—an'—nen her Ma she dot
Her little basket out, 'at Old Kriss bringed
Her wunst—one time, he did. An' nen she fill'
It full o' whole lots an' 'bundance o' dood things t'
  eat
(Allus my Dran'ma *she* says ' 'bundance,' too.)
An' so her Ma fill' little Red Riding-Hood's
Nice basket all ist full o' dood things t' eat,

Maymie's Version of Red Riding Hood.

ONE time they wuz a little=weenty girl,
An' she wuz named Red Riding Hood, 'cause her—
Her Ma she maked a little red cloak fer her
'At turnt up over her head —An' it wuz all
Jist one piece o' red cardinul 'at's like
Them dratted=long stockin's the store=keeper's got—
O'it 'uz purtiest cloak in all the world
An' all this town er anywheres they is!
An' so, one day, her Ma she put it on
Red Riding Hood, she did —one day, she did—
An' it 'uz Sundy—'cause the little cloak
It 'uz too nice to wear ist ever' day
An' all the time!—An' so her Ma she put
It on Red Riding Hood—an' telled her not

Bud's Fairy Tale.

SOME peoples thinks they aint no Fairies now
No more! — But they is, I bet! 'Cause ef
They wuzn't Fairies, nen I like to know
Who'd write 'bout Fairies in the books, an' know
What Fairies does, an' how their picture looks,
An' all an' everthing! Wy, ef they don't
Be Fairies anymore, nen little boys
'Ud jist sleep when they go to sleep an' won't
Have any dreams at all, — 'cause Fairies — good
Fairies — they're a-purpose to make dreams!
But they is Fairies — an' I know they is! —
'Cause one time wunst, when it's all Summertime,
An' don't be any fires in the stove
An' fireplace to keep warm wiv — ner don't haf
To wear old scratchy flannen shirts at all
Ner ketch yer death o' cold — an' when the big

An' tell her take 'em to her old Dran'ma—
An' not to *spill* 'em, neever—'cause ef she
'Ud stump her toe an' spill 'em, her Dran'ma
She'll haf to *punish* her!

               An' nen—An' so
Little Red Riding-Hood she p'omised she
'Ud be all careful nen, an' cross' her heart
'At she won't run an' spill 'em all fer six—
Five—ten—two-hundred-bushel-dollars-gold!
An' nen she kiss' her Ma doo'-by an' went
A-skippin' off—away fur off frough the
Big woods, where her Dran'ma she live at—
    No!—
She didn't do *a-skippin'*, like I said:—
She ist went *walkin'*—careful-like an' slow—
Ist like a little lady—walkin' 'long
As all polite an' nice—an' slow—an' straight—
An' turn her toes—ist like she's marchin' in
The Sund'y-School k-session!

                 An'—an'—so
She 'uz a-doin' along—an' doin' along—
On frough the drate-big woods—'cause her
    Dran'ma
She live 'way, 'way fur off frough the big woods
From *her* Ma's house. So when Red Riding-Hood
Dit to do there, she allus have most fun—
When she do frough the drate-big woods, you
    know.—
'Cause she ain't feard a bit o' anything!

An' so she sees the little hoppty-birds
'At's in the trees, an' flyin' all around,
An' singin' dlad as ef their parunts said
They'll take 'em to the magic-lantern show!
An' she 'ud pull the purty flowers an' things
A-growin' round the stumps.—An' she 'ud ketch
The purty butterflies, an' drasshoppers,
An' stick pins frough 'em—No!—I ist *said* that!—
'Cause she's too dood an' kind an' 'bedient
To *hurt* things thataway.—She'd *ketch* 'em, though,
An' ist *play* wiv 'em ist a little while,
An' nen she'd let 'em fly away, she would,
An' ist skip on ad'in to her Dran'ma's.

An' so, while she 'uz doin' 'long an' 'long,
First thing you know they 'uz a drate-big old
Mean wicked Wolf jumped out 'at wanted t' eat
Her up, but *dassent* to—'cause wite clos't there
They wuz a Man a-choppin' wood, an' you
Could *hear* him.—So the old Wolf he 'uz *feard*
Only to ist be *kind* to her.—So he
Ist 'tended-like he wuz dood friends to her
An' says, "Dood morning, little Red Riding-
    Hood!"—
All ist as kind!
                  An' nen Riding-Hood
She say "Dood morning," too—all kind an' nice—
Ist like her Ma she learn'—No!—mustn't say
"Learn'," 'cause *"learn'"* it's unproper.—So she say
It like her *Ma* she *"teached"* her.—An'—so she

Ist says "Dood morning" to the Wolf—'cause she
Don't know ut-tall 'at he's a *wicked* Wolf
An' want to eat her up!
          Nen old Wolf smile
An' say, so kind: "Where air you doin' at?"
Nen little Red Riding-Hood she say: "I'm doin'
To my Dran'ma's, 'cause my Ma say I might."
Nen, when she tell him that, the old Wolf he
Ist turn an' light out frough the big thick woods,
Where she can't see him any more. An' so
She think he's went to *his* house—but he hain't,—
He's went to her Dran'ma's, to be there first—
An' *ketch* her, ef she don't watch mighty sharp
What she's about!
          An' nen when the old Wolf
Dit to her Dran'ma's house, he's purty smart,—
An' so he 'tend-like *he's* Red Riding-Hood,
An' knock at th' door. An' Riding-Hood's Dran'ma
She's sick in bed an' can't come to the door
An' open it. So th' old Wolf knock' *two* times.
An' nen Red Riding-Hood's Dran'ma she says,
"Who's there?" she says. An' old Wolf 'tends-like
    he's
Little Red Riding-Hood, you know, an' make'
His voice soun' ist like hers, an' says: "It's me,
Dran'ma—an' I'm Red Riding-Hood an' I'm
Ist come to *see* you."
          Nen her old Dran'ma
She think it *is* little Red Riding-Hood,
An' so she say: "Well, come in nen an' make
You'se'f at home," she says, "'cause I'm down sick

In bed, an' got the 'ralgia, so's I can't
Dit up an' let ye in."
                            An' so th' old Wolf
Ist march' in nen an' shet the door ad'in,
An' *drowl'*, he did, an' *splunge'* up on the bed
An' et up old Miz Riding-Hood 'fore she
Could put her specs on an' see who it wuz.—
An' so she never knowed *who* et her up!

An' nen the wicked Wolf he ist put on
Her nightcap, an' all covered up in bed—
Like he wuz *her*, you know.
                                Nen, purty soon
Here come along little Red Riding-Hood,
An' *she* knock' at the door. An' old Wolf 'tend-
Like *he's* her Dran'ma; an' he say, "Who's there?"
Ist like her Dran'ma say, you know. An' so
Little Red Riding-Hood she say: "It's *me*,
Dran'ma—an' I'm Red Riding-Hood an' I'm
Ist come to *see* you."
                            An' nen old Wolf nen
He cough an' say: "Well, come in nen an' make
You'se'f at home," he says, "'cause I'm down sick
In bed, an' got the 'ralgia, so's I can't
Dit up an' let ye in."
                            An' so she think
It's her Dran'ma a-talkin'.—So she ist
Open' the door an' come in, an' set down
Her basket, an' taked off her things, an' bringed
A chair an' clumbed up on the bed, wite by
The old big Wolf she thinks is her Dran'ma—

Only she thinks the old Wolf's dot whole lots
More bigger ears, an' lots more whiskers, too,
Than her Dran'ma; an' so Red Riding-Hood
She's kind o' skeered a little. So she says,
"Oh, Dran'ma, what *big eyes* you dot!" An' nen
The old Wolf says: "They're ist big thataway
'Cause I'm so dlad to see you!"

               Nen she says,
"Oh, Dran'ma, what a drate-big nose you dot!"
Nen th' old Wolf says: "It's ist big thataway
Ist 'cause I smell the dood things 'at you bringed
Me in the basket!"

             An' nen Riding-Hood
She says, "Oh-me-oh-*my!* Dran'ma! what big
White long sharp teeth you dot!"

              Nen old Wolf says:
"Yes—an' they're thataway"—an' drowled—
"They're thataway," he says, "to *eat* you wiv!"
An' nen he ist *jump'* at her.—

             But she *scream'*—
An' *scream'*, she did.—So's 'at the Man
'At wuz a-choppin' wood, you know,—*he* hear,
An' come a-runnin' in there wiv his ax;
An', 'fore the old Wolf know' what he's about,
He split his old brains out an' killed him s' quick
It make' his head swim!—An' Red Riding-Hood
She wuzn't hurt at all!

           An' the big Man
He tooked her all safe home, he did, an' tell
Her Ma she's all right an' ain't hurt at all
An' old Wolf's dead an' killed—an' ever'thing!—

So her Ma wuz so tickled an' so proud,
She gived *him* all the good things t' eat they wuz
'At's in the basket, an' she tell' him 'at
She's much oblige', an' say to "call ad'in."
An' story's honest *truth*—an' all *so*, too!

LIMITATIONS OF GENIUS

THE audience entire seemed pleased—indeed,
Extremely pleased. And little Maymie, freed
From her task of instructing, ran to show
Her wondrous colored picture to and fro
Among the company.

                "And how comes it," said
Some one to Mr. Hammond, "that, instead
Of the inventor's life, you did not choose
The *artist's?*—since the world can better lose
A cutting-box or reaper than it can
A noble picture painted by a man
Endowed with gifts this drawing would suggest"—
Holding the picture up to show the rest.
"There now!" chimed in the wife, her pale face lit
Like winter snow with sunrise over it,—
"That's what *I'm* always asking him.—But *he*—
Well, as he's answering *you*, he answers *me*,—
With that same silent, suffocating smile
He's wearing now!"

                For quite a little while
No further speech from any one, although
All looked at Mr. Hammond and that slow,
Immutable, mild smile of his. And then
The encouraged querist asked him yet again

Why was it, and et cetera—with all
The rest, expectant, waiting round the wall,—
Until the gentle Mr. Hammond said
He'd answer with a *"parable,"* instead—
About "a dreamer" that he used to know—
"An artist"—"master"—*all*—in *embryo*.

MR. HAMMOND'S PARABLE

THE DREAMER

I

HE was a Dreamer of the Days:
   Indolent as a lazy breeze
Of midsummer, in idlest ways
   Lolling about in the shade of trees.
The farmer turned—as he passed him by
   Under the hillside where he kneeled
Plucking a flower—with scornful eye
   And rode ahead in the harvest-field
Muttering—"Lawz! ef that-air shirk
   Of a boy wuz mine fer a week er so,
He'd quit *dreamin'* and git to work
   And *airn* his livin'—er—Well! *I* know!"
And even kindlier rumor said,
Tapping with finger a shaking head,—
"Got such a curious kind o' way—
Wouldn't surprise me much, I say!"

Lying limp, with upturned gaze
Idly dreaming away his days.
No companions? Yes, a book
Sometimes under his arm he took

To read aloud to a lonesome brook.
  And schoolboys, truant, once had heard
A strange voice chanting, faint and dim—
Followed the echoes, and found it him,
  Perched in a tree-top like a bird,
Singing, clean from the highest limb;
And, fearful and awed, they all slipped by
To wonder in whispers if he could fly.

"Let him alone!" his father said
  When the old schoolmaster came to say,
  "He took no part in his books to-day—
Only the lesson the readers read.—
  His mind seems sadly going astray!"
"Let him alone!" came the mournful tone,
And the father's grief in his sad eyes shone—
Hiding his face in his trembling hand,
Moaning, "Would I could understand!
But as Heaven wills it I accept
Uncomplainingly!" So he wept.

Then went "The Dreamer" as he willed,
As uncontrolled as a light sail filled
Flutters about with an empty boat
Loosed from its moorings and afloat:
Drifted out from the busy quay
Of dull school-moorings listlessly;
Drifted off on the talking breeze,
All alone with his reveries;
Drifted on, as his fancies wrought—
Out on the mighty gulfs of thought.

II

The farmer came in the evening gray
  And took the bars of the pasture down;
Called to the cows in a coaxing way,
  "Bess" and "Lady" and "Spot" and "Brown,"
While each gazed with a wide-eyed stare,
As though surprised at his coming there—
Till another tone, in a higher key,
Brought their obeyance loathfully.

Then, as he slowly turned and swung
The topmost bar to its proper rest,
  Something fluttered along and clung
An instant, shivering at his breast—
  A wind-scared fragment of legal cap
Which darted again, as he struck his hand
  On his sounding chest with a sudden slap,
And hurried sailing across the land.
But as it clung he had caught the glance
Of a little penciled countenance,
And a glamour of written words; and hence,
A minute later, over the fence,
"Here and there and gone astray
Over the hills and far away,"
He chased it into a thicket of trees
And took it away from the captious breeze.

A scrap of paper with a rhyme
Scrawled upon it of summer-time:
A pencil-sketch of a dairymaid,
Under a farmhouse porch's shade,

Working merrily; and was blent
With her glad features such sweet content,
That a song she sang in the lines below
Seemed delightfully apropos:—

SONG

"Why do I sing—Tra-la-la-la-la!
Glad as a King?—Tra-la-la-la-la!
　　Well, since you ask,—
　　　I have such a pleasant task,
　I can not help but sing!

"Why do I smile—Tra-la-la-la-la!
Working the while?—Tra-la-la-la-la!
　　Work like this is play,—
　　　So I'm playing all the day—
　I can not help but smile!

"So, if you please—Tra-la-la-la-la!
Live at your ease!—Tra-la-la-la-la!
　　You've only got to turn,
　　　And, you see, it's bound to churn—
　It can not help but please!"

The farmer pondered and scratched his head,
　Reading over each mystic word.—
"Some o' The Dreamer's work!" he said—
　"Ah, here's more—and name and date
In his handwrite'!"—And the good man read,—
　" 'Patent applied for, July third,
　Eighteen hundred and forty-eight'!"
The fragment fell from his nerveless grasp—
His awed lips thrilled with the joyous gasp:
　"I see the p'int to the whole concern,—
　He's studied out a patent churn!"

FLORETTY'S MUSICAL CONTRIBUTION

ALL seemed delighted, though the elders more,
   Of course, than were the children.—Thus,
     before
Much interchange of mirthful compliment,
The story-teller said *his* stories "went"
(Like a bad candle) *best* when they went *out*,—
And that some sprightly music, dashed about,
Would *wholly* quench his "glimmer," and inspire
Far brighter lights.
            And, answering this desire,
The flutist opened, in a rapturous strain
Of rippling notes—a perfect April-rain
Of melody that drenched the senses through;—
Then—gentler—gentler—as the dusk sheds dew,
It fell, by velvety, staccatoed halts,
Swooning away in old "Von Weber's Waltz."
Then the young ladies sang "Isle of the Sea"—
In ebb and flow and wave so billowy,—
Only with quavering breath and folded eyes
The listeners heard, buoyed on the fall and rise
Of its insistent and exceeding stress

Of sweetness and ecstatic tenderness. . . .
With lifted finger *yet,* Remembrance—List!—
"Beautiful isle of the sea!" wells in a mist
Of tremulous. . . .

         . . . After much whispering
Among the children, Alex came to bring
Some kind of *letter*—as it seemed to be—
To Cousin Rufus. This he carelessly
Unfolded—reading to himself alone,—
But, since its contents became, later, known,
And no one *"played* so *awful* bad," the same
May here be given—of course without full name,
Facsimile, or written kink or curl
Or clue. It read:—

    "Wild Roved an indian Girl
Brite al Floretty"
          deer freind
           i now take
~~this~~ These means to send that *Song* to you & make
my Promus good to you in the Regards
Of doing What i Promust afterwards.
the *notes* & *Words* is both here *Printed* sos
you ~~kin~~ can git *uncle Mart* to read you ~~them~~ those
& cousin Rufus you can git to *Play*
the *notes* fur you on eny Plezunt day
His Legul Work aint ~~Presein~~ Pressing.
            Ever thine
        As shore as the Vine
        doth the Stump intwine
        thou art my Lump of Sackkerrine
          Rinaldo Rinaldine
           the Pirut in Captivity.

. . . There dropped
Another square scrap.—But the hand was stopped
That reached for it—Floretty suddenly
Had set a firm foot on her property—
Thinking it was the *letter,* not the *song,*—
But blushing to discover she was wrong,
When, with all gravity of face and air,
Her precious letter *handed* to her there
By Cousin Rufus left her even more
In apprehension than she was before.
But, testing his unwavering, kindly eye,
She seemed to put her last suspicion by,
And, in exchange, handed the song to him.—

A page torn from a song-book: Small and dim
Both notes and words were—but as plain as day
They seemed to him, as he began to play—
And plain to *all* the singers,—as he ran
An airy, warbling prelude, then began
Singing and swinging in so blithe a strain,
That every voice rang in the old refrain:

MOUNTAIN MAID'S INVITATION

ARRANGED BY J. E. GOULD.

1. Come! come! come! O'er the hills, free from care, In my home true pleas-ure share; Blos-soms sweet, flow'rs most rare, Come where joys are found!

Here the spar-kling dews of morn Tree and shrub with gems a-dorn, Jew-els bright, gay-ly worn, Beau-ty all a-round! Tra la la la,

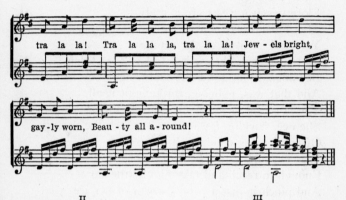

tra la la! Tra la la la, tra la la! Jew-els bright,

gay-ly worn, Beau-ty all a-round!

<table>
<tr><td>

II

Come! come! come!
Not a sigh, not a tear,
E'er is found in sadness here;
Music soft, breathing near,
  Charms away each care!
Birds, in joyous hours among
Hill and dell, with grateful song,
Dearest strains here prolong,
  Vocal all the air!
  Tra la la la, tra la la!
  Tra la la la, tra la la!
Dearest strains here prolong,
  Vocal all the air!

</td><td>

III

Come! come! come!
When the day's gently gone,
Evening shadows coming on,
Then, by love, kindly won,
  Truest bliss be thine!
Ne'er was found a bliss so pure,
Never joys so long endure;
Who would not love secure?
  Who would joys decline?
  Tra la la la, tra la la!
  Tra la la la, tra la la!
Who would not love secure?
  Who would joys decline?

</td></tr>
</table>

429

From the beginning of the song, clean through,
Floretty's features were a study to
The flutist who "read *notes*" so readily,
Yet read so little of the mystery
Of that face of the girl's.—Indeed, *one* thing
Bewildered him quite into worrying,
And that was, noticing, throughout it all,
The Hired Man shrinking closer to the wall,
She ever backing toward him through the throng
Of barricading children—till the song
Was ended, and at last he saw her near
Enough to reach and take him by the ear
And pinch it just a pang's worth of her ire
And leave it burning like a coal of fire.
He noticed, too, in subtle pantomime
She seemed to dust him off, from time to time;
And when somebody, later, asked if she
Had never heard the song before—"What! *me?*"
She said—then blushed again and smiled,—
"I've knowed that song sence *Adam* wuz a child!—
It's jes' a joke o' this-here man's.—He's learned
To *read* and *write* a little, and it's turned
His fool-head some—That's all!"

                                    And then some one
Of the loud-wrangling boys said—"*'Course* they's
     none
No more, *these* days!—They's Fairies *ust* to be,
But they're all dead, a hundred years!" said he.

"Well, there's where you're *mustakened!*"—in reply
They heard Bud's voice, pitched sharp and thin and
    high.—

"An' how you goin' to *prove* it?"

            "Well, I *kin!*"
Said Bud, with emphasis,—"They's one lives in
Our garden—and I *see* 'im wunst, wiv my
Own eyes—*one* time I did."

              "*Oh, what a lie!*"
—"'*Sh!*"

      "Well, nen," said the skeptic—seeing there
The older folks attracted—"tell us *where*
You saw him, an' all *'bout* him!"

             "Yes, my son.—
If you tell 'stories,' you may tell us one,"
The smiling father said, while Uncle Mart,
Behind him, winked at Bud, and pulled apart
His nose and chin with comical grimace—
Then sighed aloud, with sanctimonious face,—
    "*'How good and comely it is to see*
    Children and parents in friendship agree!'—
You fire away, Bud, on your Fairy tale—
Your *Uncle's* here to back you!"
              Somewhat pale,
And breathless as to speech, the little man
Gathered himself. And thus his story ran.

BUD'S FAIRY TALE

SOME peoples thinks they ain't no Fairies *now*
No more yet!—But they *is,* I bet! 'Cause ef
They *wuzn't* Fairies, nen I' like to know
Who'd w'ite 'bout Fairies in the books, an' tell
What Fairies *does,* an' how their *picture* looks,
An' all an' ever'thing! W'y, ef they don't
Be Fairies any more, nen little boys
'Ud ist *sleep* when they go to sleep an' won't
Have ist no dweams at all,—'cause Fairies—*good*
Fairies—they're a-purpose to make dweams!
But they *is* Fairies—an' I *know* they is!
'Cause one time wunst, when it's all Summer-time,
An' don't haf to be no fires in the stove
Er fireplace to keep warm wiv—ner don't haf
To wear old scwatchy flannen shirts at all,
An' ain't no fweeze—ner cold—ner snow!—An'—
   an'
Old skweeky twees got all the gween leaves on
An' ist keeps noddin', noddin' all the time,
Like they 'uz lazy an' a-twyin' to go
To sleep an' couldn't, 'cause the wind won't quit
A-blowin' in 'em, an' the birds won't stop
A-singin', so's they *kin.*—But twees *don't* sleep,

432

I guess! But *little boys* sleeps—an' *dweams,* too.—
An' that's a sign they's Fairies.

So, one time,
When I be'n playin' "Store" wunst over in
The shed of their old stable, an' Ed Howard
He maked me quit a-bein' pardners, 'cause
I dwinked the 'tend-like sody-water up
An' et the shore-'nuff crackers,—w'y, nen I
Clumbed over in our garden where the gwapes
Wuz purt' nigh ripe: An' I wuz ist a-layin'
There on th' old cwooked seat 'at Pa maked in
Our arber,—an' so I 'uz layin' there
A-whittlin' beets wiv my new dog-knife, an'
A-lookin' wite up thue the twimbly leaves—
An' wuzn't 'sleep at all!—An'-sir!—first thing
You know, a little *Fairy* hopped out there!—
A leetle-teenty Fairy!—hope-may-die!
An' he look' down at me, he did—an' he
Ain't bigger'n a *yellerbird!*—an' he
Say "Howdy-do!" he did—an' I could *hear*
Him—ist as *plain!*

Nen *I* say "Howdy-do!"
An' he say *"I'm* all hunky, Nibsey; how
Is *your* folks comin' on?"

An' nen I say
"My name ain't *'Nibsey,'* neever—my name's
Bud.—
An' what's *your* name?" I says to him.

An' he
Ist laugh an' say, " *'Bud's* awful *funny* name!"

An' he ist laid back on a big bunch o' gwapes
An' laugh' an' laugh', he did—like somebody
'Uz tick-el-un his feet!

          An' nen I say—
"What's *your* name," nen I say, "afore you bu'st
Yo'se'f a-laughin' bout *my* name?" I says.
An' nen he dwy up laughin'—kind o' mad—
An' say, "W'y, *my* name's *Squidjicum*," he says.
An' nen *I* laugh an' say—"*Gee!* what a name!"
An' when I make fun of his name, like that,
He ist git awful mad an' spunky, an'
'Fore you know, he gwabbed holt of a vine—
A big long vine 'at's danglin' up there, an'
He ist helt on wite tight to that, an' down
He swung quick past my face, he did, an' ist
Kicked at me hard's he could!

          But I'm too quick
Fer *Mr. Squidjicum!* I ist weached out
An' ketched him, in my hand—an' helt him, too,
An' *squeezed* him, ist like little wobins when
They can't fly yet an' git flopped out their nest.
An' nen I turn him all wound over, an'
Look at him clos't, you know—wite clos't,—cause ef
He *is* a Fairy, w'y, I want to see
The *wings* he's got.—But he's dwessed up so fine
'At I can't *see* no wings.—An' all the time
He's twyin' to kick me yet: An' so I take
F'esh holts an' *squeeze* ag'in—an' harder, too;
An' I says, "*Hold up, Mr. Squidjicum!*—
You're kickin' the w'ong man!" I says; an' nen

I ist *squeeze'* him, purt' nigh my *best,* I did—
An' I heerd somepin' bu'st!—An' nen he cwied
An' says, "You better look out what you're doin'!—
You' bu'st my spider-web suspenners, an'
You' got my wose-leaf coat all cwinkled up
So's I can't go to old Miss Hoodjicum's
Tea-party, 's afternoon!"

                              An' nen I says—
"Who's 'old Miss Hoodjicum'?" I says.

                                     An' he
Says, "Ef you lemme loose I'll tell you."

                                       So
I helt the little skeezics 'way fur out
In one hand—so's he can't jump down t' th' ground
Wivout a-gittin' all stove up: an' nen
I says, "You're loose now.—Go ahead an' tell
'Bout the 'tea-party' where you're goin' at
So awful fast!" I says.

                            An' nen he say,—
"No use to *tell* you 'bout it, 'cause you won't
Believe it, 'less you go there your own se'f
An' see it wiv your own two eyes!" he says.
An' *he* says: "Ef you lemme *shore-'nuff* loose,
An' p'omise 'at you'll keep wite still, an' won't
Tetch nothin' 'at you see—an' never tell
Nobody in the world—an' lemme loose—
W'y, nen I'll *take* you there!"

                             But I says, "Yes
An' ef I let you loose, you'll *run!*" I says.
An' he says, "No, I won't!—I hope-may-die!"

Nen I says, "Cwoss your heart you won't!"
                                        An' he
Ist cwoss his heart; an' nen I reach an' set
The little feller up on a long vine—
An' he 'uz so tickled to git lose ag'in,
He gwab the vine wiv boff his little hands
An' ist take an' turn in, he did, an' skin
'Bout forty-'leben cats!
                                Nen when he git
Thue whirlin' wound the vine, an' set on top
Of it ag'in, w'y, nen his "wose-leaf coat"
He bwag so much about, it's ist all tored
Up, an' ist hangin' strips an' rags—so he
Look like his Pa's a dwunkard. An' so nen
When he see what he's done—a-actin' up
So smart,—he's awful mad, I guess; an' ist
Pout out his lips an' twis' his little face
Ist ugly as he kin, an' set an' tear
His whole coat off—an' sleeves an' all.—An' nen
He wad it all togevver an' ist *th'ow*
It at me ist as hard as he kin dwive!

An' when I weach to ketch him, an' 'uz goin'
To give him 'nuvver squeezin', *he ist flewed
Clean up on top the arbor!*—'Cause, you know,
They *wuz* wings on him—when he tored his *coat*
Clean off—they *wuz* wings *under there*. But they
Wuz purty wobbly-like an' wouldn't work
Hardly at all—'cause purty soon, when I
Th'owed clods at him, an' sticks, an' got him shooed

Down off o' there, he come a-floppin' down
An' lit k-bang! on our old chicken-coop,
An' ist laid there a-whimper'n' like a child!
An' I tiptoed up wite clos't, an' I says, "What's
The matter wiv ye, Squidjicum?"

                                       An' he
Says: "Dog-gone! when my wings gits stwaight
    ag'in,
Where you all *crumpled* 'em," he says, "I bet
I'll ist fly clean away an' won't take you
To old Miss Hoodjicum's at all!" he says.
An' nen I ist weach out wite quick, I did,
An' gwab the sassy little snipe ag'in—
Nen tooked my top-stwing an' tie down his wings
So's he *can't* fly, 'less'n I want him to!
An' nen I says: "Now, Mr. Squidjicum,
You better ist light out," I says, "to old
Miss Hoodjicum's, an' show *me* how to git
There, too," I says; "er ef you don't," I says,
"I'll climb up wiv you on our buggy-shed
An' push you off!" I says.

                             An' nen he say
All wite, he'll show me there; an' tell me nen
To set him down wite easy on his feet,
An' loosen up the stwing a little where
It cut him under th' arms. An' nen he says,
"Come on!" he says; an' went a-limpin' 'long
The garden-paph—an' limpin' 'long an' 'long
Tel—purty soon he come on 'long to where's
A grea'-big cabbage-leaf. An' he stoop down

An' say, "Come on inunder here wiv me!"
So *I* stoop down an' crawl inunder there,
Like he say.
            An' inunder there's a grea'-
Big clod, they is—a' awful grea'-big clod!
An' nen he says, *"Woll this-here clod away!"*
An' so I woll' the clod away. An' nen
It's all wet, where the dew'z inunder where
The old clod wuz.—An' nen the Fairy he
Git on the wet-place: Nen he say to me,
"Git on the wet-place, too!" An' nen he say,
"Now hold yer breff an' shet yer eyes!" he says,
"Tel I say *Squinchy-winchy!"* Nen he say—
Somepin' *in Dutch,* I guess.—An' nen I felt
Like we 'uz sinkin' down—an' sinkin' down!—
Tel purty soon the little Fairy weach
An' pinch my nose an' yell at me an' say,
"Squinchy-winchy! Look wherever you please!"
Nen when I looked—Oh! they 'uz purtiest place
Down there you ever saw in all the World!—
They 'uz ist *flowers* an' *woses*—yes, an' *twees*
Wiv *blossoms* on an' *big wipe apples* boff!
An' butterflies, they wuz—an' hummin'-birds—
An' *yeller*birds an' *blue*birds—yes, an' *wed!*—
An' ever'wheres an' all awound 'uz vines
Wiv wipe p'serve-pears on 'em!—Yes, an' all
An' ever'thing 'at's ever growin' in
A garden—er canned up—all wipe at wunst!—
It wuz ist like a garden—only it
'Uz ist a *little bit* o' garden—'bout big wound

As ist our twun'el-bed is.—An' all wound
An' wound the little garden's a gold fence—
An' little gold gate, too—an' ash-hopper
'At's all gold, too—an' ist full o' gold ashes!
An' wite in th' middle o' the garden wuz
A little gold house, 'at's ist 'bout as big
As ist a bird-cage is: An' *in* the house
They 'uz whole-lots *more* Fairies there—'cause I
Picked up the little house, an' peeked in at
The winders, an' I see 'em all in there
Ist *buggin'* round! An' Mr. Squidjicum
He twy to make me quit, but I gwab *him*
An' poke him down the chimbly, too, I did!—
An' y'ort to see *him* hop out 'mongst 'em there!—
Ist like he 'uz the boss an' ist got back!—
"Hain't ye got on them-air dew-dumplin's yet?"
He says.

     An' they says no.

         An' nen he says—
"Better git at 'em nen!" he says, *"wite quick—
'Cause old Miss Hoodjicum's a-comin'!"*

         Nen

They all set wound a little gold tub—an'
All 'menced a-peelin' dewdwops, ist like they
'Uz *peaches.*—An', it looked so funny, I
Ist laugh' out loud, an' *dwopped* the little house,—
An' 't bu'sted like a soap-bubble!—an' 't skeered
Me so, I—I—I—I,—it skeered me so,—
I—ist *waked* up.—No! I *ain't* be'n *asleep*
An' *dweam* it all, like *you* think,—but it's shore
Fer-certain *fact* an' cwoss my heart it is!

A DELICIOUS INTERRUPTION

ALL were quite gracious in their plaudits of
  Bud's Fairy; but another stir above
That murmur was occasioned by a sweet
Young lady-caller, from a neighboring street,
Who rose reluctantly to say good night
To all the pleasant friends and the delight
Experienced,—as she had promised sure
To be back home by nine.   Then paused, demure,
And wondered was it *very* dark.—Oh, *no!*—
She had *come* by herself and she could go
Without an *escort*. Ah, you sweet girls all!
What young gallant but comes at such a call,
Your most abject slaves! Why, there were three
Young men, and several men of family,
Contesting for the honor—which at last
Was given to Cousin Rufus; and he cast
A kingly look behind him, as the pair
Vanished with laughter in the darkness there.
As order was restored, with everything
Suggestive, in its way, of "romancing,"
Some one observed that *now* would be the chance
For *Noey* to relate a circumstance
That *he*—the very specious rumor went—

Had been eye-witness of, by accident.
Noey turned pippin-crimson; then turned pale
As death; then turned to flee, without avail.—
"There! head him off! *Now!* hold him in his
    chair!—
Tell us the Serenade-tale, now, Noey.—*There!"*

NOEY'S NIGHT-PIECE

"THEY ain't much 'tale' about it!" Noey
　　said.—
"K'tawby grapes wuz gittin' good-'n'-red
I rickollect; and Tubb Kingry and me
'Ud kind o' browse round town, daytime, to see
What neighbers 'peared to have the most to spare
'At wuz git-at-able and no dog there
When we come round to git 'em, say 'bout ten
O'clock at night, when mostly old folks then
Wuz snorin' at each other like they yit
Helt some old grudge 'at never slep' a bit.
Well, at the *Pars'nige*—ef ye'll call to mind,—
They's 'bout the biggest grape-arber you'll find
'Most anywheres.—And mostly there, we knowed
They wuz *k'tawbies* thick as ever growed—
And more'n they'd *p'serve*.—Besides I've heerd
Ma say k'tawby-grape p'serves jes' 'peared
A waste o' sugar, anyhow!—And so
My conscience stayed outside and lemme go
With Tubb, one night, the back-way, clean up
　　through
That long black arber to the end next to
The house, where the k'tawbies, don't you know,
Wuz thickest. And 't'uz lucky we went *slow*,—

Fer jes' as we wuz cropin' to'rds the gray-
End, like, of the old arber—heerd Tubb say
In a skeered whisper, 'Hold up! They's some one
Jes' slippin' in here!—and *looks like a gun*
He's carryin'!' I *golly!* we both spread
Out flat ag'inst the ground!

                    'What's that?' Tubb said.—
And jes' then—'*plink! plunk! plink!*' we heerd
    something
Under the back-porch winder.—Then, i jing!
Of course we rickollected 'bout the young
School-mam 'at wuz a-boardin' there, and sung,
And played on the melodium in the choir.—
And she 'uz 'bout as purty to admire
As any girl in town!—the fac's is, she
Jes' *wuz,* them times, to a dead certainty,
The belle o' this-here bailywick!—But—Well,—
I'd best git back to what I'm tryin' to tell:—
It wuz some feller come to serenade
Miss Wetherell: And there he plunked and played
His old guitar, and sung, and kep' his eye
Set on her winder, blacker'n the sky!—
And black it *stayed.*—But mayby she wuz 'way
From home, er wore out—bein' *Saturday!*

"It *seemed* a good 'eal *longer,* but I *know*
He sung and plunked there half a' hour er so
Afore, it 'peared-like, he could ever git
His own free qualified consents to quit
And go off 'bout his business. When he went
I bet you could 'a' bought him fer a cent!

"And now, behold ye all!—as Tubb and me
Wuz 'bout to raise up,—right in front we see
A feller slippin' out the arber, square
Smack under that-air little winder where
The *other* feller had been standin'.—And
The thing he wuz a-carryin' in his hand
Wuzn't no *gun* at all!—it wuz a *flute,*—
And *whoop-ee!* how it did git up and toot
And chirp and warble, tel a mockin'-bird
'Ud dast to never let hisse'f be heerd
Ferever, after such miracalous, high
Jimcracks and grand skyrootics played there by
Yer Cousin Rufus!—Yes-sir; it wuz him!—
And what's more,—all a-suddent that-air dim
Dark winder o' Miss Wetherell's wuz lit
Up like a' oyshture-sign, and under it
We see him sort o' wet his lips and smile
Down 'long his row o' dancin' fingers, while
He kind o' stiffened up and kinked his breath
And everlastin'ly jes' blowed the peth
Out o' that-air old one-keyed flute o' his.
And, bless their hearts, that's all the 'tale' they is!"

And even as Noey closed, all radiantly
The unconscious hero of the history,
Returning, met a perfect driving storm
Of welcome—a reception strangely warm
And *unaccountable,* to *him,* although
Most *gratifying,*—and he told them so.
"I only urge," he said, "my right to be
Enlightened."   And a voice said: *"Certainly:—*

During your absence we agreed that you
Should tell us all a story, old or new,
Just in the immediate happy frame of mind
We knew you would return in."

So, resigned,

The ready flutist tossed his hat aside—
Glanced at the children, smiled, and thus complied.

COUSIN RUFUS' STORY

MY little story, Cousin Rufus said,
   Is not so much a story as a fact.
It is about a certain wilful boy—
An aggrieved, unappreciated boy,
Grown to dislike his own home very much,
By reason of his parents being not
At all up to his rigid standard and
Requirements and exactions as a son
And disciplinarian.
                    So, sullenly
He brooded over his disheartening
Environments and limitations, till,
At last, well knowing that the outside world
Would yield him favors never found at home,
He rose determinedly one July dawn—
Even before the call for breakfast—and,
Climbing the alley-fence, and bitterly
Shaking his clenched fist at the wood-pile, he
Evanished down the turnpike.—Yes: he had,
Once and for all, put into execution
His long low-muttered threatenings—He had
Run off!—He had—had run away from home!

446

His parents, at discovery of his flight,
Bore up first-rate—especially his Pa,—
Quite possibly recalling his own youth,
And therefrom predicating, by high noon,
The absent one was very probably
Disporting his nude self in the delights
Of the old swimmin'-hole, some hundred yards
Below the slaughter-house, just east of town.
The stoic father, too, in his surmise
Was accurate—For, lo! the boy was there!

And there, too, he remained throughout the day—
Save at one starving interval in which
He clad his sunburnt shoulders long enough
To shy across a wheat-field, shadow-like,
And raid a neighboring orchard—bitterly,
And with spasmodic twitchings of the lip,
Bethinking him how all the other boys
Had *homes* to go to at the dinner-hour—
While *he*—alas!—*he had no home!*—At least
These very words seemed rising mockingly,
Until his every thought smacked raw and sour
And green and bitter as the apples he
In vain essayed to stay his hunger with.
Nor did he join the glad shouts when the boys
Returned rejuvenated for the long
Wet revel of the feverish afternoon.—
Yet, bravely, as his comrades splashed and swam
And spluttered, in their weltering merriment,
He tried to laugh, too,—but his voice was hoarse
And sounded to him like some other boy's.
And then he felt a sudden, poking sort

Of sickness at the heart, as though some cold
And scaly pain were blindly nosing it
Down in the dreggy darkness of his breast.
The tensioned pucker of his purple lips
Grew ever chillier and yet more tense—
The central hurt of it slow spreading till
It did possess the little face entire.
And then there grew to be a knuckled knot—
An aching kind of core within his throat—
An ache, all dry and swallowless, which seemed
To ache on just as bad when he'd pretend
He didn't notice it as when he did.
It was a kind of a conceited pain—
An overbearing, self-assertive and
Barbaric sort of pain that clean outhurt
A boy's capacity for suffering—
So, many times, the little martyr needs
Must turn himself all suddenly and dive
From sight of his hilarious playmates and
Surreptitiously weep under water.
                              Thus
He wrestled with his awful agony
Till almost dark; and then, at last—then, with
The very latest lingering group of his
Companions, he moved turgidly toward home—
Nay, rather *oozed* that way, so slow he went,—
With loathful, hesitating, loitering,
Reluctant late-election-returns air,
Heightened somewhat by the conscience-made
    resolve
Of chopping a double armful of wood

As he went in by rear way of the kitchen.
And this resolve he executed;—yet
The hired girl made no comment whatsoever
But went on washing up the supper-things,
Crooning the unutterably sad song, *"Then think,*
Oh, think how lonely this heart must ever be!"
Still, with affected carelessness, the boy
Ranged through the pantry; but the cupboard-door
Was locked. He sighed then like a wet forestick
And went out on the porch.—At least the pump,
He prophesied, would meet him kindly and
Shake hands with him and welcome his return!
And long he held the old tin dipper up—
And oh, how fresh and pure and sweet the draught!
Over the upturned brim, with grateful eyes
He saw the back-yard, in the gathering night,
Vague, dim and lonesome; but it all looked good:
The lightning-bugs, against the grape-vines, blinked
A sort of sallow gladness over his
Home-coming, with this softening of the heart.
He did not leave the dipper carelessly
In the milk-trough.—No: he hung it back upon
Its old nail thoughtfully—even tenderly.
All slowly then he turned and sauntered toward
The rain-barrel at the corner of the house,
And, pausing, peered into it at the few
Faint stars reflected there. Then—moved by some
Strange impulse new to him—he washed his feet.
He then went in the house—straight on into
The very room where sat his parents by

The evening lamp.—The father all intent
Reading his paper, and the mother quite
As intent with her sewing. Neither looked
Up at his entrance—even reproachfully,—
And neither spoke.
          The wistful runaway
Drew a long, quavering breath, and then sat down
Upon the extreme edge of a chair. And all
Was very still there for a long, long while.—
Yet everything, someway, seemed *restful*-like
And *homy* and old-fashioned, good and kind,
And sort of *kin* to him!—Only too *still!*
If somebody would *say* something—just *speak*—
Or even rise up suddenly and come
And lift him by the ear sheer off his chair—
Or box his jaws—Lord bless 'em!—*any*thing!—
Was he not there to thankfully accept
Any reception from parental source
Save this incomprehensible *voicelessness?*
O but the silence held its very breath!
If but the ticking clock would only *strike*
And for an instant drown the whispering,
Lisping, sifting sound the katydids
Made outside in the grassy nowhere!
                       Far
Down some back street he heard the faint halloo
Of boys at their night-game of "Town-fox,"
But now with no desire at all to be
Participating in their sport.—No; no;—
Never again in this world would he want

To join them there!—he only wanted just
To stay in home of nights—Always—always—
Forever and a day!

                He moved; and coughed—
Coughed hoarsely, too, through his rolled tongue;
    and yet
No vaguest of parental notice or
Solicitude in answer—no response—
No word—no look. O it was deathly still!—
So still it was that really he could not
Remember any prior silence that
At all approached it in profundity
And depth and density of utter hush.
He felt that he himself must break it: So,
Summoning every subtle artifice
Of seeming nonchalance and native ease
And naturalness of utterance to his aid,
And gazing raptly at the house-cat where
She lay curled in her wonted corner of
The hearth-rug, dozing, he spoke airily
And said: "I see you've got the same old cat!"

BEWILDERING EMOTIONS

THE merriment that followed was subdued—
  As though the story-teller's attitude
Were dual, in a sense, appealing quite
As much to sorrow as to mere delight,
According, haply, to the listener's bent
Either of sad or merry temperament.—
"And of your two appeals I much prefer
The pathos," said "The Noted Traveler,"—
"For should I live to twice my present years,
I know I could not quite forget the tears
That child-eyes bleed, the little palms nailed wide,
And quivering soul and body crucified. . . .
But, bless them! there are no such children here
To-night, thank God!—Come here to me, my dear!"
He said to little Alex, in a tone
So winning that the sound of it alone
Had drawn a child more loathful to his knee:—
"And, now-sir, *I'll* agree if *you'll* agree,—
You tell us all a story, and then *I*
Will tell one."

       "But I can't."

               "Well, can't you *try?*"
"Yes, Mister: he *kin* tell *one*. Alex, tell

The one, you know, 'at you made up so well,
About the *Bear*.   He allus tells that one,"
Said *Bud,*—"He gits it mixed some 'bout the *gun*
An' *ax* the Little Boy had, an' *apples,* too."—
Then Uncle Mart said—"There, now! that'll do!—
Let *Alex* tell his story his own way!"
And Alex, prompted thus, without delay
Began.

THE BEAR STORY

W'Y, wunst they wuz a Little Boy went out
In the woods to shoot a Bear. So, he went
out
'Way in the grea'-big woods—he did.—An' he
Wuz goin' along—an' goin' along, you know,
An' purty soon he heerd somepin' go *"Wooh!"*—
Ist thataway—*"Woo-ooh!"* An' he wuz *skeered,*
He wuz. An' so he runned an' clumbed a tree—
A grea'-big tree, he did,—a sicka-*more* tree.
An' nen he heerd it ag'in: an' he looked round,
An' *'t'uz a Bear!—a grea'-big shore-'nuff Bear!*—
No: 't'uz *two* Bears, it wuz—two grea'-big Bears—
One of 'em wuz—ist *one's* a *grea'-big* Bear.—
But they ist *boff* went *"Wooh!"*—An' here *they*
come
To climb the tree an' git the Little Boy
An' eat him up!
                        An' nen the Little Boy
He 'uz skeered worse'n ever! An' here come
The grea'-big Bear a-climbin' th' tree to git
The Little Boy an' eat him up—Oh, *no!*—

THE BEAR STORY THAT ALEX
Ist Maked Up His=own=se'f"

Wy, wunst they wuz a Little Boy went out (1)
In th' woods to shoot a Bear. So, he went out
Way in the grea=big woods—he did.—An' he
Wuz goin' along—an' goin' along, you know,
An' purty soon he heerd somepin' go "Wooh!"—
Jes' thataway—"Woo=ooh!" An' he wuz skeered,
He wuz.—An' so he runned an' clumbed a tree—
A grea=big tree, he did,—a sicka=more tree.
An' nen he heerd it agin: an' he looked round,
An' 'tuz a Bear!—a grea=big shore=nuff Bear!—
No!—'tuz two Bears, it wuz—two grea=big Bears—
One of 'em wuz—ist one's a grea=big Bear.—
But they ist boff went "Wooh!"—An' here they come

It 'uzn't the *Big* Bear 'at clumb the tree—
It 'uz the *Little* Bear. So here *he* come
Climbin' the tree—an' climbin' the tree! Nen when
He git wite *clos't* to the Little Boy, w'y, nen
The Little Boy he ist pulled up his gun
An' *shot* the Bear, he did, an' killed him dead!
An' nen the Bear he falled clean on down out
The tree—away clean to the ground, he did—
Spling-splung! he falled *plum* down, an' killed him,
    too!
An' lit wite side o' where the *Big* Bear's at.

An' nen the Big Bear's awful mad, you bet!—
'Cause—'cause the Little Boy he shot his gun
An' killed the *Little* Bear.—'Cause the *Big* Bear
He—he 'uz the Little Bear's Papa.—An' so here
He come to climb the big old tree an' git
The Little Boy an' eat him up! An' when
The Little Boy he saw the *grea'-big Bear*
A-comin', he 'uz badder skeered, he wuz,
Than *any* time! An' so he think he'll climb
Up *higher*—'way up higher in the tree
Than the old *Bear* kin climb, you know.—But he—
He *can't* climb higher 'an old *Bears* kin climb,—
'Cause Bears kin climb up higher in the trees
Than any little Boys in all the Wo-r-r-ld!

An' so here come the grea'-big Bear, he did,—
A'climbin' up—an' up the tree, to git
The Little Boy an' eat him up! An' so
The Little Boy he clumbed on higher, an' higher,

An' higher up the tree—an' higher—an' higher—
An' higher'n iss-here *house* is!—An' here come
The old Bear—clos'ter to him all the time!—
An' nen—first thing you know,—when th' old Big
    Bear
Wuz wite clos't to him—nen the Little Boy
Ist jabbed his gun wite in the old Bear's mouf
An' shot an' killed him dead!—No; I *fergot,*—
He didn't shoot the grea'-big Bear at all—
'Cause *they 'uz no load in the gun,* you know—
'Cause when he shot the *Little* Bear, w'y, nen
No load 'uz any more nen *in* the gun!

But th' Little Boy clumbed *higher* up, he did—
He clumbed *lots* higher—an' on up *higher*—an'
    higher
An' *higher*—tel he ist *can't* climb no higher,
'Cause nen the limbs 'uz all so little, 'way
Up in the teeny-weeny tip-top of
The tree, they'd break down wiv him ef he don't
Be keerful! So he stop an' think: An' nen
He look around—An' here come the old Bear!
An' so the Little Boy make up his mind
He's got to ist git out o' there *some*way!—
'Cause here come the old Bear!—so clos't, his bref's
Purt' nigh so's he kin feel how hot it is
Ag'inst his bare feet—ist like old "Ring's" bref
When he's be'n out a-huntin' an' 's all tired.
So when th' old Bear's so clos't—the Little Boy
Ist gives a grea'-big jump fer *'nother* tree—
No!—no, he don't do that!—I tell you what

The Little Boy does:—W'y, nen—w'y, he—Oh,
    yes!—
The Little Boy *he finds a hole up there*
'At's in the tree—an' climbs in there an' *hides*—
An' *nen* th' old Bear can't find the Little Boy
At all!—but purty soon the old Bear finds
The Little Boy's *gun* 'at's up there—'cause the *gun*
It's too *tall* to tooked wiv him in the hole.
So, when the old Bear find' the *gun,* he knows
The Little Boy's ist *hid* round *somers* there,—
An' th' old Bear 'gins to snuff an' sniff around,
An' sniff an' snuff around—so's he kin find
Out where the Little Boy's hid at.—An' nen—nen—
Oh, *yes!*—W'y, purty soon the old Bear climbs
'Way out on a big limb—a grea'-long limb,—
An' nen the Little Boy climbs out the hole
An' takes his ax an' chops the limb off! . . . Nen
The old Bear falls *k-splunge!* clean to the ground,
An' bu'st an' kill hisse'f plum dead, he did!

An' nen the Little Boy he git his gun
An' 'menced a-climbin' down the tree ag'in—
No!—no, he *didn't* git his *gun*—'cause when
The *Bear* falled, nen the *gun* falled, too—An'
    broked
It all to pieces, too!—An' *nicest* gun!—
His Pa ist buyed it!—An' the Little Boy
Ist cried, he did; an' went on climbin' down
The tree—an' climbin' down—an' climbin' down!—
An'-sir! when he 'uz purt' nigh down,—w'y, nen
The old Bear he jumped up ag'in!—an' he

Ain't dead at all—*ist* 'tendin' thataway,
So he kin git the Little Boy an' eat
Him up! But the Little Boy he 'uz too smart
To climb clean *down* the tree.—An' the old Bear
He can't climb *up* the tree no more—'cause when
He fell, he broke one of his—He broke *all*
His legs!—an' nen he *couldn't* climb! But he
Ist won't go 'way an' let the Little Boy
Come down out of the tree. An' the old Bear
Ist growls round there, he does—ist growls an' goes
"*Wooh!—woo-ooh!*" all the time! An' Little Boy
He haf to stay up in the tree—all night—
An' 'thout no *supper* neever!—Only they
Wuz *apples* on the tree!—An' Little Boy
Et apples—ist all night—an' cried—an' cried!
Nen when 't'uz morning the old Bear went "*Wooh!*"
Ag'in, an' try to climb up in the tree
An' git the Little Boy—But he *can't*
Climb t' save his *soul,* he can't!—An' *oh!* he's
    mad!—
He ist tear up the ground! an' go "*Woo-ooh!*"
An'—*Oh, yes!*—purty soon, when morning's come
All *light*—so's you kin *see,* you know,—w'y, nen
The old Bear finds the Little Boy's *gun,* you know,
'At's on the ground.—(An' it ain't broke at all—
I ist *said* that!) An' so the old Bear think
He'll take the gun an' *shoot* the Little Boy:—
But *Bears they* don't know much 'bout shootin'
    guns:
So when he go to shoot the Little Boy,
The old Bear got the *other* end the gun

Ag'in' his shoulder, 'stid o' *th' other* end—
So when he try to shoot the Little Boy,
It shot *the Bear,* it did—an' killed him dead!
An' nen the Little Boy clumb down the tree
An' chopped his old woolly head off.—Yes, an'
    killed
The *other* Bear ag'in, he did—an' killed
All *boff* the bears, he did—an' tuk 'em home
An' *cooked* 'em, too, an' *et* 'em!
                  —An' that's all.

THE PATHOS OF APPLAUSE

THE greeting of the company throughout
    Was like a jubilee,—the children's shout
And fusillading hand-claps, with great guns
And detonations of the older ones,
Raged to such tumult of tempestuous joy,
It even more alarmed than pleased the boy;
Till, with a sudden twitching lip, he slid
Down to the floor and dodged across and hid
His face against his mother as she raised
Him to the shelter of her heart, and praised
His story in low whisperings, and smoothed
The "amber-colored hair," and kissed and
       soothed
And lulled him back to sweet tranquillity—
"An' 'at's a sign 'at you're the Ma fer me!"
He lisped, with gurgling ecstasy, and drew
Her closer, with shut eyes; and feeling, too,
If he could only *purr* now like a cat,
He would undoubtedly be doing that!

"And now"—the serious host said, lifting there
A hand entreating silence;—"now, aware
Of the good promise of our Traveler guest
To add some story with and for the rest,

460

I think I favor you, and him as well,
Asking a story I have heard him tell,
And know its truth, in each minute detail:"
Then leaning on his guest's chair, with a hale
Hand-pat by way of full endorsement, he
Said, "Yes—the Free-Slave story—certainly."

The old man, with his waddy note-book out,
And glittering spectacles, glanced round about
The expectant circle, and still firmer drew
His hat on, with a nervous cough or two:
And, save at times the big hard words, and tone
Of gathering passion—all the speaker's own,—
The tale that set each childish heart astir
Was thus told by "The Noted Traveler."

TOLD BY "THE NOTED TRAVELER"

COMING, clean from the Maryland-end
  Of this great National Road of ours,
Through your vast West; with the time to spend,
Stopping for days in the main towns, where
Every citizen seemed a friend,
And friends grew thick as the wayside flowers,—
I found no thing that I might narrate
More singularly strange or queer
Than a thing I found in your sister-State
Ohio,—at a river-town—down here
In my note-book: *Zanesville—situate*
On the stream Muskingum—broad and clear,
And navigable, through half the year,
North, to Coshocton; south, as far
As Marietta.—But these facts are
Not of the *story,* but the *scene*
Of the simple little tale I mean
To tell *directly*—from this, straight through
To the *end* that is best worth listening to:

Eastward of Zanesville, two or three
Miles from the town, as our stage drove in,
I on the driver's seat, and he
Pointing out this and that to me,—

On beyond us—among the rest—
A grovy slope, and a fluttering throng
Of little children, which he "guessed"
Was a picnic, as we caught their thin
High laughter, as we drove along,
Clearer and clearer.   Then suddenly
He turned and asked, with a curious grin,
What were my views on *Slavery?*   *"Why?"*
I asked, in return, with a wary eye.
"Because," he answered, pointing his whip
At a little, whitewashed house and shed
On the edge of the road by the grove ahead,—
"Because there are two slaves *there,*" he said—
"Two Black slaves that I've passed each trip
For eighteen years.—Though they've been set free,
They have been slaves ever since!" said he.
And, as our horses slowly drew
Nearer the little house in view,
All briefly I heard the history
Of this little old Negro woman and
Her husband, house, and scrap of land;
How they were slaves and had been made free
By their dying master, years ago
In old Virginia; and then had come
North here into a *free* State—so,
Safe forever, to found a home—
For themselves alone?—for they left South there
Five strong sons, who had, alas!
All been sold ere it came to pass
This first old master with his last breath
Had freed the *parents.*—(He went to death

Agonized and in dire despair
That the poor slave *children* might not share
Their parents' freedom. And wildly then
He moaned for pardon and died. Amen!)

Thus, with their freedom, and little sum
Of money left them, these two had come
North, full twenty long years ago;
And, settling there, they had hopefully
Gone to work, in their simple way,
Hauling—gardening—raising sweet
Corn, and pop-corn.—Bird and bee
In the garden-blooms and the apple tree
Singing with them throughout the slow
Summer's day, with its dust and heat—
The crops that thirst and the rains that fail;
Or in Autumn chill, when the clouds hung low,
And hand-made hominy might find sale
In the near town-market; or baking pies
And cakes, to range in alluring show
At the little window, where the eyes
Of the Movers' children, driving past,
Grew fixed, till the big white wagons drew
Into a halt that would sometimes last
Even the space of an hour or two—
As the dusty, thirsty travelers made
Their noonings there in the beeches' shade
By the old black Aunty's spring-house, where,
Along with its cooling draughts, were found
Jugs of her famous sweet spruce-beer,
Served with her gingerbread horses there,

While Aunty's snow-white cap bobbed round
Till the children's rapture knew no bound,
As she sang and danced for them, quavering clear
And high the chant of her old slave-days—

> "Oh, Lo'd, Jinny! my toes is so',
> Dancin' on yo' sandy flo'!"

Even so had they wrought all ways
To earn the pennies, and hoard them, too,—
And with what ultimate end in view?—
They were saving up money enough to be
Able, in time, to buy their own
Five children back.

                 Ah! the toil gone through!
And the long delays and the heartaches, too,
And self-denials that they had known!
But the pride and glory that was theirs
When they first hitched up their shackly cart
For the long, long journey South!—The start
In the first drear light of the chilly dawn,
With no friends gathered in grieving throng,—
With no farewells and favoring prayers;
But, as they creaked and jolted on,
Their chiming voices broke in song—

> " 'Hail, all hail! don't you see the stars a-fallin'?
>   Hail, all hail! I'm on my way.
>   Gideon am
>   A healin' ba'm—
>   I belong to the blood-washed army.
>   Gideon am
>   A healin' ba'm—
>   On my way!' "

And their *return!*—with their oldest boy
Along with them! Why, their happiness
Spread abroad till it grew a joy
Universal—It even reached
And thrilled the town till the *Church* was stirred
Into suspecting that wrong was wrong!—
And it stayed awake as the preacher preached
A *Real* "Love"-text that he had not long
To ransack for in the Holy Word.
And the son, restored, and welcomed so,
Found service readily in the town;
And, with the parents, sure and slow,
He went "saltin' de cole cash down."

So with the *next* boy—and each one
In turn, till *four* of the five at last
Had been brought back; and, in each case,
With steady work and good homes not
Far from the parents, *they* chipped in
To the family fund, with an equal grace.
Thus they managed and planned and wrought,
And the old folks throve—Till the night before
They were to start for the lone last son
In the rainy dawn—their money fast
Hid away in the house,—two mean,
Murderous robbers burst the door.
. . . Then, in the dark, was a scuffle—a fall—
An old man's gasping cry—and then
A woman's fife-like shriek.
                              . . . Three men
Splashing by on horseback heard

The summons: And in an instant all
Sprang to their duty, with scarce a word.
And they were *in time*—not only to save
The lives of the old folks, but to bag
Both the robbers, and buck-and-gag
And land them safe in the county jail—
Or, as Aunty said, with a blended awe
And subtlety,—"Safe in de calaboose whah
De dawgs cain't bite 'em!"
                              —So prevail
The faithful!—So had the Lord upheld
His servants of both deed and prayer,—
H<small>IS</small> the glory unparalleled—
Theirs the reward,—their every son
Free, at last, as the parents were!
And, as the driver ended there
In front of the little house, I said,
All fervently, "Well done! well done!"
At which he smiled, and turned his head,
And pulled on the leader's lines, and—"See!"
He said,—"you can read old Aunty's sign?"
And, peering down through these specs of mine
On a little, square board-sign, I read:

> "Stop, traveler, if you think it fit,
> And quench your thirst, for a-fi'-penny-bit.—
> The rocky spring is very clear,
> And soon converted into beer."

And, though I read aloud, I could
Scarce hear myself for laugh and shout
Of children—a glad multitude

Of little people, swarming out
Of the picnic-grounds I spoke about.—
And in their rapturous midst, I see
Again—through mists of memory—
An old black Negress laughing up
At the driver, with her broad lips rolled
Back from her teeth, chalk-white, and gums
Redder than reddest red-ripe plums.
He took from her hand the lifted cup
Of clear spring-water, pure and cold,
And passed it to me: And I raised my hat
And drank to her with a reverence that
My conscience knew was justly due
The old black face, and the old eyes, too—
The old black head, with its mossy mat
Of hair, set under its cap and frills
White as the snows on Alpine hills;
Drank to the old *black* smile, but yet
Bright as the sun on the violet,—
Drank to the gnarled and knuckled old
Black hands whose palms had ached and bled
And pitilessly been worn pale
And white almost as the palms that hold
Slavery's lash while the victim's wail
Fails as a crippled prayer might fail.—
Ay, with a reverence infinite,
I drank to the old black face and head—
The old black breast with its life of light—
The old black hide with its heart of gold.

HEAT-LIGHTNING

THERE was a curious quiet for a space
Directly following: and in the face
Of one rapt listener pulsed the flush and glow
Of the heat-lightning that pent passions throw
Long ere the crash of speech.—He broke the spell—
The host:—The Traveler's story, told so well,
He said, had wakened there within his breast
A yearning, as it were, to know *the rest*—
That all unwritten sequence that the Lord
Of Righteousness must write with flame and sword,
Some awful session of His patient thought.
Just then it was, his good old mother caught
His blazing eye—so that its fire became
But as an ember—though it burned the same.
It seemed to her, she said, that she had heard
It was the *Heavenly* Parent never erred,
And not the *earthly* one that had such grace:
"Therefore, my son," she said, with lifted face
And eyes, "let no one dare anticipate
The Lord's intent. While *He* waits, *we* will
      wait."
And with a gust of reverence genuine

Then Uncle Mart was aptly ringing in—
   " *'If the darkened heavens lower,*
     Wrap thy cloak around thy form;
   Though the tempest rise in power,
     God is mightier than the storm!' "
Which utterance reached the restive children all
As something humorous. And then a call
For *him* to tell a story, or to "say
A funny piece." His face fell right away:
He knew no story worthy. Then he must
Declaim for them: In that, he could not trust
His memory. And then a happy thought
Struck some one, who reached in his vest and
   brought
Some scrappy clippings into light and said
There was a poem of Uncle Mart's he read
Last April in "The Sentinel." He had
It there in print, and knew all would be glad
To hear it rendered by the author.

                       And,

All reasons for declining at command
Exhausted, the now helpless poet rose
And said: "I am discovered, I suppose.
Though I have taken all precautions not
To sign my name to any verses wrought
By my transcendent genius, yet, you see,
Fame wrests my secret from me bodily;
So I must needs confess I did this deed
Of poetry red-handed, nor can plead
One whit of unintention in my crime—
My guilt of rhythm and my glut of rhyme.—

" 'Mæonides rehearsed a tale of arms,
  And Naso told of curious meta*mur*phoses;
Unnumbered pens have pictured woman's charms,
  While crazy *I*'ve made poetry *on purposes!'*

In other words, I stand convicted—need
I say—by my own doing, as I read."

UNCLE MART'S POEM

THE OLD SNOW-MAN

HO! the old Snow-Man
    That Noey Bixler made!
He looked as fierce and sassy
    As a soldier on parade!—
'Cause Noey, when he made him,
    While we all wuz gone, you see,
He made him, jist a-purpose,
    Jist as fierce as he could be!—
      But when we all got *ust* to him,
      Nobody wuz afraid
    Of the old Snow-Man
    That Noey Bixler made!

'Cause Noey told us 'bout him
    And what he made him fer:—
He'd come to feed, that morning
    He found we wuzn't here;
And so the notion struck him,
    When we all come taggin' home
'T'ud *s'prise* us ef a' old Snow-Man
    'Ud meet us when we come!
So, when he'd fed the stock, and milked,
    And be'n back home, and chopped

472

His wood, and et his breakfast, he
   Jist grabbed his mitts and hopped
Right in on that-air old Snow-Man
   That he laid out he'd make
Er bu'st a trace *a-tryin'*—jist
    Fer old-acquaintance-sake!—
      But work like that wuz lots more fun,
       He said, than when he played!
      Ho! the old Snow-Man
       That Noey Bixler made!

He started with a big snowball,
   And rolled it all around;
And as he rolled, more snow 'ud stick
   And pull up off the ground.—
He rolled and rolled all round the yard—
   'Cause we could see the *track,*
All wher' the snow come off, you know,
   And left it wet and black.
He got the Snow-Man's *legs-part* rolled—
   In front the kitchen-door,—
And then he hat to turn in then
   And roll and roll some more!—
He rolled the yard all round ag'in,
   And round the house, at that—
Clean round the house and back to wher'
   The blame legs-half wuz at!
      He said he missed his dinner, too—
       Jist clean fergot and stayed
      There workin'. Oh! the old Snow-Man
       That Noey Bixler made!

And Noey said he hat to *hump*
  To git the *top-half* on
The *legs-half!*—When he *did,* he said,
  His wind wuz purt' nigh gone.—
He said, i jucks! he jist drapped down
  There on the old porch-floor
And panted like a dog!—And then
  He up! and rolled some more!—
The *last* batch—that wuz fer his head,—
  And—time he'd got it right
And clumb and fixed it on, he said—
  He hat to quit fer night!—
And *then,* he said, he'd kep' right on
  Ef they'd be'n any *moon*
To work by! So he crawled in bed—
  And *could* 'a' slep' tel *noon,*
    He wuz so plum wore out! he said,—
    But it wuz washin'-day,
    And hat to cut a cord o' wood
    'Fore he could git away!

But, last, he got to work ag'in,—
  With spade, and gouge, and hoe,
And trowel, too—(All tools 'ud do
  What *Noey* said, you know!)
He cut his eyebrows out like cliffs—
  And his cheek-bones and chin
Stuck *furder* out—and his old *nose*
  Stuck out as fur-ag'in!
He made his eyes o' walnuts,
  And his whiskers out o' this-

Here buggy-cushion stuffin'—*moss,*
  The teacher says it is.
And then he made a' old wood' gun,
  Set keerless-like, you know,
Acrost one shoulder—kind o' like
  Big Foot, er Adam Poe—
    Er, mayby, Simon Girty,
      The dinged old Renegade!
    Wooh! the old Snow-Man
      That Noey Bixler made!

And there he stood, all fierce and grim,
  A stern, heroic form:
What was the winter blast to him,
  And what the driving storm?—
What wonder that the children pressed
  Their faces at the pane
And scratched away the frost, in pride
  To look on him again?—
    What wonder that, with yearning bold,
      Their all of love and care
    Went warmest through the keenest cold
      To that Snow-Man out there!

But the old Snow-Man—
  What a dubious delight
He grew at last when Spring came on
  And days waxed warm and bright!—
Alone he stood—all kith and kin
  Of snow and ice were gone;—

Alone, with constant tear-drops in
　　His eyes and glittering on
His thin, pathetic beard of black—
　　Grief in a hopeless cause!—
Hope—hope is for the man that *dies*—
　　What for the man that *thaws!*
　　　O Hero of a hero's make!—
　　　　Let *marble* melt and fade,
　　　But never *you*—you old Snow-Man
　　　That Noey Bixler made!

"LITTLE JACK JANITOR"

AND there, in that ripe Summer night, once
    more
A wintry coolness through the open door
And window seemed to touch each glowing face
Refreshingly; and, for a fleeting space,
The quickened fancy, through the fragrant air,
Saw snowflakes whirling where the rose-leaves were,
And sounds of veriest jingling bells again
Were heard in tinkling spoons and glasses then.

Thus Uncle Mart's old poem sounded young
And crisp and fresh and clear as when first sung,
Away back in the wakening of Spring,
When his rhyme and the robin, chorusing,
Rumored, in duo-fanfare, of the soon
Invading Johnny-jump-ups, with platoon
On platoon of sweet-williams, marshaled fine
To bloomèd blarings of the trumpet-vine.

The poet turned to whisperingly confer
A moment with "The Noted Traveler,"
Then left the room, tripped up the stairs, and then
An instant later reappeared again,
Bearing a little, lacquered box, or chest,

Which, as all marked with curious interest,
He gave to the old Traveler, who in
One hand upheld it, pulling back his thin
Black luster coat-sleeves, saying he had sent
Up for his "Magic Box," and that he meant
To test it there—especially to show
The Children. "It is *empty now,* you know."—
He thumped it with his knuckles, so they heard
The hollow sound—"But lest it be inferred
It is not *really* empty, I will ask
Little Jack Janitor, whose pleasant task
It is to keep it ship-shape."

                    Then he tried
And rapped the little drawer in the side,
And called out sharply, "Are you in there,
    Jack?"
And then a little, squeaky voice came back,—
*"Of course I'm in here—ain't you got the key
Turned on me!"*
              Then the Traveler leisurely
Felt through his pockets, and at last took out
The smallest key they ever heard about!—
It wasn't any longer than a pin:
And this at last he managed to fit in
The little keyhole, turned it, and then cried,
"Is everything swept out clean there inside?"
*"Open the drawer and see! Don't talk so much;
Or else,"* the little voice squeaked, *"talk in Dutch—
You age me, asking questions!"*
                     Then the man
Looked hurt, so that the little folks began

To feel so sorry for him, he put down
His face against the box and had to frown.—
"Come, sir!" he called,—"no impudence to *me!*—
You've swept out clean?"

       "Open the drawer and see!"
And so he drew the drawer out: Nothing there
But just the empty drawer, stark and bare.
He shoved it back again, with a sharp click.—

"Ouch!" yelled the little voice—*"unsnap it—*
    quick!—
You've got my nose pinched in the crack!"
        And then
The frightened man drew out the drawer again,
The little voice exclaiming, *"Jee-mun-nee!*—
Say what you want, but please don't murder me!"
"Well, then," the man said, as he closed the drawer
With care, "I want some cotton-batting for
My supper! Have you got it?"

        And inside,
All muffled-like, the little voice replied,
"Open the drawer and see!"

        And, sure enough,
He drew it out, filled with the cotton stuff.
He then asked for a candle to be brought
And held for him; and tuft by tuft he caught
And lit the cotton, and, while blazing, took
It in his mouth and ate it, with a look
Of purest satisfaction.

       "Now," said he,

"I've eaten the drawer empty, let me see
What this is in my mouth:" And with both hands
He began drawing from his lips long strands
Of narrow silken ribbons, every hue
And tint;—and crisp they were and bright and
    new
As if just purchased at some Fancy-Store.
"And now, Bub, bring your cap," he said, "before
Something might happen!" And he stuffed the cap
Full of the ribbons. *There,* my little chap,
Hold *tight* to them," he said, "and take them to
The ladies there, for they know what to do
With all such rainbow finery!"

                                He smiled
Half sadly, as it seemed, to see the child
Open his cap first to his mother. . . . There
Was not a ribbon in it anywhere!
"Jack Janitor!" the man said sternly through
The Magic Box—"Jack Janitor, did *you*
Conceal those ribbons anywhere?"

                                "Well, yes,"
The little voice piped—*"but you'd never guess
The place I hid 'em if you'd guess a year!"*

"Well, won't you *tell* me?"

                                *"Not until you clear
Your mean old conscience,"* said the voice, *"and
    make
Me first do something for the Children's sake."*

"Well, then, fill up the drawer," the Traveler said,
"With whitest white on earth and reddest red!—
Your terms accepted—Are you satisfied?"

"Open the drawer and see!" the voice replied.

"Why, bless my soul!"—the man said, as he drew
The contents of the drawer into view—
"It's level-full of *candy!*—Pass it round—
Jack Janitor shan't steal *that,* I'll be bound!"—
He raised and crunched a stick of it, and
        smacked
His lips.—"Yes, that *is* candy, for a fact!—
And it's all *yours!"*
                    And how the children there
Lit into it!—O never anywhere
Was such a feast of sweetness!
                        "And now, then,"
The man said, as the empty drawer again
Slid to its place, he bending over it,—
"Now, then, Jack Janitor, before we quit
Our entertainment for the evening, tell
Us where you hid the ribbons—can't you?"
                                "Well,"
The squeaky little voice drawled sleepily—
"Under your old hat, maybe.—Look and see!"

All carefully the man took off his hat:
But there was not a ribbon under that.—
He shook his heavy hair, and all in vain
The old white hat—then put it on again:

"Now, tell me, *honest,* Jack, where *did* you hide
The ribbons?"
       "Under your hat," the voice replied.—
"Mind! I said 'under' and not 'in' it.—Won't
You ever take the hint on earth?—or don't
You want to show folks where the ribbon's at?—
Law! but I'm sleepy!—Under—unner yer hat!"

Again the old man carefully took off
The empty hat, with an embarrassed cough,
Saying, all gravely, to the children: "You
Must promise not to *laugh*—you'll all *want* to—
When you see where Jack Janitor has dared
To hide those ribbons—when he might have spared
My feelings.—But no matter!—Know the worst—
Here are the ribbons, as I feared at first."—
And, quick as snap of thumb and finger, there
The old man's head had not a sign of hair,
And in his lap a wig of iron-gray
Lay, stuffed with all that glittering array
Of ribbons. . . . "Take 'em to the ladies—Yes.
Good night to everybody, and God bless
The Children."
       In a whisper no one missed
The Hired Man yawned: "He's a vantrilloquist."

.   .   .   .

So gloried all the night. Each trundle-bed
And pallet was enchanted—each child-head
Was packed with happy dreams. And long before
The dawn's first far-off rooster crowed, the snore
Of Uncle Mart was stilled, as round him pressed

So gloried all the night. Each trundle=bed
And pallet was enchanted — Each child=head
Was packed with happy dreams, And long before
The dawn's first far=off rooster crowed, the snore
Of Uncle Mart was stilled, as 'round him pressed
The bare arms of the wakeful little guest
That he had carried home with him. . . .
                              "I think,"
An awed voice said — "No: I don't want a drink.—
I say still. — I think The Noted Traveler he
'S the inscrutibul=est man I ever see!"

                    ————

              [Curtain]

The last lines of A Child-World

The bare arms of the wakeful little guest
That he had carried home with him. . . .
                              "I think,"
An awed voice said—"(No: I don't want a
    dwink.—
Lay still.)—I think 'The Noted Traveler' he
'S the inscrutibul-est man I ever see!"

NOTES

NOTES

p. 1   THE POET OF THE FUTURE

Printed in *The Century Magazine,* January, 1889;
published in POEMS HERE AT HOME—1893, THE
LOCKERBIE BOOK—1911.

p. 3   NAUGHTY CLAUDE

Printed in *St. Nicholas,* January, 1889; published
in RHYMES OF CHILDHOOD—1890, CHILD-RHYMES
—1898, WHILE THE HEART BEATS YOUNG—1906,
THE RUNAWAY BOY—1908.

p. 4   THE ARTEMUS OF MICHIGAN

Written in February, 1889; published in GREEN
FIELDS AND RUNNING BROOKS—1892. Mr. Riley
and Mr. Nye met the jovial Hiram Y. Potts as described in the poem, and in consideration of his
inimitable drollery, they dubbed him the Artemus
(Ward) of Michigan.

p. 6   WAITIN' FER THE CAT TO DIE

Printed in *Harper's Magazine,* February, 1889;
published in RHYMES OF CHILDHOOD—1890, CHILD-
RHYMES—1898.

p. 9 THE ALL-KIND MOTHER

Printed in *The Century Magazine,* February, 1889; published in POEMS HERE AT HOME—1893, THE LOCKERBIE BOOK—1911.

p. 11 TO HATTIE—ON HER BIRTHDAY

Written just prior to February 17, 1889; published in RHYMES OF CHILDHOOD—1890. These lines were inscribed in Stevenson's *A Child's Garden of Verses,* presented to Mr. Riley's niece, Harriet Day Eitel, now Mrs. Samuel R. Wells.

p. 12 DOWN TO THE CAPITAL

Printed in *The Century Magazine,* March, 1889; published in POEMS HERE AT HOME—1893. In introducing the recitation of this poem at the second annual banquet of the Indiana Society of Chicago, December 11, 1906, Mr. Riley said:—

In the old Hoosier country down there—this is an incident that I know about personally—an old pensioner had occasion to go from the little town to the great capital, where he had an old friend who was high in office. Originally, these two men were poor young men, and had made toward "The Golden Californies"; and one of them had "struck it rich," and one had been a failure, had come home early, disgusted with the lay-out; and his friend had gone on, with his accumulated wealth, from one position to the other, until, popular and capable, and worthy of high trust, he was now a congressman at Washington;—but, in all his splendor, glad to welcome his old crippled friend who came down to see about a detail in the pension act that would enable him to gain something from the government, which, heretofore, he had refrained from asking, from really patriotic reasons. So now, returned from Washington, back at his old home in the little Hoosier town, the old crippled soldier is leaning on his crutch, telling his story to his fellow townsmen.

p. 17   JAP MILLER

Printed in *The Indianapolis Journal,* August 4, 1889; published in GREEN FIELDS AND RUNNING BROOKS—1892. The poem is fact, and the friendship between Mr. Riley and the subject of the sketch has grown in cordiality with the years. Mr. Riley has taken particular relish in the opportunities afforded to visit "Jap" Miller at Brooklyn, Indiana, now for many years his home, where as he humorously described it at the time, he was mayor, fire department head, chief-of-police and police, all combined.

p. 20   JOHN TARKINGTON JAMESON

Written in December, 1889; published in RHYMES OF CHILDHOOD—1890. These verses were written for the son of Mr. and Mrs. Ovid Butler Jameson, of Indianapolis, friends of Mr. Riley.

p. 22   HENRY W. GRADY

Dated December 23, 1889, printed in *The New York Tribune,* December 24, 1889; published in HOME-FOLKS—1900, THE LOCKERBIE BOOK—1911. Henry W. Grady [1851-1889], with whom Mr. Riley was personally acquainted, was a distinguished orator and journalist. He was the editor of *The Atlanta Constitution.*

p. 23   IN THE EVENING

Written in 1889; printed in *Lippincott's Magazine,* January, 1890; published in HOME-FOLKS—1900, SONGS OF HOME—1910, THE LOCKERBIE BOOK—1911.

p. 25   THOUGHTS ON THE LATE WAR

Printed in *The Century Magazine,* January, 1890; published in POEMS HERE AT HOME—1893. Stanza 6, 1. 4, "Durin' the army": "I have met critics who have doubted the authenticity of this phrase," says Mr. Riley. "It is good Hoosier dialect, and I have heard it time and time again."

p. 27   THE OLD BAND

Printed in *The Century Magazine,* February, 1890; published in POEMS HERE AT HOME—1893. The poem is a verity and refers to the Greenfield Saxhorn Band. The elder brother, John A. Riley, left among his papers the names of the original members and the instruments they played:—

L. W. Eastman—Leader,—E Flat
William Lindsey—Tuba
Nat Snow—Second Tenor
Samuel Warsaw Barnett—First Tenor
Nathaniel C. Meek—First Alto
William E. Hart—B Flat Cornet
Tom Richardson—Second Alto
Thomas Offutt—B Bass
William E. Ogg—Third Tenor
John A. Riley—Bass Drum

The other three members mentioned by the author played occasionally,—Bonaparte Meek and Hiram Kerns played horns and Jim Richardson the bass drum. After the war Mr. Riley himself was a member.

The "old band" was organized by Thomas Offutt and William E. Hart early in 1857; and J. Ward Walker suggested the name of L. W. Eastman, then a teacher of music living near Pendleton, as leader.

With the outbreak of the Civil War the entire band enlisted in the Eighteenth Indiana Regiment with the exception of Thomas Offutt and John A. Riley, who were too young at the time. The band boys had each contributed ten dollars toward a fund for instruments which were purchased in Cincinnati and bore the celebrated Saxhorn label. New instruments were furnished by the government when the band went to war, and the old ones were used in the organization of a second band. In 1862 the band came home on a furlough. As it approached the city limits, Thomas Offutt and John A. Riley joined in and marched into town with their old comrades, who played a spirited march written for the occasion by Eastman and entitled *Greenfield's Favorite*. The country for miles around gathered at the Dunbar Hotel to welcome the return of the "old band" and the joy felt was mingled with sighs and tears as the crowd listened to *John Brown's Body* and *John Anderson, My Jo*.

The "new band" was composed chiefly of younger men who had more "finery." It was proud in its array of splendid uniforms and in the possession of a handsome band wagon drawn by four white horses.

When Mr. Riley came to Greenfield to give his last public reading, January 21, 1896, the survivors of the "old band" met him at the station, and as the train drew up to the platform, played *Sweet Alice* and other of the old tunes. In May, 1908, L. W. Eastman, the last of the original group, passed away.

p. 30   BY ANY OTHER NAME

Printed in *The Indianapolis Journal*, March 2, 1890, with the title, *A Rose by Any Other Name;*

published in GREEN FIELDS AND RUNNING BROOKS —1892. The homely names of Bowersox and Daubenspeck are actualities of the Greenfield district, and are reiterated in the roster of old names given in *Name Us No Names No More,* Vol. V, p. 330.

p. 32
LINES FER ISAAC BRADWELL, OF INDANOPLIS, IND., COUNTY-SEAT OF MARION

Written for a friend, Isaac Bradwell, in a rescued copy of THE OLD SWIMMIN'-HOLE AND 'LEVEN MORE POEMS after the Bowen-Merrill fire of March, 1890; published in NEGHBORLY POEMS—1891. The verses are in the character of "Benj. F. Johnson," the feigned author of the book so inscribed.

p. 33 ## "THE LITTLE MAN IN THE TIN-SHOP"

Printed in *The Century Magazine,* April, 1890; published in POEMS HERE AT HOME—1893, THE LOCKERBIE BOOK—1911. The boy Riley played both the snare and bass drums in the "old band" after the war, and played them with great zest, too. Therefore he always paid particular attention to "The Little Man in the Tin-Shop" and took especial delight in him.

Last stanza, p. 34: Of the distinguished musicians here mentioned, Ole Bornemann Bull [1810-1880] was a Norwegian violinist and composer (see Mr. Riley's poem, *Ole Bull,* Vol. II, p. 247); Nicolo Paganini [1782-1840] was a celebrated Italian violinist of weird genius and Mephistophelian appearance; and Madame Parepa-Rosa [1836-1874] was an English soprano singer who married Carl Rosa.

p. 36 A SOUTHERN SINGER

Printed in *The Indianapolis Journal,* May 11, 1890; published in GREEN FIELDS AND RUNNING BROOKS—1892, THE LOCKERBIE BOOK—1911. Once, while browsing in a bookstore among the volumes of poetry, Mr. Riley came across a book that gave him a fresh and rare sense of pleasure, a specimen of art "exquisite—feeling, most delicately sensitive —and color simply vibrant with fervor." It was by an author then unknown to him, Madison Cawein, of Louisville, and its title was *Blooms of the Berry.* "I should like to know that fellow," was Mr. Riley's hearty wish. A little later the two became fast friends, comrades in poetical endeavor, and advised with each other in their work. In 1890, when Mr. Riley rewrote *The Flying Islands of the Night,* he read the last revision to Mr. Cawein, conferred with him about it, and later dedicated the book to him.

p. 38 JUNE AT WOODRUFF

Printed in *The Indianapolis Journal,* June 8, 1890; published in GREEN FIELDS AND RUNNING BROOKS— 1892, THE LOCKERBIE BOOK — 1911. Woodruff Place is an incorporated residence district within the limits of Indianapolis, and is distinguished for its wide lawns, its forest trees, its esplanades, and still more for its quiet restfulness.

p. 40 IRY AND BILLY AND JO

Printed in *The Indianapolis News,* July 5, 1890; published in GREEN FIELDS AND RUNNING BROOKS —1892. The story of this poem is true and refers to Iry and Billy Loy and their dog Jo. Mr. Will Vawter, who illustrated several of Mr. Riley's books, told him of the incident as it happened at Greenfield, and showed him the tintype of the two abashed little boys and the dog. Mr. Vawter relates the incident after this fashion:—

When about fifteen years old, I was seized with an impulse to become a great man, and with this idea in mind I ran away from home and came to Indianapolis. Shortly after my arrival in that city, and before the achievement of my purpose, I met Mr. Riley, and in making an invoice of my valuables for his kindly consideration, brought to light a little tintype of Iry, Billy and Jo. I came by the tintype in this manner. A short time after the picture had been made, Jo was killed by a train. Iry and Billy, moved to generosity by their great loss, had engaged me for three and a half dollars, as I remember now, to paint a portrait of their dog, and gave me the tintype to copy from. Mr. Riley seemed much pleased by the sturdy little figures of Iry and Billy and suggested that he should write some verses about them and that I should copy the tintype just as it was. This I did that very night in Mr. R. B. Gruelle's studio, and the result with Mr. Riley's verses was published in *The Indianapolis News* on the following Saturday to the great astonishment and delight of Iry and Billy.

p. 42   UNCLE SIDNEY'S VIEWS

Printed in *The Indianapolis Journal,* July 20, 1890; published in RHYMES OF CHILDHOOD—1890, THE LOCKERBIE BOOK—1911.

p. 43   BEREAVED

Written in July, 1890; printed in *The Century Magazine,* 1890; published in POEMS HERE AT HOME —1893, THE LOCKERBIE BOOK—1911. Mr. Riley had what seemed a psychical experience in the composition of these verses. It was at night; he could not sleep and he arose with a feeling that he must write—that he must express, in some way, the sympathy he felt for he knew not whom. And so the poem was written and, as was very unusual, set down quite rapidly, the entire composition requiring less than half an hour. A few days afterward news came that the child of his comrade, Edgar Wilson Nye, was dead. Mr. Riley at once addressed the poem to the bereaved parents, feeling that he understood what had prompted him to write it.

p. 44   THE RIDER OF THE KNEE

Published in RHYMES OF CHILDHOOD—1890, CHILD-RHYMES—1898, THE LOCKERBIE BOOK— 1911. This is the dedicatory poem to RHYMES OF CHILDHOOD and refers to "the little nephew," Edmund Henry Eitel, who is shown in the frontispiece to that volume seated upon his uncle's knee.

The preface to RHYMES OF CHILDHOOD is reproduced here because it is applicable to many of the poems that immediately follow :—

In presenting herein the child dialect upon an equal footing with the proper or more serious English, the conscientious author feels it neither his desire nor province to offer excuse.

Wholly simple and artless, Nature's children oftentimes seem the more engaging for their very defects of speech and general deportment. We need worry very little for their future since the All-Kind Mother has them in her keep.

It is just and good to give the elegantly trained and educated child a welcome hearing. It is no less just and pleasant to admit his homely but wholesome-hearted little brother to our interest and love.   J. W. R.

p. 45   THE LITTLE-RED-APPLE TREE

Published in RHYMES OF CHILDHOOD—1890, SONGS O' CHEER—1905, THE LOCKERBIE BOOK—

1911. The poem is reminiscent of the joyous childhood of the boy Riley and his brother John. "The little-red-apple tree," which shed its apples so "lavishly into the neighbor's lot," is a verity, as is also its comparison to the kindly and utterly unselfish disposition of his brother.

p. 47   UNCLE SIDNEY

Published in RHYMES OF CHILDHOOD—1890. The poet himself was frequently called "Uncle Sidney" by his child friends.

p. 48   IN THE NIGHT

Published in RHYMES OF CHILDHOOD—1890.

p. 49   THE DREAM OF THE LITTLE PRINCESS

Published in RHYMES OF CHILDHOOD—1890, THE LOCKERBIE BOOK—1911. An undated letter sent by Mr. Riley with the poem to the editor of *St. Nicholas* explains:—

The enclosed example of "such stuff as *dreams* are made of"—(for it was born of a dream, indeed) I think was suggested by the admiring contemplation of the central picture on the cover of your magazine. That has always dazed as much as pleased me, and now that my *sleep* has had to do with its interpretation I am left to confess a more complex state of bewilderment than ever. You may find no use for the poem at all, but do find out for me the artist's meaning; and, if convenient, show the verses to him, with my best compliments.

p. 52   THE SQUIRT-GUN UNCLE MAKED ME

Published in RHYMES OF CHILDHOOD—1890, CHILD-RHYMES — 1898, THE ORPHANT ANNIE BOOK—1908, THE BOY LIVES ON OUR FARM—1911.

p. 54 THE YOUTHFUL PRESS

Published in RHYMES OF CHILDHOOD—1890. The inspiration of this poem came from a boy of twelve years, George U. Tompers, of Brooklyn, New York, who printed some visiting cards for Mr. Riley on a small printing press given him by his parents. He was unable to get the entire name, James Whitcomb Riley, on the card and therefore used only the initial of the first name. Similar service for other public men brought autograph letters from Longfellow, Holmes, Whittier, and others.

p. 55 MAX AND JIM

Published in RHYMES OF CHILDHOOD—1890, WHILE THE HEART BEATS YOUNG—1906, CHILD-VERSE—1908. These lines were written for the sons of Edgar Wilson Nye, Max and Frank, the latter called "Jim."

p. 56 THE OLD HAYMOW

Published in RHYMES OF CHILDHOOD—1890, CHILD-RHYMES — 1898, THE ORPHANT ANNIE BOOK—1908, SONGS OF SUMMER—1908, THE BOY LIVES ON OUR FARM—1911, THE OLD SWIMMIN'-HOLE AND OTHER POEMS—1912.

p. 58 GUINEY-PIGS

Published in RHYMES OF CHILDHOOD—1890.

p. 59 BUSCH AND TOMMY

Published in RHYMES OF CHILDHOOD—1890, THE LOCKERBIE BOOK—1911. These verses were addressed to the sons of Mr. Riley's old friend and physician, Dr. Franklin W. Hays, with whom, on first coming to Indianapolis, he shared a room in the Vinton Block at the southwest corner of Pennsylvania and Market streets, diagonally across from *The Journal* office. One of the boys was named after another old comrade of those days, Albert Busch, while the other bears the poet's middle name. These two boys were great favorites with Mr. Riley and their spirited manners made him heartily enjoy his visits to Dr. Hays' office. See note on *A Simple Recipe,* Vol. V, p. 274.

p. 60 THE LUGUBRIOUS WHING-WHANG

Published in RHYMES OF CHILDHOOD—1890, CHILD-RHYMES—1898. The poem, as evidenced by an undated newspaper clipping (identified by Mr. Riley as his composition) originally consisted of the last three stanzas and was introduced by the following dissertation:—

SCIENCE AND POETRY

As Science advances Poetry grows fidgety. They are combative elements—no doubt about it, and, some way or other, Poetry hasn't the poise and dignity of Science, and in consequence is always ill at ease in the presence of its high, austere, and coldly-calculating contemporary. There may be exceptions to this rule, but they are as rare as a— as a—"as a day in June." And the most striking exception we call to mind is instanced in the case of Professor Startailer, who some months since was devastating the northern portion of our State with a lecture on astronomy, couched from A to izzard in poetic phrase, and every line of it rhythmically perfect, and jingling like a strand of sleigh-bells; and if you don't believe it, just listen:—

> "Fly! fly! cleave the sky;
> If man can't, pray tell me why!"

Now, we don't pretend to any profound knowledge of astronomy, but we do know poetry when we hear it, and therefore the gifted scientist has our full permission to "cleave the sky" at his very earliest convenience. In fact, we can but think he well deserves the broader field the change would afford; for here he can at best but give us a two-hundred-and-a-half program, and there he could sing on and on through all eternity.

Then, to consistently mingle these opposing qualities is too hazardous an undertaking for the ordinary bard, and hence it is that we find him continually dodging the real issues of scientific development, and more blindly than ever employing all manner of imaginative ammunition in a warfare wherein the "stern, relentless Fact" must surely prove the victor in the fray.

But poetry deserves more than a common share of credit, seeing how well it has maintained its dignity under such disadvantages. Time was when all that was necessary to make poetry acceptable was simply a casual observance of the metrical requirements, together with a lesser recognition of the requirements of perfect rhymes. And in that indulgent epoch it was no uncommon thing to find rhymical twins made of "chime" and "shine", while "roof" and "cough" and "enough" strayed hand in hand through many a flowery page of the old pastorals, and no critic was ever intrepid enough to dare protest against the strange mésalliance. We recall the opening stanza of one of these old gems, running in this wise:—

> "Jacob he had seven sons,
>   And these seven sons were brothers;
> For one of them he made a coat,
>   It was of many colors."

Now, the reader will agree that "brothers" and "colors" are not perfect rhymes, and yet we can but think that, with us, he will be slow to detect the error, being swallowed up in admiration of the adroitness of the author in luring the attention from the very flaw itself and dazzling the intelligence with the parenthetical proposition that "these seven sons were brothers," so that by the time the rhyme "colors" shall be foisted upon his esthetic senses he is either ready to absorb it without a suspicion of its spuriousness, or inwardly regret that there is in existence no authority permitting any one but a harelipped man to pronounce "brothers" "brullers."

Although Science has been making rapid inroads toward the sure annihilation of her frailer sister, Poetry still has her resources, and is idle by no means; and, indeed, in the

latest fend that she employs in her defense, Science herself
is awed, and pauses in a wild, bewildered way, not knowing where next to attack her mysterious and now almost
impalpable victim. She has refined herself, has Poetry,
and, of the true belief and assurance that she is simply that
quality which appeals to that part of ourselves we do not
understand, she is making the most of her knowledge, and
by her very coquetries is becoming more lovable and fascinating. We are drawn to her with an indefinable tenderness and sympathy, as with lifted arm she awaits the further advances of her old-time enemy, and, in a voice as
faint and far away as voices heard in dreams, twitters and
cooters to herself.

p. 62   LITTLE MANDY'S CHRISTMAS-TREE

Published in RHYMES OF CHILDHOOD—1890,
WHILE THE HEART BEATS YOUNG—1906, THE
RUNAWAY BOY—1908.

p. 66 THE FUNNIEST THING IN THE WORLD

Published in RHYMES OF CHILDHOOD—1890,
SONGS O' CHEER—1905, WHILE THE HEART BEATS
YOUNG—1906, CHILD-VERSE—1908.

p. 67   THE BUMBLEBEE

Published in RHYMES OF CHILDHOOD—1890,
CHILD-RHYMES—1898, THE RAGGEDY MAN—1907.

p. 68   A PROSPECTIVE GLIMPSE

Published in RHYMES OF CHILDHOOD—1890.

p. 69   THE OLD TRAMP

Published in RHYMES OF CHILDHOOD—1890,
CHILD-RHYMES—1898, THE RAGGEDY MAN—1907.

p. 70   THE PET COON

Published in RHYMES OF CHILDHOOD—1890,
CHILD-RHYMES—1898. The "Noey Bixler" of
these lines was a boy favorite in the poet's youth.
He is described in *A Child-World,* p. 379.

p. 72   AN IMPETUOUS RESOLVE

Published in RHYMES OF CHILDHOOD—1890,
CHILD-RHYMES—1898, WHILE THE HEART BEATS
YOUNG—1906, CHILD-VERSE—1908. In an inter-
view Mr. Riley once said:—

I recollect distinctly when I was a small boy, and from
choice spent much of my time in the kitchen rolling dough
and making miniature pies. After a while, through the
obliging assistance of the hired girl, I advanced so that I
could build a pie of legitimate size. My joy was complete
when I actually fashioned a custard pie; and then came the
feat, worthy of a sleight-of-hand performer, of getting it
into the oven without spilling. You may gather from this
that my first ambition was to be a baker, and at times I
have felt a twinge of disappointment that my juvenile ambition was not realized. I really think I would have been
a success as a baker.

See Vol. I, p. 371.

p. 73   THE HUNTER BOY

Published in RHYMES OF CHILDHOOD—1890,
THE LOCKERBIE BOOK—1911. Lines 1 to 8 of the
last stanza of this poem, completed by

> And in mists of song divine
> Veil this violin of mine!

originally appeared as Part IV of *Just a Fiddler,*

which was printed in *The Indianapolis Journal,*
April 18, 1880, as follows:—

> Not a violinist—No;
> Just a fiddler!—See, his bow
> Is too short and slack; and see,
> He drawls it so rakishly
> O'er the strings, they grate and rasp
> In the rosin's wrathful grasp,
> As in some asthmatic state
> Painful to articulate.
> And his bow-arm moves as if
> Every joint of it were stiff.
> So he saws, or, pausing, plucks
> At the strings and screws, and tucks
> The old tail-piece 'neath his chin,
> Rasps again, and rattles in.
>
> While the fingers, old and brown,
> Cut dull capers up and down
> The brief gamut of his skill,
> Who will say what raptures thrill
> In that warm old breast of his,
> All untutored as it is?
> Who will say but, in his heart,
> He is master of the art
> That not even Ole Bull
> Finds more rarely beautiful!
> So it is, this afternoon,
> Listening to the old-time tune
> He is playing—faint and clear
> Falls his soul's voice on my ear
> As it sways the bow, and sings
> To the strange, enchanted strings:—

I

> O my robin, teetering
> On thy spray with lifted wing,
> Perk thy jaunty head, and chant
> Me a rondel jubilant!
> Pipe of summer, O thou beak
> At the cherry's crimson cheek!
> Let thy light staccatoes spill
> Drippingly as water will,
> And in mists of song divine
> Veil this violin of mine!

II

O my merry boy, at play
Down the past so far away
I but see thee with the eyes
That were meant for Paradise,—
With thy glad face to the sun,
Let thy laughter overrun
The ripe lips whose crimson cleft
Seeded is with jewels, left
In the treasure-lands I know
But in dreams of long ago.

III

O my maiden, tripping through
Meadow-grasses wet with dew;
Pausing—listening to hear
If the cow-bells tattle near;
Laughing then, and faring on
In the footsteps of the Dawn,—
Sing once more thy milking-song,
Till thy sweet voice—stilled so long—
Once again shall welcome ring
To my kisses as you sing.

IV

O my Hunter! tilt the cup
Of thy silver bugle up,
And like wine pour out for me
All its limpid melody!
Pout thy happy lips and blare
Music's kisses everywhere—
Whiff o'er forest, field and town,
Tufts of tune like thistle-down,
And in mists of song divine
Veil this violin of mine!

V

This the voice that sings to me
As the old man dreamily
Trails the bow along the strings
Through the strange meanderings.
Not a violinist—No!
Just a fiddler? Yes; but O

As God's sweetest music may
Be thus wasted, let us pray
That the fiddler, through his tears,
Sees the music no one hears.

p. 75   BILLY GOODIN'

Published in RHYMES OF CHILDHOOD—1890.

p. 77   SONG—FOR NOVEMBER

Published in RHYMES OF CHILDHOOD—1890, THE LOCKERBIE BOOK—1911.

p. 79   AT AUNTY'S HOUSE

Published in RHYMES OF CHILDHOOD—1890, CHILD-RHYMES—1898, WHILE THE HEART BEATS YOUNG—1906, THE RUNAWAY BOY—1908.

p. 81   LIFE AT THE LAKE

Printed in *The Indianapolis Journal,* August 10, 1890, with the title, *Maxinkuckee;* published in MORNING—1907, THE LOCKERBIE BOOK—1911. The poem refers to a visit to Lake Maxinkuckee, Indiana.

p. 83   JOHN BOYLE O'REILLY

Printed in *The Indianapolis Journal,* August 13, 1890; hitherto unpublished in book form. John Boyle O'Reilly, an Irish-American journalist and poet, was born June 28, 1844, at Dowth Castle, County Meath, Ireland, and died at Hull, Massachusetts, August 10, 1890. At the age of nineteen he took service with the Tenth Hussars in Ireland in order to spread the revolutionary doctrines of the Fenians among the soldiers. Three years later he was sentenced to death on the charge of high treason. Because of his youth the sentence was revoked and he was sent to the colony in Australia to spend twenty years in penal servitude. He arrived there in 1868 and in the following year escaped to the United States, where in 1870 he secured a position on *The Boston Pilot,* of which he became editor-in-chief in 1874. He published *Songs from the Southern Seas*—1874; *Songs, Legends, and Ballads*—1878; *The Statutes in the Block*—1881.

Mr. Riley was always an ardent friend of John Boyle O'Reilly, to whom he owed his first introduction to the East. In a letter to Madison Cawein of August 14, 1890, Mr. Riley referred to him in speaking of the loveliness of *home,* and said:—

John Boyle O'Reilly was *driven* from his—and, dead to-day, would rather be back there, haply, than in Heaven —unless, indeed, in Paradise he finds it there in Counterpart—even to the *sunburst* in the skies—the shamrock in the fields—

> "The feeling of the breeze upon his face—
> The feeling of the turf beneath his feet—
> And no walls but the far off mountain tops!"

See, *On a Fly-Leaf in John Boyle O'Reilly's Poems,* Vol. III, p. 372.

p. 85   THE BOYS' CANDIDATE

Printed in *The Indianapolis Journal,* August 31, 1890, with the title, *The Boys' Friend;* published in RHYMES OF CHILDHOOD—1890, CHILD-RHYMES—1898, WHILE THE HEART BEATS YOUNG—1906, THE RUNAWAY BOY—1908.

p. 86   CHRISTINE

Printed in *The Indianapolis Journal,* August 31,
1890, with the title, *Wilhelmina;* published in
MORNING—1907. The quotation, l. 6, is from a
song of this name by A. Reichardt, sung to the air
of *Germania:*—

> Du liebes Aug', du lieber Stern
> Du bist mir nah', und doch so fern.

The letter in the poem was actually written, and the
incident, except for the tragic ending, is true. It
refers to a young American of Mr. Riley's acquaintance who was studying in Germany.

p. 87   OLD JOHN CLEVENGER ON BUCKEYES

Written about October, 1890, with the title,
Buckeyes; published in NEGHBORLY POEMS—1891,
at which time lines 1-20 appeared for the first time.
These verses were prepared for the Columbus,
Hocking Valley and Toledo Railway Company,
which is called from the state it traverses, *The
Buckeye Route.* They were printed in a compli-
mentary booklet issued by the passenger department, and called *A Buckeye Ballad.*

Old John Clevenger pronounces just, *jis'.* There
are several dialectic forms of the word actually
used even by the same persons, *jes', jest, jis',* and
jist. Mr. Riley prefers the form *jes',* except where
"Benj. F. Johnson, of Boone," is supposedly writing down the verses, when the form *jest* is the natural selection. The form *jis* used here represents
"Benj. F. Johnson's" reproduction of Ohio dialect.

For the child dialect form of the word, see the
note on *The Happy Little Cripple,* Vol. III, p. 342.

p. 92   MEREDITH NICHOLSON

Printed in *The Indianapolis Journal,* September 7, 1890; hitherto unpublished in book form. These lines to Meredith Nicholson, of Indianapolis, are indicative of Mr. Riley's early interested friendship for the novelist. He admired Mr. Nicholson's verse and always urged him to give his chief attention to poetry. Mr. Nicholson showed his sincere appreciation in his fine lines entitled, *To James Whitcomb Riley.*

Line 1: Keats died at the age of twenty-five. Henry Kirke White (1785-1806) whose *Remains* and biography were published by Southey in 1807, died from overstudy at the university of Cambridge. David Gray (1838-1861) was a Scotch poet, author of *The Luggie* and other poems.

p. 93   MY RUTHERS

Printed in *The Indianapolis Journal,* September 14, 1890; published in NEGHBORLY POEMS—1891. This is a "Benj. F. Johnson" poem.

p. 95   GOD'S MERCY

Written September 27, 1890; hitherto unpublished. This stanza was written by Mr. Riley in an album belonging to Miss Lulu Crawford, formerly of Greenfield. She is mentioned in *A Child-World,* p. 363, l. 17.

p. 96   THE WHITHERAWAYS

Written October 15, 1890; published in RHYMES OF CHILDHOOD—1890, THE LOCKERBIE BOOK—1911. These lines were written when the poet's good friend, George C. Hitt, set sail with his family for Europe. Mr. Hitt, then business manager of *The Indianapolis Journal*, published Mr. Riley's first book. See Vol. I, p. 379; note on the book, THE OLD SWIMMIN'-HOLE AND 'LEVEN MORE POEMS, Bibliography, Vol. VI.

p. 97   A BOY'S MOTHER

Printed in *The Century Magazine,* December, 1890; published in RHYMES OF CHILDHOOD—1890, POEMS HERE AT HOME—1893, SONGS O' CHEER—1905.

p. 98   THE RUNAWAY BOY

Printed in *The Century Magazine*, December, 1890; published in RHYMES OF CHILDHOOD (first edition only)—1890, POEMS HERE AT HOME—1893, CHILD-RHYMES—1898, WHILE THE HEART BEATS YOUNG—1906, THE RUNAWAY BOY—1908. The verses refer to one of the earliest memories of the poet's, to a time when as a child in petticoats he made a break for the open world, bitter and sore at heart. He met a great and terrible cow led precariously down the road, and was terrified by the sudden salute of an immense pig. So vivid is his recollection of the experience that when an artist once undertook to illustrate the poem, Mr. Riley drew a diagram of the lane down which he ran, and marked the spots where the cow and pig appeared and where the "big girl" found him.

p. 100   THE FISHING-PARTY

Printed in *The Century Magazine,* December, 1890; published in RHYMES OF CHILDHOOD—1890, POEMS HERE AT HOME—1893, SONGS OF SUMMER—

1908. Line 4:—Hanch's Woods was a popular picnic ground on White River when Mr. Riley first came to Indianapolis. The poet on several occasions helped entertain the children of Roberts Park Sunday-school during their outings in this grove.

p. 102   THE RAGGEDY-MAN

Printed in *The Century Magazine,* December, 1890; published in RHYMES OF CHILDHOOD—1890, POEMS HERE AT HOME—1893, CHILD-RHYMES—1898, WHILE THE HEART BEATS YOUNG—1906, THE RAGGEDY MAN—1907, CHILD-VERSE—1908. The special edition, 1907, has the following dedication:—

> To Lesley and Elizabeth
>   And Jim and Jinks and Dallas
> And Dory Ann and Bud and Seth,
>   And little Rachel Alice;
> Marcellus, Ruth and Silence—Yea,
>   And all their little brothers
> And sisters in the world to-day—
>   And all the blessèd others.

Among the children here referred to are the little nieces, Lesley Payne and Elizabeth Whitcomb Eitel; Frank ["Jim"] Nye, Edith Thomas ["Dory Ann"] Medairy, and Rachel Alice Miller,—all now young men and women.

"The Raggedy Man was not a tramp, nor was he so ragged as people usually seem to think," says Mr. Riley. "He was just a farmer boy from some neighboring family, clad in working-clothes which were patched and worn, as you well may guess when you know that eight dollars a month and 'keep' was all that such a man received for his loyal labor. He was a kindly-faced chap, often with a battered hat and always with an honest smile, who loved children genuinely, and who was loved by them as heartily."

The Raggedy Man is identical with the Hired Man of *A Child-World,* [see p. 401] and other poems.

Stanza 3, ll. 6-7: Near Greenfield in Mr. Riley's boyhood there was a farm of this homely name owned by Warner Smoot.

p. 106   OUR HIRED GIRL

Printed in *The Century Magazine,* December, 1890; published in RHYMES OF CHILDHOOD—1890, POEMS HERE AT HOME—1893, CHILD-RHYMES—1898, WHILE THE HEART BEATS YOUNG—1906, THE RAGGEDY MAN—1907, THE RUNAWAY BOY—1908. "In the old days of homely democracy the hired girl was an institution," says Mr. Riley, "and was considered as one of the family. 'Lizabuth Ann was a young girl from the neighboring country, whose father owned a large farm, and could have bought and sold my own father. He sent her to town to obtain its advantages and to get 'polished off.' She didn't consider that she demeaned herself in the least by doing the work of a servant, but rather felt gratified and proud to have the advantages of town life. She dressed as well as other girls, though, of course, with no great style or show. Simply, she was a good wholesome girl who loved the members of the family, especially the children, who, in turn, loved her."

'Lizabuth Ann is a character identical with Floretty in *A Child-World,* p. 401.

p. 108   THE BOY LIVES ON OUR FARM

Printed in *The Century Magazine,* December, 1890; published in RHYMES OF CHILDHOOD—1890,

Poems Here at Home—1893, Child-Rhymes—1898, The Orphant Annie Book—1908, The Boy Lives on Our Farm—1911.

p. 109   THE SONG OF THE BULLET

Printed in *The Indianapolis Journal,* December 13, 1890; published in Poems Here at Home—1893, The Lockerbie Book—1911. This poem was one of the few which Mr. Riley "dashed off." On the night of its composition he went to bed in good time but found himself sleepless. The idea of the poem came to him, he took pencil and paper and rapidly worked out the fancy into the words as they stand. After that he made a transcript in ink. By this time he was so enthusiastic that he wanted to see it in print immediately. He dressed and took it to *The Journal* office, where he arrived after midnight. Mr. Harry S. New, then city editor, had already sent the editorial page to be stereotyped, and suggested that the poem could be printed just as well in a later issue. Mr. Riley persuaded him to "send down" for the editorial page and have the poem inserted and a new stereotype made. Few poems have had so rapid a voyage from composition to the public; certainly no other poem of Mr. Riley's has; nor any other, with the possible exception of *If I Knew What Poets Know* (Note Vol. I, p. 403), was composed with such rapidity.

p. 110   CHRISTMAS GREETING

Written December 24, 1890; printed in *The World* (New York), December 25, 1890; hitherto unpublished in book form. The original form of the lines was a letter telegraphed by request "To the Editor of the New York World" and dated, Indianapolis, December 24, 1890. In the column where it appeared were greetings from Oliver Wendell Holmes, Mark Twain, Joel Chandler Harris, George William Curtis, Frank R. Stockton, Ella Wheeler Wilcox, Kate Field, Elizabeth Stuart Phelps, John P. Newman, J. H. Kinsman and David Swing.

p. 111   UNCLE WILLIAM'S PICTURE

Printed in *The Century Magazine,* January, 1891; published in POEMS HERE AT HOME—1893.

p. 113   ERASMUS WILSON

Printed in *The Pittsburgh Commercial Gazette,* January 30, 1891; published in NEGHBORLY POEMS —1891. These verses are in the character of "Benj. F. Johnson," who pays the tribute to the author's friend, the "gentlest, finest soul on earth," Erasmus Wilson. He conducted a pleasant, gossipy department in *The Pittsburgh Dispatch* under the caption of *The Quiet Observer,* and later published a volume with this title.

p. 117   BACK FROM TOWN

Printed in *The Century Magazine,* February, 1891; published in POEMS HERE AT HOME—1893.

p. 119   TUGG MARTIN

Written in February, 1891; published in GREEN FIELDS AND RUNNING BROOKS—1892.

p. 123   TO RUDYARD KIPLING

Written at Denver, Colorado, February 16, 1891; hitherto unpublished in book form. These lines are a reply to an appreciation. In 1891 Mr. George C. Hitt called on Mr. Kipling in England and on Mr. Riley's behalf presented him with a copy of RHYMES OF CHILDHOOD. Mr. Kipling's reply, through his kindly courtesy, is here printed for the first time:—

To J. W. R.

Your trail runs to the westward,
  And mine to my own place;
There is water between our lodges,
  And I have not seen your face.

But since I have read your verses
  'Tis easy to guess the rest,—
Because in the hearts of the children
  There is neither East nor West.

Born to a thousand fortunes
  Of good or evil hap,
Once they were kings together,
  Throned in a mother's lap.

Surely they know that secret—
  Yellow and black and white—
When they meet as kings together
  In innocent dreams at night.

By a moon they all can play with—
  Grubby and grimed and unshod—
Very happy together,
  And very near to God.

Your trail runs to the westward,
  And mine to my own place:
There is water between our lodges,
  And you can not see my face.—

And that is well—for crying
  Should neither be written nor seen,
But if I call you Smoke-in-the-Eyes,
  I know you will know what I mean.

Nov. 20, '90.   RUDYARD KIPLING.

p. 125   DECORATION DAY ON THE PLACE

Written prior to April 7, 1891; published in
Neghborly Poems—1891. The author is "Benj.
F. Johnson." The poem was first given to the public at a reading in the Grand Opera House, Indianapolis, April 7, 1891, in which Bill Nye, A. P. Bur-
bank and Mr. Riley participated. In introducing
the reading of these lines at a banquet of the Society of the Army of Tennessee, in Chicago, October 8, 1891, Mr. Riley said:—

And may I offer yet another instance of the common
patriot's worth; this from the homely fact of life itself,
not alone conspiring in my neighborhood, but yours. The
scene of it is set upon the farm—the old home place where
a race of patriots has been reared. There is the old an-
cestral roof, with the old locusts looming all about it, with
the old sweet blossoms on them, and the old bees droning
there; the old dooryard, the old porch and the old dog
sleeping in the sun; the old well-sweep; the little garden
patch, and the old orchard just beyond, made sacred as the
family burial-ground. The old house is very full of quiet
now. Sometimes an old man comes out and sits upon the
porch and looks wistfully across the fields to where the
road to town goes by. Sometimes an old woman comes out
and sits there with him, saint-like and silent. They see
sometimes a neighbor driving by, and know him by his
horses; sometimes they see go by—in early morning generally—two, three, five, sometimes as many as a dozen dif-
ferent wagons, and then they know there is "a big day" in
town. Maybe an old settlers' meeting, a political rally, or
Decoration Day. Vague rumors reach them of these alien
affairs; but they are always interested to hear of them—
especially of Decoration Day, since it seems particularly
sacred to this old home-keeping couple, who have never yet
attended this annual service made so much of by the people of the town. Their Decoration Day experiences the old
man might sum up like this.

p. 127   TOWN AND COUNTRY

Printed in *The Indianapolis Journal,* April 10,
1891, with the title, *The Sooburbs,* signed "Benj. F.

Johnson"; published in NEGHBORLY POEMS—1891.
The following introduction by Mr. Riley preceded
the poem in *The Journal:*—

BENJ. F. JOHNSON OF BOONE AGAIN HEARD FROM

To the Editor of the Indianapolis Journal.

Respectud 'Sir—A town feller, from in around your bailywick somers, lectchurd fer us t'other night at Little Bethel
on "The Fewd of Rich and Pore"; and whilse the conger-
gation, sich as it was, was a-siluntly dispursin' I made free
to put a bug in his ear.

Says I to him, says I—"They's another topick I'd like
to heer you treat of," says I, "an' that's the fewd of 'town-
fops' and 'country-jakes'."

"Will you e-looseidate a little furder?" says he; and I
done so to the best of my abilities:

Says I: "The country element is jest as good as the
town element, and vicey-versy," says I, "and both," I says,
"is eviduntly ekal in the favor of the Good Bein'," says I.

"Grantud," he says.

"Then," says I, "why don't we like each other and mix
more and neghbor as we ort?"

Says he, "My friend, you have give me a new thought
and a meaty one. What is your idy of the answer to your
question?"

Says I, "That question, in my jedgment, can only be set
at rest when these two contendin' factchuns," says I,
"agrees ammuckably to compermise in some terrytorial way
—er, in other words," says I—"when your city people comes
half-way and moves into the sooburbs, whare we can git
at 'em comfortable, then we'll not scroople," says I, "to
come the other half."

It was these thoughts, therefore, in a nutshell, Mr. Editor, that give rise to the follerin' lines in my head which
I call *The Sooburbs*.

p. 129　　　　　THE FIRST BLUEBIRD

Printed in *The Indianapolis Journal,* April 19,
1891, with the title, *The First Boone County Bluebird,* signed, "Benj. F. Johnson"; published in
NEGHBORLY POEMS—1891, SONGS O' CHEER—1905.

p. 130 LINES TO PERFESSER JOHN CLARK RIDPATH

Written in April, 1891; published in NEGHBORLY POEMS—1891. John Clark Ridpath [1840-1900] was educated at Asbury University, now DePauw, where he was professor of history, 1869-1885. He edited *The Arena,* 1897-1898, published a number of volumes of United States history, biographies of Garfield and Blaine, and a *History of the World.* He largely secured the endowment for DePauw University. Mr. Riley wrote these lines for the celebration of Dr. Ridpath's fiftieth birthday, held a year late, April 26, 1891. The historian and the poet were early friends and corresponded for years. See *John Clark Ridpath,* Vol. V, p. 152.

p. 134 ELIZABETH

Written April 30, 1891; printed in *The Indianapolis Journal,* May 1, 1891, with the title, *Elizabeth Meredith Steele (Sepulture, May 1, 1891);* published in GREEN FIELDS AND RUNNING BROOKS —1892, THE LOCKERBIE BOOK—1911. Elizabeth was the daughter of Thomas J. Steele, managing editor of *The Indianapolis Journal.* Mr. Steele relates that on April 30, 1891, he was called to *The Journal* office and, while there, found Mr. Riley seated at a desk in a small room. "I saw he was preparing a poem, but I didn't know the subject thereof. He took me by the hand and in a tone of tenderest sympathy said, 'Don't say a word; I know just how you feel.' And that was all. At that time I had known him a good many years, and my little daughter, who was about the office frequently, had come to know him well, and was a favorite with him."

At the time of her death she was thirteen years old. She was buried on the first of May and was thus a May-day queen.

p. 136 SONGS OF A LIFE-TIME

Written probably in June, 1891; published in His Pa's Romance—1903, The Lockerbie Book—1911. These lines appeared as the proem to a volume of poems bearing the same title, published by Sarah T. Bolton, copyrighted 1891. She was born at Newport, Kentucky, December 18, 1814, and died in Indianapolis, where she had lived most of her life, on August 4, 1893. She wrote *Paddle Your Own Canoe, The Union Forever, Left on the Battlefield* and many other popular and patriotic poems.

p. 137 AN OLD MAN'S MEMORY

Published in Neghborly Poems (as proem)—1891, Songs o' Cheer—1905. By "Benj. F. Johnson, of Boone."

p. 139 US FARMERS IN THE COUNTRY

Published in Neghborly Poems—1891, as the proem to the section entitled *Neghborly Poems on Friendship, Grief and Farm-Life, by Benj. F. Johnson, of Boone.*

p. 141 ON A DEAD BABE

Published in Neghborly Poems—1891.

p. 142   "MYLO JONES'S WIFE"

Published in NEGHBORLY POEMS—1891, FARM-
RHYMES—1901, THE PRAYER PERFECT AND OTHER
POEMS—1912.

p. 145
A PEN-PICTUR' OF A CERT'IN FRIVVOLUS OLD
MAN

Published in NEGHBORLY POEMS—1891.

p. 148   THOUGHTS ON A PORE JOKE

Published in NEGHBORLY POEMS—1891.
Other thoughts on poor jokes were expressed by
Mr. Riley in an editorial in *The Indianapolis Jour-
nal,* September 15, 1881 :—

TRILLPIPE ON PUNS

In both the voice and manner of Mr. Trillpipe there was
a tang of satire, as he said: "Now I don't want you to
understand me to say that I don't like puns—especially bad
puns—but I do claim that puns is undoubtedly the worst
possible thing that ever broke out on the human system—
as fer as any hopes of even escapin' the awful results of
the disease is concerned. That's adzackly what I mean.
O! a man may pun and pun along for years and years, and
think he's a-comin' through all right, but I've allus noticed
that fate keeps her eye on him jest the same, and sneaks
along in his very tracks, on'y waitin' fer a poetical climax,
don't you understand, to jest naterly swoop down and
swipe that man clean off o' the face o' the earth! You see,
I've watched the thing fer time out o' mind, and I'm here
to say that I have never saw a single exception to the rule
—not one!

"Had a nephew onc't that had a tetch of it, along about
nineteen er twenty. Don't know where the boy caught the
blame thing—and, in reality, as I say, it wasn't no bad case
at all—jest a sort o' 'veryloid,' you might say; but it grad-

ully kep' a-growin' and a-growin' till he couldn't talk at all
without a-betrayin' the most alarmin' symptoms of his
affliction. They even sent him off to college, hopin' he'd
improve there, but it only seemed to aggervate the case,
'cause he come back home on a velocipede one vacation,
got off at the front door, went in to a five o'clock breakfast with the folks, and while his patient old mother was
a-makin' some excuse about the surprise he'd give 'em, and
a-sayin' that their butcher had lied to 'em about the last
steak he'd sent—and the steak was a trifle stale that
mornin', owin' to the hot weather, mebby—the boy sided in
with the meat man, fer no other reason on earth but to
ring in—'You butcher self in his place;' and when his
father, without p'tendin' to catch on, says—'Well, but, my
son, they's no excuse fer the man a-sellin' tainted meat!'
the boy says—'Ice chest a-goin' to observe that ef it ain't-et
where's the difference, anyhow?' and smilin'ly that boy
went out and straddled his velocipede—rode right square
down to the crick and run off o' the bridge. Didn't drownd
—wasn't enough worter for that—but he struck a big hump
backed bowlder sort o' at the aidge o' the bank, and broke
both legs, and mummixed hisse'f up generally, and crawled
back home a cripple fer life.

"And then I knowed a feller onc't," continued Mr. Trillpipe, "that had made a speciallity of jest layin' around
where folks were talkin', and fer years and years had been
listenin' to other people's business for no other object on'y
to build puns out o' whatever new word he could get on to.
Well, sir, there was a crowd of us one evening up in a
private office, and this feller was amongst us, sayin' nothin',
as usual, but layin' fer a chance. Finally a telegraph was
brought in fer the proprietor, and in lookin' over it he
found that it had been delayed or somepin', and so he was
a-puttin' the messenger boy through some cross-questions
regardin' the thing, and got purty hot over the boy's answers, till at last, not bein' able to get ahead of the kid, he
told him jest to get out of there, which the boy did, with
a partin' salute of some kind that bored the feller clean to
the red. And then he jest kep' on a-givin' it to the boy, till,
finally, this other feller I was a-tellin' of sort o' turned
round and gaped and says, says he: 'O let up on the little
kuss, the boy's gone now, anyhow,' he says, 'and you'd
orto be willin' to let boy-gones be boy-gones.' Well, sir,
although that pun was really enjoyed and laughed at, bad
as it was, it was on'y the pre-curser, as you might say, of
gloom and sorrow, fer it wan't more'n two minutes from

that time that a slab of plastern, as big as a table top, jest sort o' let loose of the ceilin', and drove that feller blame nigh through the floor. Reckon Providence saw that we was a-goin' to let him git away from us, and jest spotted him once fer luck. Busted his head all up so's they didn't get done a-shavin' and sowin' it up and salvin' it over fer six weeks.

"Then they was another feller that I knowed well: sharp as a tack and keen as a whistle. Young lawyer he was, and engaged to the hightonedest girl in the town. Went to dance one night up in Melodian Hall, and was the happiest man on the floor—till about one o'clock in the mornin' he was suddenly missed, and when they went to look fer him, they found a feller jest a-shoulderin' him to bring him back up-stairs, and the feller explained that his foot slipped at the top of the stairs five minutes before jest as he—this young lawyer, you understand—was a-urgin' his friend to jine the revel, er as he had called it, 'A feast of resin and a flow of sole!'

"And then there was the poetical feller who once quoted the follerin' lines:—

> 'I stood on my head at midnight
> When the clock was strikin' the hour,
> And my heels rose over the city
> Behind the dark church tower,'—

—claimin' it was wrote, of course, by Long-fellow.—See? And that fellow went in the army and got killed with a cannon-ball.

"But the worst case I know of," continued Mr. Trillpipe, "the very worst case of pun, was a feller 'at hired a livery rig and drove seven mile with a friend jest to git this one off. P'intin' to a farmhouse at the side of the road, he told his friend that the owner of all that splendid farm, and all them unharvested crops, was a-layin' at the p'int of death. Of course, his friend was inclined to moralize on sich a subject, and naturally thought that of all times fer a man to die that was the worst. 'Yes,' says the feller, a-startin' to turn the team around fer town ag'in, 'the only consolation the old feller's got now is that all these fields of unreaped grain here he can buck-wheat to his children.' And jest then the horses shied at somepin', and whirled and started, head up in the clouds and tail over the dash! La! —Well, the feller's friend come out of it without no special damage, but the feller that fired the pun," concluded

Trillpipe, with a sleight-of-hand motion of his thumb and a sudden upward movement of the eyes—"The feller, I say, that fired the pun—T-s-s-s-s-t!"

p. 149   EVAGENE BAKER

Published in Neghborly Poems—1891.

p. 151
ON ANY ORDENARY MAN IN A HIGH STATE OF LAUGHTURE AND DELIGHT

Published in Neghborly Poems—1891, Songs o' Cheer—1905.

p. 152   THE HOODOO

Printed in *The Indianapolis Journal,* September 10, 1891, with the title, *Benj. F. Johnson on Skates;* published in Green Fields and Running Brooks —1892.

p. 153   CUORED O' SKEERIN'

Printed in *The Indianapolis Journal,* September 12, 1891; published in Poems Here at Home— 1892.

p. 155   OLD WINTERS ON THE FARM

Printed in *The Indianapolis Journal,* September 13, 1891; published in Green Fields and Running Brooks—1892, Farm-Rhymes—1901.

p. 156   "COON-DOG WESS"

Printed in *The Indianapolis Journal,* September 23, 1891; published in Neghborly Poems—1891.

p. 161   GOIN' TO THE FAIR

Written for the Indianapolis Flower Mission Fair
and printed in the booklet, *Golden Rod,* sold at that
fair, November 3, 1891; published in POEMS HERE
AT HOME—1893.

p. 163   THE WATCHES OF THE NIGHT

Printed in *The Independent,* November 16, 1891;
published in GREEN FIELDS AND RUNNING BROOKS
—1892, THE LOCKERBIE BOOK—1911. Stanza 4,
with this title, was printed in *The Indianapolis
Journal,* April 5, 1891.

p. 165   OSCAR C. McCULLOCH

Printed in *The Indianapolis Journal,* December
12, 1891; published in HOME-FOLKS—1900, THE
LOCKERBIE BOOK—1911. The poet's good friend,
Oscar C. McCulloch, who was for a score of years
pastor of Plymouth (Congregational) Church, Indianapolis, was born in Fremont, Ohio, July 2, 1843,
and died at Indianapolis, December 10, 1891. In
Indianapolis he was known as the leader and or-
ganizer of many charities, among which were the
Charity Organization Society, the Children's Aid
Society, and the Summer Mission for Sick Children.
An achievement that he took great pride in was
the organization of the Dime Savings and Loan
Association, since this carried out his idea of help-
ing people to self-reliance and therefore self-respect.
Mr. Riley always admired him for his cheering and
inspiring doctrine.

p. 166
WHAT CHRIS'MAS FETCHED THE WIGGINSES

Printed in *The Louisville Times,* December 31, 1891; published in GREEN FIELDS AND RUNNING BROOKS—1892. The scene is laid among the poor whites of the mountains of the central South.

p. 179 ## THE GUDEWIFE

Printed in *Lippincott's Magazine,* January, 1892; hitherto unpublished in book form.

p. 180 ## RIGHT HERE AT HOME

Printed in *The Indianapolis Journal,* February 7, 1892; published in GREEN FIELDS AND RUNNING BROOKS—1892.

p. 182 ## LITTLE MARJORIE

Printed in *The Indianapolis Journal,* March 13, 1892; published in POEMS HERE AT HOME—1893, THE LOCKERBIE BOOK—1911. Little Marjorie, aged four, the daughter of Mr. Riley's friend, William C. Bobbs, died March 6, 1892. Her death came very suddenly, so suddenly that it seemed the poet must have had some intuition of its approach. But a few hours elapsed after her death before a messenger came to the parents bearing this tribute.

p. 183 ## KATHLEEN MAVOURNEEN

Printed in *The Indianapolis Journal,* April 16, 1892; published in HIS PA'S ROMANCE—1903, THE LOCKERBIE BOOK—1911. Frederick Nicholls

Crouch, as the subheading indicates, set to music the verses of Louisa Macartney Crawford with a very exquisite melody. He was born in London, July 31, 1808, began his musical career before he was ten years old, made a tour of the United States in 1849, and during the Civil War served in the Confederate army. He wrote many favorite melodies of which *Kathleen Mavourneen* and *The Soldier's Grave* were the most popular. Death came to him August 19, 1896.

p. 185   OLD JOHN HENRY

Printed in *The Indianapolis Journal,* April 17, 1892; published in Poems Here at Home—1893.

p. 187   BEING HIS MOTHER

Printed in *Lippincott's Magazine,* June, 1892; published in Green Fields and Running Brooks —1892, The Lockerbie Book—1911. These lines were written for Mr. Riley's friend, William Carey, of *The Century Magazine,* whose home he visited. Carey's tender, devoted affection for his mother, as well as hers for her son, affected the poet deeply.

p. 188   GREEN FIELDS AND RUNNING BROOKS

Published as the proem in Green Fields and Running Brooks—1892.

p. 189   SOME SCATTERING REMARKS OF BUB'S

Published in Green Fields and Running Brooks—1892, Rhymes of Childhood (not in first edition)—1898, While the Heart Beats Young— 1906, Child-Verse—1908, The Orphant Annie Book—1908, The Boy Lives on Our Farm—1911.

p. 190   BY HER WHITE BED

Published in GREEN FIELDS AND RUNNING
BROOKS—1892, THE LOCKERBIE BOOK—1911.

p. 191   HOW JOHN QUIT THE FARM

Published in GREEN FIELDS AND RUNNING
BROOKS—1892, FARM-RHYMES—1901.

p. 199   HIS MOTHER'S WAY

Published in GREEN FIELDS AND RUNNING
BROOKS—1892.

p. 200   THE HOOSIER FOLK-CHILD

Published in GREEN FIELDS AND RUNNING
BROOKS—1892, THE LOCKERBIE BOOK—1911.

p. 203   THEIR SWEET SORROW

Published in GREEN FIELDS AND RUNNING
BROOKS—1892, AFTERWHILES—1898, LOVE-LYRICS
—1899, THE LOCKERBIE BOOK—1911.

p. 204   DAWN, NOON AND DEWFALL

Published in GREEN FIELDS AND RUNNING
BROOKS—1892, SONGS O' CHEER—1905, SONGS OF
SUMMER—1908.

p. 205   LONGFELLOW

Published in GREEN FIELDS AND RUNNING
BROOKS—1892, AFTERWHILES (not in first edition)

—1898, THE LOCKERBIE BOOK—1911. In his early lectures Mr. Riley paid this tribute to Longfellow :—

The happiest forms of poetic expression are cast in simplest phraseology and seeming artlessness. The student of poetic composition is not long in finding that the secret of enduring verse lies in the spontaneity of expression, and the grace of pure simplicity. Longfellow has furnished many notable examples, first among which I would class the poem, *The Day Is Done.* It is like resting to read it. It is like bending with uncovered head beneath the silent benediction of the stars. It is deep and warm and generous in religious fervor; it is infinitely sorrowful, and yet so humanely comforting throughout, one can but breathe a blessing on the kindly heart from which is poured this—

> . . . "Feeling of sadness and longing,
> That is not akin to pain,
> And resembles sorrow only
> As the mist resembles the rain."

See *In the Dark,* Vol. I, p. 411, *Longfellow's Love for the Children,* Vol. III, p. 25, and its note.

p. 206   THE VIGIL

Published in GREEN FIELDS AND RUNNING BROOKS—1892, THE LOCKERBIE BOOK—1911.

p. 207   THE QUARREL

Published in GREEN FIELDS AND RUNNING BROOKS—1892, THE LOCKERBIE BOOK—1911.

p. 209   JOHN BROWN

Published in GREEN FIELDS AND RUNNING BROOKS—1892, THE LOCKERBIE BOOK—1911. John Brown [1800-1859], famous abolitionist, led the attack on Harper's Ferry, October 16, 1859, and, aided by twenty men, took some forty prisoners. The following day the party was captured. John Brown was tried, and on December 2, 1859, was hanged. He met his death with serene composure.

p. 210   GO, WINTER!

Published in GREEN FIELDS AND RUNNING BROOKS—1892, THE LOCKERBIE BOOK—1911.

p. 211   THANKSGIVING

Published in GREEN FIELDS AND RUNNING BROOKS—1892, THE LOCKERBIE BOOK—1911.

p. 213   AUTUMN

Published in GREEN FIELDS AND RUNNING BROOKS—1892, SONGS O' CHEER—1905, THE LOCKERBIE BOOK—1911.

p. 217   JOHN ALDEN AND PERCILLY

Published in GREEN FIELDS AND RUNNING BROOKS—1892.

p. 220   THE RHYMES OF IRONQUILL

Written during the summer of 1892; published in HOME-FOLKS—1900. *The Rhymes of Ironquill* is a book by Eugene F. Ware [1841-1911] poet, soldier, lawyer and politician. He was a man admired greatly by Mr. Riley, as evidenced by an extensive correspondence as well as by this poem.

p. 223 THE CURSE OF THE WANDERING FOOT

Printed in *The Indianapolis Journal,* August 7, 1892; published in GREEN FIELDS AND RUNNING BROOKS—1892, THE LOCKERBIE BOOK—1911. This poem was originally introduced by the following:—

"While I perceive," said the kindly man to the tramp, "that you are a sober fellow and not averse to the sound performance of any nominal work that may be intrusted to your hands, I am somewhat curious to know why you do not invite some continuous employment and settle down to that steadfastly, and cease utterly your unprofitable rovings."

"Most willingly would I do the thing suggested," replied the tramp, "but that in such an effort I would assuredly prove a disappointment to any who might so seek to befriend me. I am not of the caste that may abide. I was born otherwise. Despite myself I must be moving always— on and on. It is my fate—a ban—a curse—leastwise, half bitterly, I often call it so—the curse of the wandering foot."

p. 225   AS MY UNCLE USED TO SAY

Printed in *The Indianapolis Journal,* August 28, 1892; published in GREEN FIELDS AND RUNNING BROOKS—1892, SONGS OF HOME—1910.

p. 227   WHITTIER—AT NEWBURYPORT

Written following the death of Whittier, September 7, 1892; published in HOME-FOLKS—1900, THE LOCKERBIE BOOK—1911.

p. 228   ROSAMUND C. BAILEY

Written at the death of Mrs. Leon Bailey, of Indianapolis, September 24, 1892, printed in *The In-*

dianapolis News, October 1, 1892; hitherto unpublished in book form. Mrs. Bailey was a talented singer, and on several occasions appeared on the same platform with Mr. Riley.

p. 229 TENNYSON

Printed in *The Critic,* October 15, 1892, subtitled *England, Oct. 5, 1892;* hitherto unpublished in book form. Mr. Riley found his very first inspiration in the works of Tennyson and has written much verse in imitation of him. See *Old Hec's Idolatry,* Vol. II, p. 12, *Wind of the Sea,* Vol. V, p. 254.

p. 230 MRS. BENJAMIN HARRISON

Written in memory of Caroline Scott Harrison, who died October 25, 1892, in the White House; hitherto unpublished in book form. She was a kind noble woman, distinguished both publicly and privately for all qualities of gracious womanhood.

p. 232 THE POEMS HERE AT HOME

Printed in *The Century Magazine,* November, 1892; published as the proem in POEMS HERE AT HOME—1893.

Stanza 5: *The Lady's Amaranth* was a journal of essays, anecdotes, stories, poetry, etc., published twice a month by Joseph Tore, Philadelphia. The "Treasury" book is *The Golden Treasury of Songs and Lyrics,* collected by Francis Turner Palgrave. "Night Thoughts" is Edward Young's *The Complaint or Night Thoughts.* Thomas Moore wrote the poem *Lalla Rookh.*

p. 234   LITTLE COUSIN JASPER

Printed in *The Century Magazine,* December, 1892; published in POEMS HERE AT HOME—1893. These verses are reminiscent of little Bob Martin. He was not a cousin of the poet's, but simply a visitor at Greenfield, who "bragged" of his home in Rensselaer, Jasper County, Indiana, until the boy Riley grew sick at heart. In his twenty-second year the latter saw Rensselaer for the first time and had an opportunity to compare it with Greenfield,—but comparisons are odious, as the poem goes to show.

p. 236   THE DOODLE-BUGS'S CHARM

Printed in *The Century Magazine,* December, 1892; published in POEMS HERE AT HOME—1893.

p. 238   "HOME AG'IN"

Printed in *The Century Magazine,* December, 1892; published in HOME-FOLKS—1900, HOME AGAIN WITH ME—1908. The special edition of 1908 is dedicated "To William C. Bobbs."

p. 240, l. 24: "Buckwheat-notes" refers to the style of notes used in the early music. They were three-cornered.

p. 240, last line: "The Grape-Vine Swing" was a song by Samuel Minturn Peck, set to music by F. Snow Knowlton.

p. 241, l. 6: *Hunters of Kentucky,* an old song, not now obtainable.

p. 244, l. 4: *The Vacant Chair,* words by H. S. Washburn, music by G. F. Root. *Franklin Square, Song Collection,* No. 3.

p. 244, l. 4: *Tenting on the Old Camp Ground,* words and music by Walter Kittredge. *Our Familiar Songs* compiled by Helen K. Johnson.

p. 246 THE SPOILED CHILD

Printed in *The Century Magazine,* December, 1892; published in POEMS HERE AT HOME—1893.

p. 247 THE BEE-BAG

Printed in *The Century Magazine,* December, 1892; published in POEMS HERE AT HOME—1893.

p. 249 THE TRULY MARVELOUS

Printed in *The Century Magazine,* December, 1892; published in POEMS HERE AT HOME—1893.

p. 250 OLD CHUMS

Printed in *The Critic,* January 7, 1893; published in POEMS HERE AT HOME—1893, THE LOCKERBIE BOOK—1911.

p. 251 "THIS DEAR CHILD-HEARTED WOMAN THAT IS DEAD"

Written following the death of Flora Walsh Hoyt, wife of Charles H. Hoyt, the playwright, January 22, 1893; published in ARMAZINDY—1894, THE LOCKERBIE BOOK—1911. She was a popular actress in her day and was distinguished for her kindly and cheery personality as well.

p. 252 "HOW DID YOU REST, LAST NIGHT?"

Dated "Atlanta, Ga., April 14, 1893," printed in *The Atlanta Constitution,* April 16, 1893; published in ARMAZINDY—1894, SONGS OF HOME—1910. This poem was composed while Mr. Riley was on the train en route to Atlanta, Georgia, where he was to deliver a lecture. It was written on a sheet of brown wrapping paper and was given after the reading at DeGive's Opera House to his friend, Frank L. Stanton.

p. 254 TO—"THE J. W. R. LITERARY CLUB"

Reproduced in facsimile, May 6, 1893, in a special number of *The Dawn,* the school magazine of The Indianapolis High School (Shortridge) ; hitherto unpublished in book form. The poet was prompted to write these lines when informed that a literary club at the high school had been named after him.

p. 255 OUT OF THE DARK AND THE DEARTH

Written after receiving a copy of *The Dawn* of May 6, 1893, referred to in the preceding note; printed in facsimile in the issue of the same magazine October 26, 1893, with the title, *After the Dark the Dawn,* published in *Spirk and Wunk Rhymes, Rounds and Catches* in THE FLYING ISLANDS OF THE NIGHT—1900, THE LOCKERBIE BOOK—1911.

p. 256   LITTLE DAVID

Written following the death of little David Cobb, June 2, 1893; published in ARMAZINDY—1894, SONGS O' CHEER—1905, THE LOCKERBIE BOOK—1911. "The Little Boy That Sleeps" is engraved on the child's tombstone.

In an article in *The Delineator,* September, 1908, Mabel Potter Daggett gives a photograph and the story of little David :—

There was a little boy lived next door. His name was David. And David had a spine that was crooked and crippled with rheumatism; and he was eleven years old. But his great ambition was to be a soldier. All the little boys around Lockerbie Street he used to gather daily in his front yard for training and he was the captain of the regiment. Always as Mr. Riley went by he would ask, "Well, and David, how's the regiment to-day?" Once at first, he had come along and found the boys in some altercation and had inquired, "What's it all about?" And David answered, "Why, sir, you see they all want to be officers, and it don't leave me any privates."

But the drilling went on. And one day David said wistfully as he walked by the poet's side, "Mr. Riley," and then very softly, "Mr. Riley, did you ever know a crooked soldier?"

"Oh, yes," promptly answered Mr. Riley, "and he was a very fine soldier, such a fine soldier indeed! David, do you see that robin over there? I declare spring's here, and I never knew it. Did you?" Afterward, when David was gone, it was to his mother that Mr. Riley wrote the beautiful poem about "The Little Boy That Sleeps."

And little David used to draw pictures most anywhere, pictures of soldiers and flags and stacks of arms. And there was one under the south parlor window. It was one day after David went to sleep that workmen came briskly into Lockerbie Street with ladders and pails of paint. And Mr. Riley called, as he walked by, "Oh, Mrs. Cobb, you going to have the house painted?"

And she said, "Yes, Mr. Riley, it's looking pretty bad this spring, and we just thought we must." Then the poet caught his breath hard and said, "Oh, but I wouldn't like to paint those out." And he was looking at David's soldiers.

p. 257   HOME AGAIN

Published in POEMS HERE AT HOME—1893, LOVE-LYRICS—1899, entitled *A Very Youthful Affair* in the latter.

p. 258   A SEA-SONG FROM THE SHORE

Published in POEMS HERE AT HOME—1893, THE LOCKERBIE BOOK—1911.

p. 260 THE DEAD WIFE

Published in POEMS HERE AT HOME—1893, THE LOCKERBIE BOOK—1911.

p. 261 TO ELIZABETH

Written July 9-10, 1893; hitherto unpublished in book form. Mrs. Charles E. Coffin, of Indianapolis, formerly Elizabeth Holloway, was held in high regard by the community in which she lived and upon her death tributes were paid her by Mr. Albert J. Beveridge, Mary Hartwell Catherwood and Dr. Joseph A. Milburn.

Lines 1-4: Mr. Riley's mother's name was Elizabeth.

p. 262 ARMAZINDY

Printed in The Indianapolis Journal, September 5, 1893, published in ARMAZINDY—1894.

p. 272 THREE SINGING FRIENDS

Written in November and December, 1893; published, in the order of the friendships to which the sonnets refer, in ARMAZINDY—1894, THE LOCKERBIE BOOK—1911.

LEE O. HARRIS

Printed in *The Indianapolis Journal*, December 3, 1893, with the title, *Master and First Song-Friend*, subtitle, *Lee O. Harris*. Captain Lee O. Harris (1839-1909) was Mr. Riley's teacher in the old Masonic Hall school and Greenfield Academy. When The Indiana State Teachers' Association held their "Riley Day" in Tomlinson Hall, Indianapolis, December 28, 1905, the poet in a response paid this tribute to his early friend :—

The last teacher I remember, was and is,—a man of many gifts, a profound lover of literature and a modest producer in story and in song, in history, and even in romance and drama; although his life-effort was given first of all to education. Most happily living to-day and hale and vigorous, he has but very recently retired from high and honorable office in my native county. To him I owe possibly the first gratitude of my heart and soul, since, after a brief warfare, upon our first acquaintance as teacher and pupil, he informed me gently but firmly that since I was so persistent in secretly reading novels during school hours he would insist upon his right to choose the novels I should read, whereupon the "Beadle" and "Munro" dime novels were discarded for such genuine masterpieces of fiction as those of Washington Irving, Cooper, Dickens, Thackeray and Scott; so that it may be virtually recorded that the first study of literature in a Hoosier country school was (perhaps very consciously) introduced by my first of literary friends and inspirers, Captain Lee O. Harris, of Greenfield.

See *Father William,* Vol. I, p. 198; *A Summer Sunrise,* Vol. I, p. 218; *James Whitcomb Riley,* Vol. I, p. 370; *A Ballad from April,* Vol. II, p. 313; *Lee O. Harris,* Vol. V, p. 432.

BENJ. S. PARKER

Printed in *The Indianapolis Journal,* December 10, 1893, with the title, *The Clearer Hail,* subtitle, *Benjamin S. Parker.* Between Mr. Riley and Benjamin S. Parker, the poet, there was an early friendship rich in mutual inspiration. It began in August, 1875, when the latter, through the good report of Captain Lee O. Harris, was prompted to ask Mr. Riley to send him a selection from his verses. They pleased Mr. Parker, who expressed enthusiastic approval. With this encouragement began a friendship that was characterized by deep and affectionate sympathy and more than once Mr. Riley referred to Mr. Parker in the phrase, "O gentlest of my friends." On February 18, 1883, Mr. Riley wrote the following letter in verse to his friend:—

Dear Parker—Ah! but let me call
You "Ben,"—it sounds more jovial
And just, and holds with sacred love
The "Rare Ben" you remind me of.—
And, come to think, the gentlest names
That ever jingled in with Fame's
Were "Dan" and "Will," and "Rob" and
   "Tom"—
The Genesis your own is from.
And so I hail you thus, Dear Ben:
It seems that Fortune, now and then,
Forgets her fickleness, and makes
Amends to those she first forsakes,
And even winds her arms about
The very chap she use to flout.
So now I see, by *The Review,*
The goddess making up to you;
And standing by, as one who may
Seem looking just the other way,
I watch her take the hand that I
Have thrilled to grasp in days gone by,
Half jealous, as I see her press
It with the selfsame tenderness,
Yet glad and proud to know the hand
Is hers, at last, to *understand*:—
The hand that has so often crept
Along the page while others slept,
And all the night for you held naught
But wakefulness and weary thought:
The hand that wavered and grew wan
On its long journey toward the dawn,
That still must break upon your sight
As drear and barren as the night:
The hand that wrote of smiling skies,
Pressing the lids of rainy eyes
Between the lines of joy and glee
Born out of gloom and agony.—

But lo, the hand that wrote the song
" 'Tis Morning and the Days Are Long"
Is white from finger-tip to wrist
For purest kisses ever kissed.—
May Fortune's kisses—those of Fame—
And those of every singer's name
Most dear swarm round your pencil-tip
With this one from the writer's lip!
And now—if your new Love agrees—
Spare me the palm I want to squeeze
An instant yet, the while I call
You "Ben"—It seems so just withal!

See *To Benj. S. Parker,* Vol. V, p. 434.

JAMES NEWTON MATTHEWS

Printed in *The Indianapolis Journal,* November 19, 1893, with the title, *To a Western Singer,* subtitle, *James Newton Matthews.* Dr. James Newton Matthews [1852-1910], a physician and the "Poet of the Prairies," was loved of all who knew him. He was born in Indiana, and educated at De Pauw University, but lived most of his life in Mason, Illinois. His verse is preserved in *The Lute of Life.* Mr. Riley and he corresponded extensively and exchanged letters in verse. See Vol. III, *To James Newton Matthews,* p. 240; *When We Three Meet,* p. 301; *In Days to Come,* p. 384, and their notes. Dr. Matthews paid this tribute to Mr. Riley:—

TO RILEY

I

I borrow half my zeal from you,
　My brother—you who soar and sing,
Like some impatient skylark thro'
　The welkin with unwearied wing;
With eager ear I turn to hear
Your song so dewy-sweet, so clear,

So silver-silken, like a skein
  Of passion tangled in a tune,
Or like the tinkle of the rain
  Upon the lily-lands of June,
  Or like the low and limpid rune
Of lotus-scented streams that creep
Among the hooded hills of sleep,
  Forever 'neath the falling moon.

II

Few singers since the world began,
  My comrade, e'er blew such a tone
Of joyance from the Pipe of Pan,
  As your warm lips have lately blown;
  No grief unknown, no old-world moan,
Finds voice in you; your songs are new
As April lilacs, dashed with dew;
Your themes are common, but your thought
Gleams like a frightened firefly caught
  In tangles of a trellised vine.
Or like a flashing jewel brought
  To light from some deserted mine;
  Your heart's a chalice, brimmed with wine
Distilled from many a field and wood;
No kinder draught the gods have brewed
  Than this you pour, O bard benign!
  Strange spirit, wrought of shade and shine,
You meet and master every mood.

p. 274   AT HIS WINTRY TENT

Written early in December, 1893; published in
HOME-FOLKS—1900, THE LOCKERBIE BOOK—1911.
Samuel Richards, the artist, was born April 22,
1853, and died November 30, 1893. Mr. Riley met
him at Anderson and the two became close friends.
They took long walks in those days and together
dreamed over their aspirations. Richards went to
Munich to study and won international renown as
a painter.

p. 275   UP AND DOWN OLD BRANDYWINE

Printed in *The Cosmopolitan,* May, 1894; published in ARMAZINDY—1894, FARM-RHYMES—1901, SONGS OF SUMMER—1908. Brandywine is the creek on the eastern edge of Greenfield containing "the old swimmin'-hole." "Kingry's mill" formerly stood on its banks.

p. 277, st. 8, l. 2: "Old Irvin" Hunt and Aunt Jane Hunt, who were born slaves, were the first two negroes to come to Greenfield and they lived in a little cottage on the banks of Brandywine. "Old Irvin was a great fisherman," says Mr. Riley, "and was able to catch fish, we said, where there weren't any."

p. 279   WRITIN' BACK TO THE HOME-FOLKS

Published in ARMAZINDY—1894, SONGS OF HOME —1908.

p. 281   WE DEFER THINGS

Published in ARMAZINDY—1894. This originally appeared in a letter to Mrs. D. M. Jordan, of Richmond, Indiana. The letter has been lost except for one sentence in which Mr. Riley refers to an occasion when he had, with others, been a guest at her home: "That happy time must be had over again—when— Great Heavens! what a world of 'spaces' and 'm quads'!" Then followed the verses. Mrs. D. M. Jordan, a poet, was later the subject of his lines, *The Silent Singer,* p. 328.

p. 282   FOR THIS CHRISTMAS

Published in ARMAZINDY—1894. See *"God Rest You, Merry Gentlemen,"* an old Christmas poem by an unknown author.

p. 283 TO A POET-CRITIC

Published in Armazindy—1894.

p. 284 A NOON LULL

Published in Armazindy—1894.

p. 285 RABBIT IN THE CROSS-TIES

Published in Armazindy—1894.

p. 286 WHEN LIDE MARRIED *HIM*

Published in Armazindy—1894, Love-Lyrics —1899.

p. 288 "RINGWORM FRANK"

Published in Armazindy—1894.

p. 289 THE YOUTHFUL PATRIOT

Published in Armazindy—1894.

p. 290 PONCHUS PILUT

Published in Armazindy—1894.
p. 291, last stanza: Mr. Riley says: "In the early days the country hotel usually had a cupola with a bell in it to call guests to meals. It was a common saying that the bell said 'pig tail done.' "

p. 292 SLUMBER-SONG

Published in Armazindy—1894, Songs of Summer—1908, The Lockerbie Book—1911.

p. 293   THE CIRCUS PARADE

Published in Armazindy—1894, Songs of Summer—1908, Down around the River and Other Poems—1911. See note on *The Circus-Day Parade,* Vol. II, p. 439.

p. 295   FOLKS AT LONESOMEVILLE

Published in Armazindy—1894.

p. 296   THE THREE JOLLY HUNTERS

Published in Armazindy—1894. Compare the old rhyme beginning, "There were three jovial Welshmen."

p. 298   THE LITTLE DOG-WOGGY

Published in Armazindy—1894.

p. 300   CHARMS

Published in Armazindy—1894.

p. 302   A FEW OF THE BIRD FAMILY

Published in Armazindy—1894.

p. 303   THROUGH SLEEPY-LAND

Published in Armazindy—1894, Songs of Home—1910, The Lockerbie Book—1911.

p. 305   THE TRESTLE AND THE BUCK-SAW

Published in Armazindy—1894.

p. 306   THE KING OF OO-RINKTUM-JING

Published in Armazindy—1894.

p. 307   THE TOY PENNY-DOG

Published in Armazindy—1894.

p. 308   JARGON-JINGLE

Published in Armazindy—1894.

p. 309   THE GREAT EXPLORER

Published in Armazindy—1894.

p. 310   THE SCHOOLBOY'S FAVORITE

Published in Armazindy—1894, Songs o' Cheer —1905. See *Thanksgiving Day* by Lydia Maria Child, *Modern Music Series, First Book,* by Eleanor Smith.

p. 313   ALBUMANIA

Published in Armazindy—1894.
The poet's impromptu lines on the blotter, written in October, 1895, for the Flower Mission Fair, may be appropriately included here:—

From Pad to Verse

Thinnest blotter's necessary
As the thickest *dictionary.*

Blotter, paper, pen and ink—
Themes to scheme, and thoughts to think.

Best friend of the porest spellers
Is the *blotter*, tell the fellers.

All we think in ink that's bad
May be *blotted* with a *pad*.

Even Eve's most cautious daughter
Trusts her secrets to the *blotter*.

Forgers do their plotting bad
When they use a *blotting-pad*.

Such its power, thrones might totter
At disclosures of the *blotter*.

When you write to thoughtful men,
Use the *blotter* more than pen.

"Do your writing and *erot*-ing,"
Said the *pad*, "I'll do the *blotting!*"

Blotters are *turned down*, I guess,
Oft for drink-ink to excess.

Said the young man to the *blotter*,
"*There!* b'george! I've good as *got* her!"

All your unbelief and doubt
Write in full, then—blot it out!

p. 315   THE LITTLE MOCK-MAN

Published in Armazindy—1894.

p. 317   SUMMER-TIME AND WINTER-TIME

Published in Armazindy—1894.

p. 318   HOME-MADE RIDDLES

Published in Armazindy—1894. Queries for
answers to the riddles have shown that the subtitle is not always understood: "All but the
answers" composed,—i. e., there are no answers.

p. 320   THE LOVELY CHILD

Published in Armazindy—1894, Songs o' Cheer
—1905, The Lockerbie Book—1911.

p. 321   THE YELLOWBIRD

Published in Armazindy—1894, Songs of Summer—1908, The Lockerbie Book—1911.

p. 322   SAD PERVERSITY

Published in Armazindy—1894, with the title,
Envoy.

p. 323   A FEEL IN THE CHRIS'MAS-AIR

Printed in *The Cosmopolitan,* December, 1894;
published in Home-Folks—1900, Songs of Home
—1910.

p. 325   MISTER HOP-TOAD

Dated, April, 1895; printed in *St. Nicholas,* November, 1895; published in Home-Folks—1900,
Songs o' Cheer—1905.

p. 328   THE SILENT SINGER

Dated April 29, 1895; printed in *The Indianapolis
Journal,* May 1, 1895; published in Home-Folks—
1900, The Lockerbie Book—1911. Mrs. D. M.
Jordan, of Richmond, Indiana, [1833-1895] was
the author of *Rosemary Leaves* and a great number of uncollected poems. A sketch of her life
appears in *Poets and Poetry of Indiana,* by Benj.
S. Parker and Enos B. Heiney (p. 438). Mr.
Riley admired her verse and occasionally corre-

sponded with her, as witness the following lines
from an undated letter :—

> Dear singing friend, your genial rhyme
> Is warm to me as summer-time,
> And sweet and glad with music, too,
> As when the skies are softest blue,
> And all the birds that sing in tune,
> And all the flowers that bloom in June
> Blend in one song and one perfume,
> As sweet as even Heaven might spare,
> Were I this moment entering there.

p. 331 THE GREEN GRASS OF OLD IRELAND

Printed in *The Century Magazine,* August, 1895;
published in HOME-FOLKS—1900.

p. 333 A PEACE-HYMN OF THE REPUBLIC

Written for the 29th Encampment of the G. A.
R., held at Louisville, Kentucky, September 12,
1895; published in HOME-FOLKS—1900, THE LOCK-
ERBIE BOOK—1911. On the occasion referred to
Mr. Riley read this poem with the following intro-
duction :—

In attempting any answer to the invitation to prepare a
fitting poem for an occasion so memorable in our history
as the present, the writer has felt that he could only trust
to the long prior inspiration of another—that inspiration
evoked by the once—alas !—exact opposite of the sectional
feelings and conditions of to-day. Then, high above the
havoc of the Civil War, rang out *The Battle Hymn of the
Republic!* Now, in faintest echo, yet most grateful fervor,
is offered this poem.

p. 335 MY DANCIN'-DAYS IS OVER

Printed in *The Century Magazine,* November,
1895, with the title, *His Dancin' Days;* published
in HOME-FOLKS—1900, SONGS OF HOME—1910.

See note, *My Fiddle,* Vol. II, p. 464.

Stanza 2, l. 3: "Gray Eagle" is an old and much-loved "fiddle tune" named for a famous running horse. Published in Harding's *All-Round Collection of Jigs, Reels and Country Dances.*

p. 338　　　　　EUGENE FIELD

Written immediately following the death of the poet, November 4, 1895; published in Home-Folks —1900, The Lockerbie Book—1911. The poetry of Field was much admired by Mr. Riley.

p. 339　　　　　DREAM-MARCH

Printed in *St. Nicholas,* December, 1895, with the title, *Dream March of the Children;* published in The Book of Joyous Children—1902.

p. 341　　　　A CHRISTMAS MEMORY

Printed in *Life,* Christmas, 1895; published in The Book of Joyous Children—1902.

p. 344　　　　TO ALMON KEEFER

Written in December, 1895; printed in *The Hancock Democrat,* December 24, 1895; hitherto unpublished in book form. Almon Keefer, of Greenfield, to whom Mr. Riley refers in an inscribed volume of A Child-World as "the beloved hero of my childhood days," received a copy of *Tales of the Ocean* with this poem written therein for Christmas, 1895. Mr. Riley had found the old edition while rummaging about in a bookstore. The title page reads:—

"Tales of the Ocean" and Essays for the Forecastle: Containing matters and incidents Humorous, Pathetic,

Romantic and Sentimental. Illustrated with numerous engravings.

"... and, he will tell
Strange tales, good Sir, that, by my halidon,
Will make you ope your ears and marvel much—
Or haply laugh an hour by Shrewsbury clock."

—OLD PLAY.

By Hawser Martingale, Boston: J. L. Locke & Co.

See *A Child-World,* p. 375, l. 27.

p. 346   LITTLE MAID-O'-DREAMS

Printed in *The Ladies' Home Journal,* February, 1896; hitherto unpublished in book form.

p. 348   EDGAR WILSON NYE

Printed in *The Indianapolis Journal,* February 23, 1896; published in HIS PA'S ROMANCE—1903, THE LOCKERBIE BOOK—1911. Edgar Wilson Nye, "Bill" Nye, an American humorist and lecturer, was born at Shirley, Maine, August 25, 1850, and died at his home near Asheville, N. C., February 22, 1896. He wrote *A Guest at the Ludlow, Comic History of the United States,* and *Comic History of England,* and contributed some of his cleverest skits to *Nye and Riley's Railway Guide.* He appeared on the platform with Mr. Riley for several seasons and the two were close friends. See *To Edgar Wilson Nye,* Vol. III, p. 413.

When told of Nye's death, Mr. Riley wrote the following for the press:—

Especially favored, as for years I have been, with close personal acquaintance and association with Mr. Nye, his going away fills me with a selfishness of grief that finds a mute rebuke in my every memory of him. He was unselfish wholly, and I am broken-hearted, recalling the al-

ways patient strength and gentleness of this true man, the
unfailing hope and cheer and faith of his child-heart, his
noble and heroic life, and pure devotion to his home, his
deep affections, constant dreams, plans, and realizations. I
can not doubt but that somehow, somewhere, he continues
cheerily on in the unspoken exercise of these same ca-
pacities.

p. 349   CASSANDER

Printed in *The Ladies' Home Journal,* June, 1896;
published in HOME-FOLKS—1900.

p. 353   A CHILD-WORLD

Published as a book in 1896.

A Child-World is a poem reminiscent of the
poet's own happy youth, home and playmates. It
was conceived very early in 1896 and completed
prior to June of that year, except for several sec-
tions written many years before, as will be indi-
cated. It was dedicated to Mr. and Mrs. Charles
L. Holstein, at whose home it was written. A letter
to the author's brother, John A. Riley, dated February 12, 1896, tells how the poem was begun:—

But, someway I *feel* your early recovery and utter resto-
ration, and this forecast you will accept the fact of—however vague and mysterious its basis—just as your letter has
given evidence to me of a like mental and spiritual condition with us twain, the last two weeks.—i. e.—You have, in
that time been continually recalling our old home, our long-
vanished youth, and the dear father and mother who so
loved us, and who were so loved by us that we may not
doubt but they are still with us, though we see them not—
loving us ever the same—and being loved by us ever and
ever the same. The selfsame theme and thoughts have
steadfastly, for the last two weeks, been haunting me.—So
that at last I felt impelled to set about a Child poem of a
whole book's length—and the which, God bless it! I have
very happily started and advanced in many pages. More
than this *now* I can not tell you—but we are *all* embraced
in the simple history, though under names known only to

the family—since I find it necessary, in order to accommodate the *very modest* writer, that he also must appear in *third* person. And now, if you want to boost a fellow along, think up and set down any and all little incidents—like the one you have just unconsciously furnished me of *going,* in midwinter, clean to "Old Irvin's Spring."—The Bixlers—particularly "Noey," and Almon Keefer—the Loehr-boys—et al.

John A. Riley responded with a letter of generous proportions, from which selections are quoted in these notes.

The setting of the poem is the author's birthplace, the little town of Greenfield, Indiana, at the time of the story a village of but three hundred inhabitants, and a very happy example of the peaceful rural democracy existing prior to these present days of big cities and restless commercialism. As Mr. W. D. Howells pointed out, in reviewing the poem [reported in *The Indianapolis Journal,* November 12, 1896] :—

From beginning to end it moves through the world of childhood, the childhood of that vanished West which lay between the Ohio and the Mississippi, and was, unless memory abuses my fondness, the happiest land that ever there was under the sun. There were no very rich nor very poor in that region, which has since become the very hotbed of millionairism, but an equality of condition never matched before or since, so that the picture of the peaceful, kindly life in one village family, which Mr. Riley gives, is the portrait of all village family life then and there.

The characters in the story are the poet's own father and mother; his older brother John, called "Johnty"; the poet himself, called by his old nickname "Bud"; his sister, Elva May, called "Maymie"; his younger brother Humboldt, called "Alex"; his younger sister Mary Elizabeth, called "Lizzie"; and also his early childhood friends. See Vol. I, p. 367.

p. 354   PROEM

The last stanza expresses a favorite speculation of
the poet's. In an interview printed in *The New
York Evening Sun,* October 11, 1912, he says:—

"Of course, one can speculate as to what Heaven will be
like. It doesn't do any harm to speculate upon the sort of
place that Heaven will be and the sort of life that is lived
there. The field isn't limited—you can imagine that anything can take place there; anything, anything, anything!
For instance, you might imagine, if you choose, that things
would go on there about as they do here on earth—with
some exceptions. I can't think of many improvements that
might be made. It may be that each one of us will be as-
signed certain things to do, certain daily tasks; one duty for
one person, another duty for another. And then, when we
had accomplished the tasks set out for us on six days of the
week, the Head Gardener maybe would allow, on the sev-
enth day, each one of us to choose for himself the thing
he wanted to do most of all. A fellow might get permission, for example, to go back to any period of his life on
earth and live a whole day over again. Think of it! Suppose a fellow were allowed to go back to any one of the
days of his boyhood he might choose—might have the
whole, long, joyous day before him again; be happy, ragged,
barefooted, with everything back as it used to be—even to
the stone-bruise on his heel. To have over again one of
those dewy mornings of fifty years ago!

This poem is, indeed, a "joyous day" of the poet's
past lived over again.

p. 355   THE CHILD-WORLD

Mr. Gavin L. Payne reports this interview with
Mr. Riley in *The Indianapolis Journal,* October 11,
1896, where this mention is made of the National
Road:—

It was a great highway to me in those days. To us children it was the highway that led to all the wonderful places
on the inhabitable globe. Our childish imagination didn't

carry us much further than the reaches of that old road; it was the main artery of the whole living world. Children nowadays—and even the grown folks—know but little of the part that the old National Road played in making our mighty West. You know it was constructed by the government, from Cumberland, Md., and in the early days the settlers traversed it—overland to "The Illinoiy" and the Territories still beyond. As late as the days when I was a boy the wagon-trains went by, and what wonderful sights they were to us! My father's house faced the road to the south. The artist has the old house pictured [in the frontispiece] just as it was then.

p. 357, l. 13: "An apple-tree." See *The Little-Red-Apple Tree,*" Vol. III, p. 45.

p. 358, l. 5: "When the old cat died." Compare *"Waitin' fer the Cat to Die,*" Vol. IV, p. 6.

p. 358   THERE WAS A CHERRY TREE

Published with the above title in SONGS O' CHEER —1905, and THE LOCKERBIE BOOK—1911.

p. 358, last line: The white-winter-pearmain is a light green apple shaped not unlike a pear.

p. 361   THE OLD HOME-FOLKS

In the copy of A CHILD-WORLD which the author sent to his brother was this inscription:—

For—
John A. Riley—the boy "Johnty" of this veracious book.—
From his loving brother "Bud"—
—James Whitcomb Riley.
Indianapolis, Oct. 7, 1896.

In this book of simple rhyme
Spare your scythe, old Father Time!—
"Scy' no mow!"—for two old men
Here are little boys again—
"Johnty" now and "Bud" are they
Just as in their Childhood's day.

p. 363, l. 3: The grandmother was Margaret Slick Riley, wife of a pioneer, Andrew Riley, then deceased, with whom she had traveled from their birthplace in Bedford County, Pennsylvania, to Ohio and at last to Indiana. She was a great lover of children, and being a persistent reader, was for this reason actually called the "historicul-est one" by "Bud".

p. 363   THE WILLOW

First printed in *The Indianapolis Journal,* May 3, 1885; published also in THE LOCKERBIE BOOK—1911, when the second stanza was first inserted.

p. 364, l. 1: The brother John speaks thus of "Maymie" in his letter to the author, March 15, 1896: "Sister Elva was a very pretty child and I have often heard Uncle Joe say she was 'the most beautiful child he ever saw.' " She resembled her mother more than any other member of the family.

p. 364, l. 17: Ella and Lu Crawford lived just east of the Riley home. See *God's Mercy,* p. 95, and its note for another mention of Miss Crawford.

p. 364, l. 29: "Alex" was named for his father, and his full name, though never used, was Alexander Humboldt Riley.

p. 365, l. 11: Among Alex' "seben Uncles" was John Slick Riley, who had gone South early in life and during the War became a surgeon in the Confederate army, while his brother Reuben, the poet's father, served as captain on the northern side. John Slick Riley was captured and imprisoned in Alton, Illinois, whence he escaped and paid a secret visit to his mother, the grandmother in this poem. It was at her house that the author first saw him.

p. 365, l. 21: "Baby Lizzie" is Mary Elizabeth,

Mrs. Frank C. Payne, who, except for her brother, is the only member of the family surviving.

p. 367, l. 1: See Vol. I, for photographs of the father and mother, and also of the old home. See Vol. I, p. 367-368, for mention of the father and mother.

p. 368   THE CHILD-HEART

Written prior to April, 1895.

p. 372, l. 1: The cheery "Cousin Rufus," later Capt. Riley's law partner, is Judge William Rufus Hough, who still lives at Greenfield. See note *Out to Old Aunt Mary's,* Vol. III, p. 521.

p. 372, l. 21: *Baron Münchhausen,* R. E. Raspey's famous fiction, published in 1785.

p. 372, l. 22: *The Swiss Family Robinson,* the celebrated narrative of shipwreck on a desert island by Rudolphe Wyss.

p. 372, l. 19: When a boy of fourteen Mr. Riley found his ideal in his uncle, Martin Whitten Riley, the father's youngest brother. He was in the printing business at Indianapolis, but came to Greenfield frequently. "On his visits home," says Mr. Riley, "he would take me walking in the woods, where nobody could hear us, and would there declaim to me. He loved to use big words. When my Uncle John, who served in the Confederacy and was captured, was paying a fugitive visit to Greenfield, following his escape from a federal prison in Illinois, Uncle Mart harangued with especial fervor on the inadvisability of giving him up to the authorities. 'What, would you have your kinsman *incarcerated* in the gloomy dungeons of the North!' he said."

Martin Riley was a humorist and versifier as well. People said the boy Riley wanted to be like his Uncle Mart, and the former felt proud of the charge, though denying it with scrupulous modesty.

All of Uncle Mart's quotations are glibly taken from the old *Type Foundry Specimen Book,* a copy of which Mr. Riley's friend, John Mitchell, of Greenfield, has preserved.

p. 375, l. 7: The two latter of these boyhood chums are mentioned in *A Retrospect.* See note, Vol. I, p. 392.

p. 375, l. 14: Almon Keefer was for years a compositor on *The Hancock Democrat.* See *To Almon Keefer,* p. 344, in which *"Tales of the Ocean,"* p. 376, l. 27, is mentioned.

p. 375, l. 7: Jim Offutt, the little brother of Judge Grandison Offutt, "was a beautiful boy," says Mr. Riley, "as strong and tough as a pine knot."

p. 376, l. 9: "Bee Lineback was a great hunter. He never missed a shot if he aimed at a rabbit, quail, robin or sparrow. In fact he had a reputation as a crack shot not only throughout the county but in Indianapolis as well. When a little boy I wrote a rhyme about him:—

> He takes his fun,
> He takes his gun,
> Takes down the railroad track;
> He then takes aim,
> Takes up his game,
> And takes a Bee-Line back."

p. 377, l. 11: *"The League of the Miami,"* says Almon Keefer, "was an old novel printed in pamphlet form and written by Emerson Bennett. It had the regulation hero and heroine to be found in all old-fashioned novels. Their persecutor was the captain of an organized band of horse-thieves, who operated under the name of '*The League of the*

'Miami.' The 'Bonnie Gray' business was a pass-
word to gain entrance to the secret stables of the
band. Mr. Riley and other boys of his age, George
A. Carr and myself among them, used to play *The
League of the Miami* in the old barn which still
stands behind the Riley homestead in Greenfield."

p. 379   WHILE THE HEART BEATS YOUNG

Printed in *The Ladies' Home Journal,* August,
1896; published in SONGS O' CHEER—1905, WHILE
THE HEART BEATS YOUNG—1906, THE LOCKERBIE
BOOK—1911.

p. 380, 1. 10: "Noah Bixler," says Mr. Riley,
"who was between my age and that of my brother
John, was a big, lubberly, rosy-cheeked boy. He
died in my father's Company at Rich Mountain,
Virginia, of homesickness, for when he enlisted it
was the first time he had ever been away from
home. He wasn't wounded,—it was simply homesickness. 'The stout old hair trunk Noey put on
wheels' [p. 382, 1. 9] was one of those curious old-
fashioned things used by the early travelers, made
out of calf- or cow-hide, with the hair on it and big
brass-headed nails studded all over it." John A.
Riley in a letter to his brother, March 15, 1896,
says :—

Noah was a typical country boy, long and sprangling. He
got the name around the town of "Noah-burnt-biscuit."
His perpetual efforts at whistling a tune and his constant
failure to come within a mile of it were almost pathetic.
He was a great boy for pets and his pet coon, as well as
a fox or two and also sundry hawks and owls, together
with his ability to make friends with and drive any kind
of a horse, made him quite a hero in our boyish eyes at
times. The corn poppings and candy pullings given by
Sally and Noah were hours of great glee.

p. 387, l. 9: "The Noted Traveler," says Mr. Riley, "was such a man as was often seen in those days,—a mysterious politician on some errand in the cause of abolition, for this story has its setting some years prior to the Civil War. Those were serious days for the abolitionists, and my father had to walk quite cautiously, for it was a dangerous thing in that day to be what was called 'a black republican.' This 'Noted Traveler' came to secrete himself with father and talk abolition or the underground railway, which was very active in Indiana at that time."

p. 388   A PROSPECTIVE VISIT

p. 389, l. 4: "Noah's rhyme," says Mr. Riley, "is a true one. In fact, the whole story is true, though it is colored up here and there, and yet, it is a simple tale without many flourishes of the pen."

p. 390   AT NOEY'S HOUSE

p. 391, l. 4: "Jason" represents a relative of Noah's not of the immediate family.

p. 393, l. 7: Johnty's story of the dog was first printed in *The Danbury News,* April 8, 1874, with the title, *That Little Dorg.*

p. 396   THE LOEHRS AND THE HAMMONDS

p. 396, l. 2: "The Loehrs" were a large family, several of whom still live at Greenfield.

p. 396, l. 17; "Will Pierson"—Dr. William Morris Pierson, now of Morristown, Indiana, to whom *Friday Afternoon* is dedicated. Vol. I, p. 92.

p. 397, l. 5: "The Hammonds"—fanciful characters, but very natural ones, visitors from the city.

p. 398   IN THE WARM HEALTH-GIVING WEATHER

p. 398: First printed in *The Ladies' Home Journal,* December, 1895, with the title, *At the Gate.*

p. 401   THE HIRED MAN AND FLORETTY

"The Hired Man" is elsewhere called "The Raggedy Man". See note, p. 509.

"Floretty" is elsewhere called " 'Lizabuth Ann." See p. 510.

p. 403, l. 25: "Then sleep no more," from an old song.

p. 406, l. 1: The quotation is from the old song, *Do They Miss Me at Home,* which Mr. Riley described in the poem, *A' Old Played-Out Song,* Vol. III, p. 311.

p. 408   THE EVENING COMPANY

The names of those mentioned in the first few lines are genuine. Ella and Mary Mathers lived opposite the Riley home. Nelly Millikan was afterward Mrs. George B. Cooley. See *A Letter to a Friend,* Vol. I, p. 133; *A Dream Unfinished,* Vol. I, p. 264.

p. 408, ll. 7-8: *Ever of Thee,* words by Foley Hall, music by G. Linley.

p. 408, l. 10: "War Barnett"—Samuel Warsaw Barnett was a member of "The Old Band." See note, p. 490.

p. 409, l. 13: Hatton's *Simon the Cellarer* is published in *The Treasury of Song for the Home Circle,* arranged by D. H. Morrison.

p. 410, ll. 7-8: *Polly Hopkin's Waltz, Rickett's Hornpipe*—popular instrumental music of those days. The former appears in *The Musicians' Om-*

nibus Number One; the latter appears in Harding's
*All-Round Collection of Jigs, Reels and Country
Dances.*

p. 412   MAYMIE'S STORY OF RED RIDING-HOOD

First printed in *The Indianapolis Saturday Herald,* June 15, 1878, in No. II of *The Respectfully
Declined Papers of the Buzz Club;* since thoroughly
revised.

p. 421   MR. HAMMOND'S PARABLE

Mr. Riley sent these verses, then entitled *A Destiny,* to *Hearth and Home,* and received from that
magazine his first check, amounting to either six
or eight dollars. They were printed in the issue of
April 10, 1875. Thus encouraged he forwarded
another poem, but the manuscript was returned
with the explanation that the magazine had been
discontinued. *A Destiny* was one of the poems sent
to Longfellow. See *James Whitcomb Riley,* Vol. I,
pp. 376-7, Notes Vol. I, pp. 412-13. The word
prone criticized by Longfellow, was changed to
limp, stanza 2, l. 1.

p. 425   FLORETTY'S MUSICAL CONTRIBUTION

p. 425, l. 14: Also called *Weber's Last Waltz.*
p. 425, l. 15: *Beautiful Isle of the Sea,* words by
George Cooper, music by J. R. Thomas.

p. 428   MOUNTAIN MAID'S INVITATION

A facsimile of the old music is reproduced opposite page 126 in the Bowen-Merrill edition—1896.

p. 432   Bud's Fairy Tale

First printed in *The Indianapolis Saturday Herald,* December 3, 1879, with the title, *Trillpipe's Boy.* This is the story that Mr. Riley's brother, Humboldt, used to tell. For other Trillpipe stories in prose, see *The Judkins' Papers,* Vol. VI.

p. 432, l. 4: "Ed Howard,"—Dr. Edward Bruce Howard, of Greenfield.

p. 442   Noey's Night-Piece

The incident is a verity.

p. 442, l. 3: "Tubb Kingry," George Kingry, the fat boy of the town, son of the miller. See *Kingry's Mill,* Vol. III, p. 355.

p. 446   Cousin Rufus' Story

This is Judge Hough's own story retold.

p. 454   The Bear Story

This story is one of Mr. Riley's most popular readings. He first gave it at a Roberts Park M. E. Church social for the children, October 1, 1874. It was published in Child-Rhymes—1898, While the Heart Beats Young—1906, The Runaway Boy—1908.

p. 462   Told by "The Noted Traveler"

The story told by "The Noted Traveler" is based on one of the traditions current at Zanesville, Ohio. Its site is the old rock spring on the National pike east near Greenwood cemetery, where the colored people whose heroic lives are commemorated by the story, lived.

p. 465, l. 25: *Gilead*—evidently. The quotation is from an old song of "Uncle Mart's."

p. 469   HEAT-LIGHTNING

p. 470: "Uncle Mart's" experiments with rhyme are illustrated by this incident which Mr. Riley takes pleasure in recalling: One day a girl came into his printing establishment and asked him to write some poetry in an album of multicolored leaves, pink, blue, green, etc., covered with love and every tender passion drawn from all sentimental treasure-houses. "Uncle Mart" chose a grass-green leaf and wrote:—

> "I will write some
> In your album."

He then roared with laughter.

p. 470, ll. 2-5: The quotation is from the old *Type Founders' Specimen Book*.

p. 470, l. 16: *The Indianapolis Sentinel* with which he was connected.

p. 471, ll. 1-4: A garbled quotation from the *Specimen Book,* changed where italicized,—originally *porpoises* in last line.

p. 472   UNCLE MART'S POEM

p. 475, ll. 6-7: Big Foot, an Indian, who had a savage fight with Adam Poe, the associate of Daniel Boone. Simon Girty [1741-1818], a contemptible renegade known as "the white Indian," who aroused the redskins of the Central West against the pioneers, and led them at the Battle of Blue Lick, Kentucky, where he was opposed by Daniel Boone.